Agonistic Mourning

Incitements

Series editors
Peg Birmingham, DePaul University
and Dimitris Vardoulakis, Western Sydney University

Editorial Advisory Board
Étienne Balibar, Andrew Benjamin, Jay M. Bernstein, Rosi Braidotti, Wendy Brown, Judith Butler, Adriana Cavarero, Howard Caygill, Rebecca Comay, Joan Copjec, Simon Critchley, Costas Douzinas, Peter Fenves, Christopher Fynsk, Moira Gatens, Gregg Lambert, Leonard Lawlor, Genevieve Lloyd, Catherine Malabou, James Martel, Christoph Menke, Warren Montag, Michael Naas, Antonio Negri, Kelly Oliver, Paul Patton, Anson Rabinbach, Gerhard Richter, Martin Saar, Miguel Vatter, Gianni Vattimo, Santiago Zabala

Available
Return Statements: The Return of Religion in Contemporary Philosophy
Gregg Lambert

The Refusal of Politics
Laurent Dubreuil, translated by Cory Browning

Plastic Sovereignties: Agamben and the Politics of Aesthetics
Arne De Boever

From Violence to Speaking Out:
Apocalypse and Expression in Foucault, Derrida and Deleuze
Leonard Lawlor

Agonistic Mourning: Political Dissidence and the Women in Black
Athena Athanasiou

Interpassivity: The Aesthetics of Delegated Enjoyment
Robert Pfaller

Derrida's Secret: Perjury, Testimony, Oath
Charles Barbour

Resistance and Psychoanalysis: Impossible Divisions
Simon Morgan Wortham

Visit the series web page at: edinburghuniversitypress.com/series/incite

Agonistic Mourning

Political Dissidence and the Women in Black

Athena Athanasiou

EDINBURGH
University Press

Edinburgh University Press is one of the leading university presses in the UK. We publish academic books and journals in our selected subject areas across the humanities and social sciences, combining cutting-edge scholarship with high editorial and production values to produce academic works of lasting importance. For more information visit our website: edinburghuniversitypress.com

Edinburgh University Press Ltd
The Tun – Holyrood Road, 12(2f) Jackson's Entry, Edinburgh EH8 8PJ

Typeset in Bembo
by R. J. Footring Ltd, Derby, UK, and

Printed and bound by CPI Group (UK) Ltd, Croydon, CR0 4YY

A CIP record for this book is available from the British Library

ISBN 978 1 4744 2014 3 (hardback)
ISBN 978 1 4744 2016 7 (webready PDF)
ISBN 978 1 4744 2015 0 (paperback)
ISBN 978 1 4744 2017 4 (epub)

Contents

Acknowledgements

As this book is the outcome of a protracted and meandering course, I have accrued, to be sure, several deep-seated debts over the past few years. Much as the figure of 'debt' inevitably retains an uncanny resonance with the abusive economy of financialisation, the dominant grand narrative of our time, having the opportunity to reaffirm my abiding indebtedness here is an incommensurable pleasure and responsibility beyond the order of debt. Although it is arguably impossible to recount, reckon, and do justice to all of them, in their singularity, this book would not have been possible without the kindness, wit, insight, and accompaniment of many people who have helped me see it through to its completion; who were there at many key moments and provided timely comfort and inspiration along the way. I 'owe' them the incalculable reliance on what exceeds the proper apparatuses of 'debt'.

Above all, I wish to thank all *ŽuC* – Women in Black activists who graced me with their trust and shared their stories with me during my time in Serbia. I would never have been able to carry out this research project without their courage, commitment, hospitality, and comradeship. They deserve more acknowledgement and gratitude than I can possibly offer them here. I want to specifically thank Bojan Aleksov, Đorđe Balzamović (Žole), Hana Ćopić, Daša Duhaček, Nađia Duhaček, Ildiko

Erdei, Fika Filipović, Senka Knežević, Saša Kovačević, Nataša Lambić, Goran Lazin, Zinaida Marjanović, Jadranka Milićević, Lepa Mlađenović, Dragan Protić (Prota), Ljiljana Radovanović, Slavica Stojanović, Barči Tabački, Miloš Urošević, Marija Vidić, Adriana Zaharijević, and Staša Zajović. They all never tired of letting me know that their collective and dissident *mal d'archive* was all worth it. I thank them for consistently teaching me anew the performative and profoundly transformative scope of re-sponsiveness. This politics of responsiveness, imbued as it is with collective stories of contrapuntal displacement and resistance to border violence, sets the stage for the pages to follow. And although comparisons should be drawn only in the most cautious way, it is precisely this call for responsiveness to war, loss, refugee, and asylum rights that has been acutely recurring in these times of necropolitics at the borderscapes of a 'fortress Europe', increasingly overtaken by nationalism, authoritarianism, and deepening economic inequalities. Indeed, as Adorno put it in his 1959 text 'The meaning of working through the past': 'Nationalism today is at once both obsolete and up-to-date' (Adorno 2005).

I am grateful to Staša Zajović who supported this work by her way of re-inscribing resistance in a 'singular plural' experience of ex-position: singularity inextricably interconnected to plurality. I am particularly thankful for the unwavering camaraderie and disarming generosity of Saša Kovačević – also exquisite language instructor, beyond the purview of translation. I am most appreciative of the insight and vision of Rada Drezgdić, Daša Duhaček, Ildiko Erdei, Orli Fridman, Obrad Savić, Slavica Stojanović, and Adriana Zaharijević. Special thanks to Adriana Zaharijević for reading parts of the manuscript with delicate attention. Photographers Vesna Pavlović and Srdjan Veljović have my sincere appreciation for kindly allowing me to use their photographs. I am grateful to Petar Bojanić, director of the Institute for Philosophy and Social Theory at the University of Belgrade, for offering me institutional hospitality in Serbia during the course of my research. The assistance of Jelena Vasiljević was gracious and much appreciated. Theodora Vetta deserves mention as well for her generosity in sharing anthropological knowledge and inventive advice in practical matters of everyday life while in Belgrade.

Heartfelt thanks go to Penelope Papailias, brilliant friend and interlocutor, for reading, commenting, and brainstorming substantively and patiently with me over the course of fashioning and refashioning my thoughts; she read the manuscript and gave generously of her time to contribute detailed feedback, editorial insight, and rigorous advice. Another dear friend, Olga Taxidou, not only read particular chapter drafts with acumen, but she has been a long time, essential, and solicitous interlocutor throughout writing: I am most grateful for her multi-layered, poetic, and theatrical readings of my work but also for her advice and encouragement when uncertainty erupted. I also thank the anonymous Press readers for their incisive and prescient comments, which were enormously helpful as I revised. The faults that have remained are my own.

My indebtedness to Judith Butler is immeasurable. Her work over the years has engaged and prompted my thinking in many thorough ways, as this book shows. She offered an extraordinarily close reading and characteristically astute comments, which strengthened the book. I cannot thank her enough for the gift of that resonant response but also for sustaining my work with her luminous intellectual engagement. I have been consistently moved and motivated by her keen insight and emotional generosity.

Over the years, I have profited greatly from the exhilaration of challenging conversations with Costas Douzinas, stalwart ally and trenchant interlocutor. I would also like to express my appreciation to an incomplete array of friends and interlocutors:

Giorgio Agamben, Etienne Balibar, Petar Bojanić, Sanja Bojanić, Joanna Bourke, Rosi Braidotti, Wendy Brown, Susan Buck-Morss, Heath Cabot, Eduardo Cadava, Steve Caton, Jane Cowan, Veena Das, Olga Demetriou, Penelope Deutscher, Mary Ann Doane, Didier Fassin, James Faubion, Anne-Marie Fortier, Zeynep Gambetti, Stathis Gourgouris, Sarah Green, Michael Herzfeld, Marianne Hirsch, Maria Hlavajova, Lynne Joyrich, Elke Krasny, Apostolos Lambropoulos, Isabell Lorey, Michael Löwy, Sandro Mezzadra, Yael Navaro-Yashin, Mariella Pandolfi, Neni Panourgiá, Dimitris Papanikolaou, Tuija Pulkkinen, Rayna Rapp, Lynne Segal, Igor Štiks, Liana Theodoratou, Amanda Third, Eleni Varikas, and Elisabeth Weed. Their intellectual solidarity and indispensable friendship have stimulated my own thinking in inestimable ways, some of which are hopefully evinced throughout this book. I can't thank Dimitris Vardoulakis enough for the creative encouragement and vigorous insight he offered throughout.

I would like to thank everyone who graciously talked to me about this project, asked tough questions, and made suggestions at different stages of its development. They all helped me clarify my thinking on several issues. I am especially grateful to audiences, faculty, and staff of academic institutions where I was invited to present versions of these chapters. They are too numerous to recount here, but I wish to thank everyone involved with these institutions for their support. Special thanks are due to Tuija Pulkkinen for her warm hospitality, both practical and intellectual, at the University of Helsinki and the Graduate Program in Gender Studies. I have very fond memories of lively conversations with the PhD students of the Program. My enduring appreciation also goes to Eleni Varikas and Michael Löwy for providing me with a congenial institutional environment at the Centre de Reserches Sociologiques et Politiques de Paris and a home in Paris: they have been an ongoing source of perceptiveness and friendship. Olga Taxidou and Igor Štiks offered a hospitable and stimulating setting at the University of Edinburgh, in the context of 'The *Bacchae* Project' and the symposium 'Theatre, Citizenship and the Law'. I thank for their invitations: Elke Krasny and the Academy of Fine Arts in Vienna; Andrea Hubin and Kunsthalle Wien; Adriana Zaharijević and the Group for Social Engagement Studies; Petar Bojanić and the Institute for Philosophy and Social Theory in Belgrade; Sanja Bojanić and the Center for Advanced Studies of Southeastern Europe at the University of Rijeka; María José Gámez Fuentes and the University Jaume I in Castellón; Margarita Tsomou and the Kampnagel Internationales Sommerfestival in Hamburg; Yael Navaro-Yashin and Umut Yildirim for their panel 'The affects of displacement' at the 2011 American Anthropological Association meetings in Montreal. Fortunately, friends were there when institutions were short of supportive capability: Eleana Yalouri and Karl Strobl offered generous hospitality in London. I owe a felt debt to my friends and colleagues from the working group 'Rethinking vulnerability: Feminism and social change', directed by Judith Butler, at the Centre for the Study of Social Difference, Columbia University: Meltem Ahiska, Sarah Bracke, Elsa Dorlin, Başak Ertür, Zeynep Gambetti, Nacira Guénif-Souilamas, Rema Hammami, Marianne Hirsch, Elena Loizidou, Leticia Sabsay, Nükhet Sirman, and Elena Tzelepis. Our conversations and interactions have provided welcomed intellectual stimulation, which has allowed me to refine my arguments.

My colleagues at Panteion University and other academic institutions in Greece provided support for which I am most grateful. Among them I acknowledge Dimitra Gefou-Madianou, Gerasimos Makris, Eleni Papagaroufali, Giorgos Tsimouris, Eleana Yalouri, and all my colleagues at the Department of Social Anthropology at Panteion, who have helped create a lively academic environment in harsh circumstances. Eleni

Papagaroufali's steadfast support has been invaluable over the years and at key stages along the way. Special thanks to: Sia Anagnostopoulou, Grigoris Ananiadis, Aristide Antonas, Eirini Avramopoulou, Alexandra Bakalaki, Aristides Baltas, Dimitris Christopoulos, Kyrkos Doxiadis, Giorgos Fourtounis, Gerasimos Kakoliris, Mina Karavanta, Alexandros Kioupkiolis, Christina Koulouri, Gerasimos Kouzelis, Ioanna Laliotou, Antonis Liakos, Dimitra Makrinioti, Akis Papataxiarchis, Stefanos Pesmazoglou, Gina Politi, Evgenia Sifaki, Angeliki Spiropoulou, Michalis Spourdalakis, Yannis Stavrakakis, Triantafyllos Triantafyllidis, Fotini Tsimbiridou, Constantine Tsoukalas, Dina Vaiou, Lina Ventoura, and Vassiliki Yiakoumaki for longstanding friendship and intellectual companionship. Many thanks to my colleagues at the collective of the journal *Historein* for all the excitement of shared work and conviviality at earlier stages of this research. I thank Soula Marinoudi for her generous assistance in the transcriptions and Leandros Kyriakopoulos for the index. To the inquisitiveness and provocative questions of my undergraduate, graduate, and PhD students I owe the sheer joys of teaching, listening, and intellectual experimenting.

I am grateful to Edinburgh University Press editor Carol Macdonald for believing in this project and for steering it at every step. My sincere appreciation extends to the series editors Dimitris Vardoulakis and Peg Birmingham for their unstinting care with my work. I thank Ersev Ersoy for diligently working with me to prepare this manuscript, James Dale for seeing it through production, and Barbara Eastman for her skillful copy-editing.

I owe a great debt to Elena Tzelepis for the intellectual stimulation and thoughtful presence she dedicated to this book. Finally, to my family and (of) friends: Costas Athanasiou, Mikela Hartoulari, Anthi Veli, and Kika Haralambidou have provided me with consistent and tangible emotional support.

Introduction

Undoing Grief as 'Feminine Language'

In diverse responses to national, colonial, and postcolonial traumas of our times, the politics of mourning has always been premised upon gender, kinship, and national normativity. However, a troublesome displacement of the discursive genealogy of female mourning as a national and familial/maternal duty is enacted in the politics of the transnational feminist and antimilitaristic movement Women in Black. The group brings forth the political restlessness and promise at the heart of mourning those socially instituted as impossible to mourn within the biopolitical archives of territory, nation, and war. In the various places where they have staged actions, these activists set up networks of commemorative solidarity and camaraderie with the 'other' community, or the others of a fractured community, who have been officially turned into 'enemies' and violently disavowed as such. My question in this book is: How might mourning turn from a language of proper gendered and national identification into a disruptive performative catachresis expelled by and actively opposed to the very intelligibility of the political and its gendered, economic, ethnic, and racial configurations? And further, how does the radical mourning for the lost other engage the endless complexities and complicities that are inherent in the unequal relations of address-ability and response-ability?

Through an anthropological account of the urban feminist and antinationalist movement Women in Black of Belgrade (*Žene u Crnom* or *ŽuC*), I seek to explore how these activists open onto spaces for challenging conventional divisions between the affective and the political, between the political and the performative, as well as between body and language. In attending to the ways in which they cross and blur these borders, I am concerned with what the ambivalent affective politics of mourning does to the idealisation of national culture as a 'sanitized space of sentimental feeling' (Berlant and Warner 1998: 549), whereby national culture is taken to be a public affect of comfort and belonging, with all its ethnocentric, heteronormative, and familialist ramifications. This book traces how the practices of trans-border commemoration refigure and reactivate the political in the border regimes of military rule and ethno-national violence, as well as in post-war moral economies of 'transitional', transnational reconciliation. How might we account for the political performativity through which mourning turns from a universal(ising) trope of humanist metaphysics into a *dispositif* of a post-identity, post-humanist collective agonism within embattled contexts of transnational distribution of life and death? How could we capture the performative power implicit in processes of turning the impossibility of mourning into an incalculable and unquantifiable political potentiality that appropriates and, at once, deconstitutes its interpellating terms and contests state-nationalist authoritarianism? And, finally, what is the challenge that the critical methodology of this feminist political movement in post-Yugoslavia presents for the available theoretical and political vocabularies of agonism?

Countering the normative ideals of war sacrifice and national affinity that are founded upon kinship symbolics of blood, *ŽuC* enacts intimate assemblies and relational life-worlds that expose the foreclosures through which public affectivity is constituted. In the context of sanctioned narratives and memories of the disintegration of socialist Yugoslavia and its aftermath, they staged vigils for unqualifiable losses, creating critical spaces for responsiveness and dissent – or responsiveness *as* dissent. They gave and continue to give space for what leaks out of the cracks of the authoritative engine of national memory and might be transformed into a means of dissent and protest. Their mode of protest is about accounting for loss – loss of others, real and imagined communities, sense of belonging in the world – that haunts the common intelligibility of memorable life. At the same time, their protest is about responding to those irrecoverable and irreconcilable losses through reckoning the unequal conditions of grievability and the impossibility of taking the lost or traumatised other within oneself.

How to mourn impossibly, then? And what to do politically through the possibility of impossible mourning? For Jacques Derrida, it is only through the impossibility to mourn that one can possibly engage with the dead other. But it is precisely through this aporia that he unsettles the logic of possible/impossible. He has suggested that 'impossible mourning' is marked by 'cryptic incorporation' (1986: xxi), whereby the dead remain discretely incorporated, entombed within the spirits of the living and, at the same time, they remain encrypted, irrecoverable, and untranslatable, as the 'otherness of the other' person resists the available means and processes of representation in mourning. And so it is a matter of responsibility towards the other to respect this resistance (1989). Derrida has notably addressed the double bind inherent in the work of remembering the dead other, as the mourner carries the dead within her or himself while at the same time recognising that the dead person was someone else – indeterminate and uncontainable. So, the work of mourning – or the putting of mourning to work – emerges as a question of how 'to leave the dead alone' without 'abandoning' them: 'a double injunction, then, contradictory and unforgiving' (Derrida 2001: 225). Given that this insight raises an issue at the centre of this book, I want to extend it by asking how this double bind is embodied in the feminist politics of dissident mourning under circumstances of sovereign regulation of otherness. My interest is in considering how contingent and unfinished histories of recounting, witnessing, and mourning are implicated in the gendered, colonial, postcolonial, national and racialised configurations of sovereign violence. Above all, it is my aim to track the troubled political performativity that re-appropriates the discursive formation of mourning and memory in order to turn it into a site of agonistic contestation. The feminist collectivity I worked with performs trans-border affectivity in the face of ethnic and gendered foreclosures that 'have made certain kinds of losses ungrievable' (Butler 1997a: 185). And so I take up Derrida's work on the impossible work of mourning along with Judith Butler's problematic of mourning as a layered figure of political catachresis critically engaging with the hierarchies of grievability (2000), in order to consider mourning-work as both foreclosed and open to political potential. Drawing on Butler's work on the exclusive intelligibility of the memorable, this study seeks to illustrate how the political subjectivity of *ŽuC* turns grief, in its involutions and alterities, into a performative resource for a politics of dissent. Considering the forces of unavowability that foreclose and sustain the work of mourning, it grapples with the ways these activists attend to the aporias – or the lack of clear and open passages that gives rise to other passages – of mourning to displace the sovereign impassibility of the border.

Biopolitics, Sovereignty, Nationalism

In the context of the wars in the former Yugoslavia and their aftermath, *ŽuC* has been concerned with the forces of nationalist sovereignty, which have conjured a biopolitical economy of enmity to create ethnically homogeneous populations and territories. The collective has been specifically intervening in this biopolitical production of modes of subjection and realms of disposability. The disposable subdivision of inhumanity, with all its racial, ethnic, and gender inflections, has been figured by the disregarded, abjected, wounded, or erased body of the 'inappropriate other' (Trinh 1986–7) – the one belonging to the other community, declared as 'enemy', and construed as absolute, mortal danger. The conjunction of biopolitics and sovereignty is crucial here in its relevance to the question of war, as the purpose of power is to inscribe war 'in the bodies themselves of each and everyone of us' (Foucault 1980: 90). So, to use Foucault's terms, especially in his more refined analysis in the series of lectures entitled *Society Must be Defended* (2003a), sovereign power does not vanish with the 'advent' of biopolitics, although it tends to lose its ceremonial and phantasmagoric aura in favour of its integration into the fabric of social norms, managerial tactics, and subjectifying processes. As I will further elaborate in the chapters of this book, the purpose of biopolitics to 'make live', that is, to preserve life, necessarily involves the violence of 'letting die' (typically associated with the juridical function of sovereignty), which is exercised on specific, dangerous, and disposable elements either inside or outside the national population; at the same time, the unaccountable injunction of sovereign power to take life does not dissolve entirely into sites of normalising power, but rather its fatal self-referentiality and self-justification persists as it is performatively re-inscribed and re-articulated in intense governmental concerns with the regulation of the national population's biological survival and reproductive capacity (Butler 2004; Derrida 2005a; Kelly 2004; Rose and Rabinow 2006; Stoler 1995; Vardoulakis 2013).

While the time of sovereignty may have 'passed', by the problematic standards of a single, universal, and epoch-centred periodisation, it is precisely through this genealogy of fading out that it endures in 'administering' life and producing subjects and power effects in national and transnational contexts. Wendy Brown has notably indicated that practices of sovereign border-work thrive in our 'post-Westphalian' times, as barriers marking national boundaries are raised to wall out such pariahs as asylum seekers, refugees, and economic migrants; these walls, however, are markers of receding sovereignty (2010). At the same time, the waning of the modernist conceit of sovereignty does not amount to the disappearance of sovereign power, but rather elicits 'openly and aggressively rather than passively theological' responses (2010: 62). Indeed, the theological premise of political sovereignty is fundamental to the compensatory practices of barricading and circumvallation. Contemporary desire for walling involves a contradiction between the inefficiency of walls to secure borders and their efficiency in subjectifying through the fantasy of impermeable state sovereignty. So the question, for us here, becomes not so much whether or not sovereignty 'works' but how it does things precisely by not working 'properly', or by (un)working differently and differentially; how the phantasmatic fading out or shiftiness of sovereignty becomes the occasion for a further and subtler elaboration of power, powerlessness, and subjectivation.

In *Society Must be Defended* (2003a), Michel Foucault has addressed the intertwined emergence and genealogy of sovereignty and nationhood. More specifically, he has focused on the ways in which sovereign power and biopower become mutually implicated in the demarcation, preservation, and securitisation of a national population, in a process profoundly marked by the historico-political discourses of race. Modern state racism affects the ways in which wars take place and are legitimised, as

> wars are no longer waged in the name of a sovereign who must be defended; they are waged on behalf of the existence of everyone; entire populations are mobilized for the purpose of wholesale slaughter in the name of life necessity: massacres have become vital. (Foucault 1981: 137)

In effect, as power is exercised at the level and in the name of population, race, and life (ibid.), wars are waged so that the life necessity (of some) can be safeguarded. Modern power determines which lives and ways of life are to be saved and which ones will be left to die.

Reading the 'animated traces' of sovereignty in realms of advanced liberal state power through Foucault's claim that 'the end of sovereignty is circular: the end of sovereignty is the exercise of sovereignty' (1991: 95), Judith Butler offers a nuanced account of power that addresses the production of sovereignty as an effect of the suspension of the rule of law. She writes: 'Sovereignty becomes that instrument of power by which law is either used tactically or suspended, populations are monitored, detained, regulated, inspected, interrogated, rendered uniform in their actions, fully ritualized and exposed to control and regulation in their daily lives' (2004: 97). As sovereignty comes to be resurfaced and reanimated in the field of governmental management of populations 'with the vengeance of an anachronism that refuses to die' (Butler 2004: 54), Butler adds crucially, 'it seems important to recognize that one way of "managing" a population is to constitute them as the less than human without entitlement to rights, as the humanly unrecognizable' (2004: 98). What this suggests is that the power of managing populations sets the formative and also differential and deforming tenets of human intelligibility in ways that cannot be subsumed under a clear-cut distinction between a restrictive/juridical and a productive/discursive modality of power. Therefore, 'juridical power is a kind of dissimulated or concealed productive power from the start', and 'the shift, the inversion, is within power, not between two historically or logically distinct forms of power' (Butler 1996: 65). Butler explains that Foucault's distinction between sovereignty and governmentality is analytic rather than temporal: it is through this possibility of convergence that she analyses the anachronism of sovereignty's resurrection within the managerial field of governmentality: 'governmentality is the condition of this new exercise of sovereignty in the sense that it first establishes law as a "tactic" something of instrumental value, and not "binding" by virtue of its status as law' (2004: 62). In this sense, normalising productive power does not offer a safe refuge from thanatopolitical power. In Butler's words, again: 'The technological aim to preserve life, then, becomes the silent sanction by which this dissimulated killing silently proceeds' (1996: 74).[1]

Following Butler's idea of 'spectral sovereignty' (2004: 61), then, for me the question concerns the ways in which sovereign power 'silently proceeds' and operates productively and differentially as biopower, demarcating liveable life and rendering thanatopolitics 'vital' (in Foucault's terms) through gendered, sexualised, ethnic and racial frames, in contemporary international frameworks of nationalist conflict, imperialist intervention, and unequal distribution of recognisability. In a context of surging nationalisms and imperialist arbitration, warring parts of Yugoslavia were exchanging aggressive representational strategies, which evoked the category of 'enemy' cast as the invading force of evil. This matrix of enmity, enfleshed in forming and differentiating disposable bodies and thus determining who must live and who must die, echoes Achille Mbembe's work on 'necropolitics', where he asks: 'What place is given to life, death, and the human body (in particular the wounded and slain body)? How are they inscribed in the order of power?' (2003: 12). *Jus ad bellum*, the possibility (and prerogative) of waging war against those cast as enemies, is a key means of animating and performing sovereignty, in all its spectral yet carnal dimensions: 'War, after all, is as much a means of achieving sovereignty as a way of exercising the right to kill', as Mbembe aptly puts it (2003: 12). Pondering late-modern colonial occupation through Foucault's account of the calculus of biopower and its reliance on the technology of race and racism, he insists, with Giorgio Agamben (1998), on the irrevocable coextensiveness of sovereignty and exposure to death: death establishes the normative basis of sovereignty, which denotes 'the capacity to define who matters and who does not, who is *disposable* and who is not' (Mbembe 2003: 27). The political activism at hand evinces a preoccupation with contemporary regimes of sovereignty in its intimate relationship to governmentality, whereby what is at stake is the biopolitical regulation and management of life and death both in contexts of national culture and in those marked by a presumed declining hegemony of the project of nationhood (Rose 2001).[2]

Here I am concerned more specifically, however, with the possibility of contesting the power assemblage of sovereignty, biopolitics, and nationalism. Even more explicitly, the aim is to illustrate the gendered aspect of the biopolitical tenet of power's involving the production and description of intelligible bodies of those subjected to it and subjectified by it. Thus, the focus is on the ways in which political subjects 'women', historically subjected as such through the body and its discursive demands, come to embody disruptively the thoroughgoing power assemblage of sovereignty, biopolitics and nationalism, and, along with it, the monolithic, normative matrices of gender and sex. The collective subjectivity of Women in Black, ŽuC in post-Yugoslavia, enacts the agonistic possibility of post-nationalist and counter-nationalist modes of belonging (Butler in Butler and Spivak 2011), in coming to be formed and performed through embodied practices of resignifying the gendered and nationalised sign of public mourning, and mobilising it for purposes radically different from its authorised originary framework. Belonging, in all its national and gendered preconditions, is thus displaced; in effect, it is performed as displaceable. The political subjects with whom I worked use mourning as a means to acknowledge inconvenient plurality as opposed to absolutist homogeneity; to publicly acknowledge the disposable victims of the 'other side', those marked as abject and dehumanised ethnic enemy, instead of solely those of 'their own side':

> Women wear black in our countries to show the grief for death of the loved ones. We wear black for the death of all the victims of the war. We wear black because people have been thrown out of their homes, because women have been raped, because cities and villages have been burnt and destroyed. (Women in Black statement, 10 June 1992, cited in Mladjenović and Hughes 2001)

Especially during the preparations for the Yugoslav wars (1991–9) that entailed the breakup of the country, the *ŽuC* radical re-inscription of mourning was a timely and de-authorising response to the avalanche of media images of grieving women at historical as well as contemporary graveyards, and the manipulation of these representational strategies to call for reparation for the sake of the nation (Slapšak 2002: 155). That popular imagery of feminised, idealised mourning was indicative of the ways in which nationalism is produced and staged through sentimental narratives of loss and mourning. Nationalism is rendered visible, imaginable, and indeed desirable, through a melodramatic language of victimisation, in its metonymic association with the biopolitics of nationalised and normalised femininity-in-mourning. Against this backdrop of intensified 'national sentimentality', in Berlant's terms (1997), which in my context is emblematised by mourning mothers as the *par excellence* traumatised national subjects, ŽuC feminist anti-war activism creates an affective scene for a counterintuitive political culture of responding to trauma beyond and against its gendered and ethno-national foreclosures. While ŽuC recalls essentialising and normalising codes of grief, theirs is not the mourning prescribed by authorised national narratives; in contrast, their mourning is situated in opposition to the militaristic death-culture, or what ŽuC activist Staša Zajović identifies as the 'cult of necrophilia (expressed in slogans such as 'the frontiers of Serbia are where Serbs are buried')' (1993: 26). ŽuC upsets the grounds of mourning as a founding scene of feminine qua maternal properness in nationalism. Adriana Zaharijević, who joined ŽuC after the war and is today a scholar of philosophy at the University of Belgrade, addressed the subversive force of this performative mourning thus:

> ŽuC mourning is subversive. The public standing in the centre of the city offers an alternative meaning to the black colour and, in fact, the act of mourning itself. Yes, women wear black when they mourn. But ŽuC activists mourn otherwise. Conventional mourning is done with crying, it has to be heard. In the way of ŽuC, however, activists (women but also men, as in ŽuC there have always been men too) are standing without weeping, just standing in silence. They are standing not shouting destructive slogans or saying 'give us back our sons'. Perhaps this happens because many ŽuC women are not mothers themselves or, if they are, they do not put particular emphasis on motherhood. Quite the contrary, we have to critically rethink motherhood and so desist from thinking motherhood in nationalistic terms.

For Adriana, *ŽuC* mourning is performatively subversive in its dislodging the discursive premises of public grief and grievability. It 'mourns otherwise', as she puts it. As much as mourning conveys a concern with intimacy, it can also work to prevent one from acknowledging the grief of another through hierarchical identifications that regulate the matrix of the memorable and circumscribe its scope of intimacy. It is because of this circumscribed intimacy of grievability, in Judith Butler's terms, that mourning is one of the most fetishised modalities of intimate sociality for all patriotisms and familialisms. Being anchored in interconnecting grids of gender, kinship, and nation–state normativity, the 'hierarchy of grief' entails the possibility of war (Butler 2004: 32). In exposing such conflictual articulations and exclusionary norms, these activists embody a radical stance toward memory that cannot be reduced to literal or figurative practices of digging up the past and burying or exhuming the dead. There is more to their practices than remembering those officially expunged from the homeland of memorability – not only 'their' dead but also the dead of the 'other side'. They also seek to displace and actively remake the biopolitical norms that regulate which bodies, subjects, and collectivities are admissible to established spaces of intelligibility, including the space of political subjectivity and public protest. Hence, far from signalling a retreat from politics, these subjects come collectively into play in animating the possibility for an experience of the political as agonism (Honig 2013; Mouffe 2000; also Crimp 1989, 2004). In so doing, they challenge conventional liberal sensibilities of politics (Cvetkovich 2003; Mahmood 2005).

From this perspective, the core theoretical question of this book is about agonistic grievability as performed through the strategies of feminists who enact grief and memory despite and against the biopolitics of warfare and its concomitant interpellating lines of heteronormative bloodline kinship and militarist national sovereignty. How should we tackle the *ŽuC* engagement with a politics of contested grievability as a dissident politics of the present, then? And how might we understand their desire for the political as a means to refiguring political life beyond sovereign accounts of subjectivity and agency?

Clearly, such questions pertaining to the interrelation of mourning and becoming other have emerged in the context of different renditions of 'activism of mourning', that is, public and collective enactments by which trauma is addressed in all its affective, social, and political dimensions. The ways in which AIDS activism in the 1980s conjured the inscriptional space of mourning – that is, the AIDS Memorial Quilt and 'die-ins' in major places of public administration – have brought into relief the forms of trauma generated by the social death of homophobia, thereby forging not only a collective recognition but also affective networks of camaraderie built on a queer archive of testimony. Such antinormative enactments of mourning have called into question the identification of mourning with political inertia in the wake of losing a public language to mourn and in the face of political, social, and psychic preclusions that regulate the space and time of the memorable. Douglas Crimp has exemplified the political urgency of understanding how and why gay people's grief is rendered unrecognisable (1989). Arguably, *ŽuC* partakes in this fraught genealogy of political enactments of mourning, whereby public grief emerges as a performative practice of protest with intense, albeit ambivalent, sensuous suggestiveness (Butler 1997a; Crimp 2004; Edelman 2004; Eng and Kazanjian 2003; Sosa 2011, 2014; Taylor 1997).

I argue throughout this book that the *ŽuC* agonistic reappropriation of displaced mourning, which remains excessive to its formal limits and normative preconditions, exposes the biopolitical limits of official commemoration and thus potentially reconfigures the conditions of in/justice from the vantage point of affecting, and being affected by, others. A performative poetics of responsiveness is at work as these feminists refuse the post-war closure of mourning and keep it open to the contingency of a different future. This performative modality of counter-memory is probably the only place where mourning is not 'at home'. It forms a scene of address not subsumed under the naturalising hold of the familiar and the familial. In figuring what Ann Cvetkovich calls the 'affective life of politics' (2003), this is about performing mourning without mourning. Ultimately, this, I would venture, is about a performative and transformative engagement with the political, which induces other presents and futures by rendering possible what it simultaneously crosses out.

Researching the Affective Life of a Political Subjectivity

Why do loss and mourning matter politically, after all? How might working on the register of uneven grievability attend to the experience of becoming a political subject engaged in pursuits of critical agency? And how does one research such political subjectivity of dissident feminist mourning with respect to national and transnational structures of recognisability? It is in considering these overarching questions that I ponder, propelled and compelled by my ethnographic material, what it means to act politically in performing a mode of non-sovereign, agonistic subjectivity in opposition and resistance to the logics of coercion, abjection, racism, and militarism. However, let me make clear from the start that the notion of non-sovereign subjectivity I seek to elaborate here, while clearly involving the modalities of mutual susceptibility and vulnerability, does not refer to a subjectivity identifying with, or reduced to, suffering and destitution. Nor should it be equated to self-negation, although it decisively relies on relationality and it questions the liberal devices of individual, unilateral selfhood. Rather, in the context at hand, it indicates a performative mode of subjectivation which is always already intersubjective (see also Ziarek 2013).

Although my point is indeed to remain critical of self-sufficient unity, indivisible oneness, and absolute self-authorisation, qualities in which the 'ontotheology of sovereignty'[3] is anchored, I certainly do not mean to do away with all sovereignty *tout court*, especially insofar as it is tied to collective claims of popular sovereignty and courageous, revolutionary struggles of self-determination. The perspective I am offering here might enjoin us to re-inscribe self-determination as determination by and with the other, as an interminable and indeterminate finding of oneself with/in the other. So my point is to ask how we might think of sovereignty differently: namely, alongside the intricacies of finitude. The notion of finitude enables us to do so, and, as I argue here, in ways that open (rather than close) the space of the political. That said, the performative point of my critique is to call for a concept of political subjectivity and the political in general, one which would require a troubled notion of top-down sovereignty, or, put differently, which may generate trouble in sovereignty. Such trouble in sovereignty foregrounds a subject of agonistic politics that always remains to come.

The trouble in sovereignty – as a central category of modern political thought – has been efficiently occasioned by various strands of critical theory. Hannah Arendt, for one, has evoked a non-sovereign classical form of politics as well as non-sovereign quality of freedom. Sovereignty, conceived as a politically pernicious force of 'self-sufficiency and mastership' that is contradictory to plurality (1998: 234), undercuts a public-political realm and functions through mechanisms of exclusion and containment.[4] Derrida shares with Arendt the attempt to get away from a thinking that reduces the political to the assumptions and principles of sovereignty. If Arendt turns toward classical, pre-sovereign forms of politics to evoke a non-sovereignty that would designate a plurality acting in concert, Derrida enquires into the political future of democracy as always deferred and yet presents iterative and disruptive potential in the here and now (1994, 2005a). In examining the history of the concept of sovereignty in its inseparable but contradictory relation to democracy, he delineates it as a form of power which is situated above the law and which decides on what is 'proper' for the established and fixed category of 'human'. In this context, 'non-sovereignty' defines the impossible – albeit transformative – possibility for democracy without sovereignty, or *démocratie à-venir* ('democracy to come') (1994, 2005a).[5] As an alternative order of politics, Derrida considers the possibility of a 'vulnerable non-sovereignty' (2005a: 157). Nevertheless, he acknowledges, not without certain ambivalence, that, although sovereign power is undemocratic, it is unavoidable for even democratic governance, and that 'the *cracy* of the demos' is required 'for democracy to be effective' (2005a: 100). But might democracy be ever 'effective' without accounting to a horizon of the possibility for a 'vulnerable non-sovereignty'? To pose the question of how not to succumb to the lure of the sovereign logic of power and politics does not seek to lay claim to a perfectly pure, uncompromising, and indivisible non-sovereignty. To be sure, that would arguably replicate the logic of sovereignty. Rather, the point is, I would submit, to generate idioms of *actual* responsiveness to the horizon of 'vulnerable non-sovereignty', as the performative force that allows democracy to take place. In registering a restless ambivalence vis-à-vis sovereignty, which is consonant with Arendt's own ambivalent attitude, Derrida has notably argued that:

In a certain sense, there is no contrary of sovereignty, even if there are things other than sovereignty. Even in politics (and

the question remains of knowing if the concept of sovereignty
is political through and through) the choice is not between
sovereignty and non-sovereignty, but among several forms of
partings, partitions, divisions, conditions that come along to
breach a sovereignty that is always supposed to be indivisible
and unconditional. (2009: 115)[6]

I bring up Derrida's analysis because it seeks to call into question
the logic of sovereignty without formulating a sovereign fiction
of pure, auto-affective, and unconditional non-sovereignty,
or, in his words, 'without ending up with a depoliticization, a
neutralization of the political . . . but an other politicization, a
re-politicization and therefore another concept of the political'
(2009: 75). The possibility of undoing the unitary and absolute
logic of sovereignty articulates an undecidable but necessary
possibility of imagining and devising a democratic politics not
determined by sovereignty.

In thinking of democracy in agonistic terms and as being
involved in a struggle with sovereignty and its structural violence, Dimitris Vardoulakis probes into the question of whether
it is possible to conceive of a space that is distinct from, or not
encompassed under, sovereignty. The arising conundrum is akin
to what he calls 'the ruse of sovereignty', whereby the challenge to sovereign power works to reanimate the mechanism of
exclusion and thus to affirm sovereignty (2017). Is it possible,
then, to provide an alternative account of political agonism, one
that would desist from taking sovereignty as an absolute presupposition for politics without reverting to the metaphysics of
a pure space outside sovereignty? And, in more grounded terms,
is it possible to resist the logic and the imaginary of sovereignty
without reaffirming the 'ruse of sovereignty'?

Although sovereignty is not immune to critique and
resistance, it resists its resistances. It can work best through its apparent failings. Either as indivisible and invulnerable self-mastery

of the subject or as an autarchic modality of power, sovereignty makes difference and sharing impossible. Or, to put it in the terms of my interlocutors, sovereignty renders itself beyond any accountability to the other. And yet, as the political subjects of this study have shown, sovereignty is not invulnerable but instead is a site of polyvalent performative forces, challenges, and critical embodiments. One cannot simply oppose or overcome all sovereignty and sovereignty in general, however (Derrida 2005a: 158). In her reading of Arendt and Derrida's accounts of political authority and resistibility, Honig has put it aptly:

> Like her [Arendt], he [Derrida] refuses to allow the law of laws to be put, unproblematically, *above* man, but he recognizes, more deeply than does Arendt, that the law will always resist his resistance. His unwillingness to passively accept that is a commitment to politicization, resistibility, and intervention. (1993: 110)[7]

In this vein, and in an attempt not to overcome sovereignty but rather to decentre its ever-shifting logic as a perennial and inevitable arbiter of the political, what I am looking for is not a metaphysics of the outside and the beyond, which would be exemplified in an idea of pure non-sovereignty, either pre-sovereign or post-sovereign. Rather, what motivates me is an interminable demand not to succumb to the self-authorising, self-mystifying logic of sovereignty as the only possible form of, and normal basis for, (the subject of) politics. Thus, in addressing the commemorative agonism of the activists with whom I worked, I seek to account for the possibility of non-sovereign political agency (Mahmood 2005; Markell 2003; Zerilli 2005): a notion of agency that is not bound to an antecedent sovereign self, not attributable and not reducible to the individual's internal possession. Instead, it remains immanent to power, socially involved, formed and compromised. It is at once finite and contingent, potent and vulnerable, powerful and destituted of its sovereign status: a sovereignty without sovereignty. Occasionally, it becomes other than sovereignty, distinct but not 'liberated' from it, even taking the risk of re-inscribing its logic by engaging with it, and even resisting it. Such political vision of agency resonates with what Butler calls 'dissent' when she suggests that the thought of dissent might be considered 'the inverse of the thought of sovereignty' (2009: 793). As I will elaborate in subsequent chapters, dissent, construed as a way of 'elaborating a certain exercise of freedom' (Butler 2009: 791) through objecting to existing authoritative constructions of intelligibility, is crucial to how *ŽuC* activists perform their non-sovereign agonism.

From the perspective of the political subjects with whom I worked, who engage with sovereign authority in advancing non-sovereign political ways, freedom is not defined in terms of self-mastery and sovereign will, but rather as enactment of plurality and relationality outside oneself and along with others in the public space (Butler 2011; Nancy 1994). It is from this perspective that I ask here whether and how sovereignty might be rethought and re-politicised in light of collective claims of political self-determination and freedom. On this register of analysis, freedom is precisely what 'throws the subject into the space of the sharing of being. Freedom is the specific logic of the access to the self outside of itself . . .' (Nancy 1994: 70). How is one to think the political, then, beyond the logic of mastery (Derrida 2005a; Nancy 1994) and through the principle of becoming outside oneself and for one another, while affirming the agonistic at every turn? What transformative imaginaries of the political would be prompted by the irreducible plurality of non-sovereign dispositions as they transpire in the 'agonistic *topos*' (Taxidou 2004: 8) of mourning? I pursue such framing questions in the present volume through the perspective of feminist anti-war collective standing within and against the contexts of nationalism and war in the former Yugoslavia: a war which rested upon intertwined gendered, sexualised, and ethnicised domains of sovereignty (Žarkov 2007).

This book is an anthropological account of a feminist political collectivity, which seeks to recuperate the political from the organising principle of sovereignty. It takes glimpses within, and strives to make sense of, the affective lives and powers of political activism, as they transform the world by engaging with but not being totalised by sovereign authority. In conducting fieldwork with the *ŽuC* in Belgrade, I became deeply concerned with and enmeshed in their lived experiences, practices of subjectivation, ideas of collective action, lines of allegiance, folds of political imagination, routes and bonds of comradeship. I was moved and motivated to consider how their activist work, as a feminist response to political war cultures, re-inscribes the eventualities of political trauma and trauma politics. The subjects of this study become outside themselves: both in the sense of being exposed to another and in the sense of dispositions implicated in dissent, such as political grief and passion (Butler 2004: 24). I am interested in bringing a conception of the subject as ek-static and dispossessed to bear on the constitution of activist political subjectivity, a figure typically understood through the apparatus of self-contained sovereign subject and with masculinist undertones. It is this affective register of becoming and embodying 'beside oneself', in Butler's terms, that redirects the logic of sovereign authority and sets the scene for the *ŽuC* cross-border affective work: their commemoration of the annihilated victims of the 'other side', their ongoing relation with the displaced people, their acts of camaraderie, and their alliance with the 'enemy' community.

My research does not by any means account for the whole scene of anti-war collectivities in what became the former Yugoslavia. This book draws its material from fieldwork I conducted with the *ŽuC* movement since my initial short stay in Belgrade in the spring of 2005 until 2012. After our first encounter in person in May 2005, I met again members of *ŽuC* in Jerusalem, where we had gone to attend an international conference of Women in Black, in August 2005. At an outdoor terrace located on the Mount of Olives overlooking Jerusalem, where the workshops were held under a canopy on those hot days of August, I had the chance to spend some time with Staša Zajović, Lepa Mlađenović, and other members of the *ŽuC* movement. We marched together through the streets of Bil'in in protest against the construction of the Separation Wall, we were on the same bus going to Ramallah, and we stood together in protest against militarisation, singing *the Internationale*, at the notorious checkpoint of Qalandia. Amidst workshops, bus journeys to the West Bank, and anti-occupation demonstrations at military checkpoints, we talked about anti-war feminist activism in the former Yugoslavia and we promised to keep in touch.

Although I was already aware of their feminist political interventions in the violent breakup of Yugoslavia, I remember being especially 'touched' by that encounter of ours in Jerusalem. For me, their political claims and theorising, but perhaps especially their foregrounding of a particular sentient and bodily modality of dissent, portended unexpected and compelling perspectives on some of the key questions that occupy current feminist and left-wing political movements, as well as various strands in social and political theory. I was interested in the ways in which their account of political organisation and self-determination did not seem to presuppose, but rather to decentre the regulatory identifications and representational politics that typically sustain conceptions of political agency. I was also intrigued by the key themes that constitute the distinctive 'trademarks' of their political work: responsiveness, cross-border acts of grief, and becoming the enemy in the face of national mobilisation.

Although I was deeply affected by their passionate political commitment, and I was certainly able to connect with them through the conduits of my own feminist history, it was, however, also a stimulating sense of challenge that inspired my eagerness to engage anthropologically with the political movement. The outset of this project had found me in the aftermath of health woes, while its concluding phase found me enmeshed in the quotidian anxieties precipitated by global neoliberal capital in the form of a fierce economic crisis, a context also marked by newly devised pursuits of collectivity and dissent. And so I posed for myself the question of why and how the crises in which we find ourselves make us strive to get hold of alternative temporalities. Ultimately, this question proved to be my modest –and rather hopeful – point of entry into an affective politics of revolutionary melancholia that, escaping standard conceptions of both 'revolutionary' and 'melancholia' but also countering Freud's rendition of melancholia as a mode of 'pathological mourning',[8] encapsulates a long-standing, passionate refusal to conform to the existing order of things; it indicates continuous, open-ended engagement with loss and its enduring resources for political action. Thus, I seek here to foreground a specific aspect of the critical agency at hand: namely, the affective intensities and urgencies – such as anxieties and desires – involved in the transvaluation of the socially and politically afflicted injuries into revolutionary possibilities.

Ever since our initial encounter in Palestine, I have visited Belgrade often. I undertook intensive, long-term field research in 2010, when I got involved in the *ŽuC* actions in a more systematic way. Since that extended stay, I have conducted several follow-up research visits and maintained regular communication through email and mutual visits with some of my interlocutors. I have interacted with *ŽuC* activists in various forms and in multifaceted intersecting occasions: intellectual work, street actions, and everyday sociality. In the course of my fieldwork, I attended and actively participated in gatherings, events, street actions, campaigns, and workshops. I followed the traces of their horizontal self-organisation and connectivity, within a network composed of local groups in Serbia and other former Yugoslav republics, as they were animated by strategies of collaboration and translation. We travelled together to attend workshops and events held in several places in Serbia. I spent time with them at the *ŽuC* office premises, located at the Green Market area in Old Belgrade. This apartment is the hub of the group's activist life, where public actions are planned, meetings and workshops are held, visitors and long-distance members of the group are received, and transnational communication is carried out. I have also cherished the time following planned events, when we engaged in more relaxed and intimate conversations, often over *rakija*, or when a heated political discussion would give its place to articulations that escaped the formal linearity of a narrative and occasionally led to the singing of antifascist Yugoslav songs. Those spontaneous and momentary gatherings created the critical space for lived and imagined worldscapes, stories, insights, reflective attachments, humour, affirmation, mutual inspiration, tensions, and intensities to emerge and indicate, sometimes fleetingly, multilayered histories of entwined affective bonds and political commitment. I listened to the stories my friends wanted to tell and I acknowledged the silences that often punctuated those narrations, but I deliberately tried to resist being another person who asks them to 'share their war story'. Just being with them, travelling with them to places, participating in street actions, and sharing palpable and ephemeral spaces of the 'ordinary' offered me valuable resources for grasping the affective nuance of their activist life.[9]

In talking with me, in open-ended interviews, oral histories but also informal conversations, my interlocutors often addressed the iniquities of war and post-war nationalism, but they also stressed, almost unanimously, the affirmative and redemptive impact that their activist engagement and camaraderie had on their lives; the steadfast sustenance they found in one another and in their collectivity. Thus, I became interested in exploring not only the articulation of trauma in and through activism in the wake of normalised political violence, but also the emotional intensities – that is, commitment, hope, exhaustion and endurance – involved in the actual labour of political involvement. In tackling the mutual complicity of trauma and activism, I take inspiration from Ann Cvetkovich's (2003) ethnographic archive of interviews with lesbian activists who worked with ACT UP/ New York during the late 1980s and early 1990s. Although at the outset of her research she sought to attend to the traumatic component of activism itself, because of the emotional intensities and disappointments that usually come with it retroactively, the oral histories of her interlocutors challenged this idea and revealed the ways in which their enduring attachments to such emotional intensities had generated affective spaces for sustaining activist involvement.

Most of my interlocutors belonged to the urban educated classes and they came from various socio-economic backgrounds. Many were veterans of left-wing Yugoslav dissidence, and all of them identified as antifascists. Some were brought up in families that had resisted fascism and shared with me stories about partisan mothers, grandmothers, and others who had fought – for 'their country' – with the Antifascist Front of Women (*Antifašistički Front Žena*, AFŽ), an anti-Nazi resistance movement that was founded in 1942. The legacy of women's participation in the antifascist Resistance and female partisan fighters' (*partizanke*) contribution to the political freedom of women (especially given that their memory was eclipsed during the era of socialism) seemed to signal my interlocutors' passionate feminist and antifascist commitment as constituting a crucial component of their own political subjectivity and history.

The activists with whom I worked came from Serbian and ethnically mixed backgrounds. Yet, they resist being identified as Serbs (*Srpkinje*), an ethno-national identification that had long become, for them, a synonym of nationalism and war culture, which have sedimented in their lives and relations. Thus, activism is, for them, a way of *unbecoming* (national) subjects. Most of them consider themselves 'nationless' and did not claim any particular nationality precisely because of the violences and exclusions through which the authorised categories of national self-identification had been consolidated. Others look to locate themselves in the rifts of reified and routinised regimes of identification. In responding to my question once whether she misses Yugoslavia, Slavica replied affirmatively:

> If there is any kind of human need to feel close to a country, this is not so much a question of belonging but of being able to say I am from there. Yes, I love that country, I would spontaneously identify it as my country. But I don't need that any more. And I didn't want to pay any price to the war. Now, when someone provokes me, I say 'I am from Yugoslavia. I was born in Socialist Federal Republic of Yugoslavia.' I don't give up Yugoslavia. When I want to avoid saying 'I am from Serbia', I say 'I am from Belgrade.' Žarana Papić used to say 'I am from Vojvodina', she had this idea of local, regional identity. Or, she would say 'I am a sociologist.'

Slavica referred to the ways in which herself but also her late friend Žarana Papić (1949–2002), a Sarajevo-born pioneering figure of the feminist movement in Yugoslavia and founding member of the Belgrade Women's Studies Center, deployed strategies of national self-disidentification in terms of giving up and not giving up the available categories of national self-identification.

Their own sense of the world, and sense of sharing a world, involves critically re-appropriating Yugoslavia while casting off from the 'common sense' of unequivocal national belonging.

Such categories of self-identification arose as volatile objects of suspension in my conversation with Fika Filipović, a *ŽuC* activist in her eighties. As much as ethnic attachments became reordered and reoriented in her storytelling, *ŽuC* emerged consistently in our conversation as an anchoring point for her. 'The fact that I was from Bosnia played a role in my decision to join *ŽuC* and in my loyal openness to their commitments', she recounted, and added: 'They gave me air to breathe.' Indeed, one can feel this fresh air in looking at the famous photograph of her holding a huge rainbow flag, which has become iconic of *ŽuC* street politics. Relishing Fika's generous hospitality at her home once, I was also offered the chance to follow her hearty narrations through different sites, temporalities, identities, and displacements. She seemed to find keen joy in talking about her participation in the 2007 calendar of the queer collectivity 'Queeria' (*Kvirija*). The edition was called 'Friends' (*Prijatelji*) and featured images of activists from different antiracist groups. 'I am very proud of this photo', she said, as I was admiring her remarkable calendar portrait on the wall, depicting her dressed up in lively colours, as 'July' – admittedly a stark contrast to her usual activist black attire of the demonstrations. Fika was born in Mostar and she became a *ŽuC* activist in 1994, during a *ŽuC* demonstration for Sarajevo. As she was sitting on a bench in Belgrade's Republic Square, she noticed a group of women wearing black, standing in silence, and holding banners calling for solidarity with people in Bosnia. She approached them and decided instantly to join the assembly, at the beginning as a gesture of solidarity to her childhood town – she had just learned from an Italian channel about the bombing of the Mostar bridge. She has stayed with the movement ever since.

Also from Bosnia, from Banja Luka, Zinaida Marjanović moved to Belgrade over ten years before the war. She identifies as 'a Bosnian who lives in Serbia', in an ethnically mixed marriage. She recounted Yugoslavia's breakup as a critical event of loss in the history of her and her family:

> Yugoslavia's falling apart has been costing me till now. It felt as though everything fell apart. Especially because we used to live in Bosnia all together. But, due to the war, I should now be one thing and my kids should be another. I don't know what exactly my husband is supposed to be. We were all Yugoslavs once and before the war I used to declare myself as such. But now we have been put in a position where we should declare our nationality. What is more, we are compelled to declare nationality with reference to religion. Although I do not admit it yet, I am now living in three states: in Bosnia, in Croatia and here.

At another point of our conversation, she added: 'I miss Yugoslavia. After the war, I cried everywhere I would go. I miss it and cannot stand all these borders. I feel deeply insulted and injured by the country's disintegration.' Another activist, Snežana Tabački, whom her friends call Barči, is a retired architect who comes originally from Macedonia and moved to Belgrade to go to school and then to university:

> All those years, I never noticed a problem with nationalist tension. I used to believe in Yugoslav multiculturalism. However, even before Milošević's ascension to power, I could recognise what would follow. As someone who belongs to a different ethnic community, I was able to sense the revival of nationalism. This made me feel scared, as I did not belong to the dominant group. Later on, when Milošević came to power, things got even worse with the enhancement of nationalism: I started receiving abusive phone calls that I should go back to Skopje. Now, I have buried deep in myself the dream of

the former Yugoslavia. We had it and we destroyed it. Tito's Non-Aligned Movement was a powerful political idea in its historical context. It was a wonderful feeling that your country was not subdued by none of the dominant political blocs – either NATO or Warsaw.

Most of my interlocutors considered the Serbia of Slobovan Milošević to be the force that killed Yugoslavia. One way or the other, the affects of belonging and unbelonging – ethno-national or otherwise – proved to be one of the fraught sites of questioning in this fieldwork rather than one of its fixed and determinate identity markers. The activists with whom I worked renounced the logic of ethno-national univocity, and assumed the abjected position of 'disloyalty' as a non-self-identical sign of disobedience. Saša Kovačević, *ŽuC* activist and political scientist, with whom I became good friends during fieldwork, posited disloyalty both in terms of contesting ethno-national identitarian regulation and in terms of assuming critical political subjectivity:

> We, the traitors, are the pride of Serbia. We don't do what we are prescribed to do: either lamenting at the tombs or being nurses. In other words, we refuse to clean the dirt left behind by men. No, nothing new can emerge this way. We do a deeper work, changing these roles. We have performed small miracles in some regards. As far as I am concerned, I do not belong to anything and anyone, only to *ŽuC*.

Saša's story, as she narrated it to me, was a story of ambivalent and precarious unbelonging. She was born in Croatia and, after her father's death, she, her mother, and her sister moved to Montenegro, where her mother came from. She described a conflicted background and a traumatic shift:

> Everything was upside down there. Montenegro is as black as it sounds. For me and for all the women there. Friends of my

mother's, living close to us, killed themselves. I was trying to protect my elder sister. And so, when the war started, I found myself living one war at home, against the patriarchal stereotypes, and another out. There was nowhere a place for me.

As she told me many times, her activism had to do with this sentiment of being out of place. For her, *ŽuC* re-inhabited and estranged the place of home, as both kinship and homeland, by expropriating its gender-marked foreignness and homelessness. Her own self-understanding of her position in *ŽuC* involved the unconventional poetics of bodies emerging out of place and affirming relationality with others situated out of place. Saša lived out of place and transfigured this estrangement and broken lineage into a politics of critical belonging and passing:

> When Yugoslavia disintegrated, I was left with no country, because I was born in Croatia. I was in the same situation as all the thousands of refugees. Within a night, I was left with no citizenship. I applied and had to wait, like everyone else, for five years. I was for five years with that little piece of paper that certified that I had filed the application. I was travelling with it, in times when people were kidnapped from trains and buses. My name sounds both Serbian and Croatian. One could say, 'she is Croatian, get rid of her'.

Saša described her embodying a state of 'not being at home' as a performative motor for her activist attachment in the wake of loss. She found a 'home' at *ŽuC*, a home beyond the gender-marked property and propriety of an idealised 'common place':

> I knew there was no future for me here. But I was hoping that women like me would find one another somewhere. And we finally did. The war had just broken out. My stance toward the war was already the one that I later found in *ŽuC*: courage and anger. When I came across the group in 1992, I was able to put

the two under one name. I had been tired of being alone. I was no longer the mad woman, the one who asks a lot or who does not know what she wants. I found a home at the moment that everything was falling apart. For me, *ŽuC* is clearly a relation of the heart.

In the face of political violence and loss, new forms of public intimacy emerged, beyond conventional accounts and lineages of kinship (Sosa 2014).

In addition to being a critical means to build new affiliations of political subjectivity, the imposed – but also, in a way, self-assumed – exile also became a site of the affective encounters that the embodied and situated condition of fieldwork entails. I met the *ŽuC* activists in a space marked by common political and intellectual commitments. But also, given their critical stance vis-à-vis Serb nationalism, on the one hand, and the official Greek position in favour of the Serb side in the Yugoslav conflict, on the other, we met at a space of mutual estrangement from 'our own' forms and norms of national sociability. Thus, inhabiting intricate registers of insider/outsider anew, together we journeyed along trajectories of exilic subjectivity and mutual involvement in feminist activism and left politics, beyond and despite ethno-national prescriptions. On a more affective realm, our encounter was determined by historically shaped intricacies of loss and comradeship.

My interlocutors were between the ages of twenty and seventy, mostly but not exclusively women: anti-war activism is not uniquely appropriate for women, in the *ŽuC* critical imagination. And yet, although this is not technically an all-women's group, its members – women and men – insist on the self-appellation *Žene u Crnom*, '*Women* in Black'. In this respect, rather than a foundational identity category, gender emerged as a nuanced site of critical sensibility and cross-identification in their political activism. In redeploying the term 'women', these activists occupy, in a politically affirmative and distinctly feminist fashion, a mark that had been used by conventional national cultures to either fix female subjects in the inscriptional space of patriotic motherhood or abject those unruly and resistant to such idealised commands. The signifier 'women', for Women in Black, is mobilised not in a merely instrumental manner, but rather as a site of critical resignification through which to call into question the sedimented legitimacy of these interpellating prescriptions. In this sense, 'women' for them has been — and still is — the rallying point of a consequential resistance to nationalist matrices of normalisation and abjection. Many of the women activists with whom I talked have a long history in feminist activism, having been involved in women's and feminist groups since the 1970s. Some were members of the collectivity Women and Society, which the Yugoslav government had condemned and accused of being an 'enemy of the state' and 'pro-capitalist' (Mladjenović and Hughes 2001; Mršević 2000). They retain vivid reminiscences of the seminal international conference 'Comrade Woman' ('Drug-ca Žena') held in Belgrade, at the Student Cultural Centre, in 1978, under the famous motto 'Proletarians of the world, who washes your socks?' That conference is now deemed as the outset of the Yugoslav feminist movement. Feminist, lesbian, and antifascist activist Lepa Mlađenović, for one, was among those young activists who had attended that historic gathering. Since, Lepa participated in almost all feminist events organised throughout Yugoslavia in the 1980s: in 1986, she initiated the first self-awareness feminist group in Belgrade, and in 1991 she took part in the formation of the Women in Black against War. A few of my interlocutors, *ŽuC* activists, had worked together to set the foundations and establish autonomous spaces of leftist feminist thought and praxis in Yugoslavia, besides and beyond the state-sponsored configuration of 'equality' between women and men. As Adriana Zaharijević puts it, the political positionality of Yugoslav feminists vis-à-vis 'state-feminism' was one of dissidence; a dissidence which, although it might be regarded as 'benevolent' compared to feminists of the newly formed states after the breakup of Yugoslavia, was a precursor of the activism of the 1990s (2013: 9–10; also Bilić 2012).

As members of the *ŽuC* movement have recounted to me, most of them have a long record of feminist, antinationalist, and anti-war action. Since the mid-1980s, even before the inception of *ŽuC*, they were founders and members of Women and Society, while since 1991 they have actively taken part in the work of the Centre of Antiwar Action. Some of my interlocutors belonged to the first generation of the Women's Studies Center, which was initiated in 1992, with an experimental one-semester course starting, symbolically, on 8 March. Others were too young to have participated in those collectivities directly, and, as inheritors of histories of conflict, took up different aspects and temporalities of the changing but persistent antinationalist feminism. In a conversation with me, Adriana Zaharijević, who was too young to be active in the movement during the 1990s and joined *ŽuC* after the war and Yugoslavia's disintegration, addressed the pervasiveness of the military logic in every aspect of everyday life:

> In the 90s, even though I was very young, it was impossible for me, for anyone for that matter, not to feel the war in the air, in one's immediate environment. For example, when I was in the eighth grade, a rascal once waited for me outside the building I was living and enforced in my hand a grenade – only later I realised it was deactivated.

During the Yugoslav wars of succession, my interlocutors supported, or got involved in, different feminist projects such as the Women's Studies Center, the Autonomous Women's Centre against Sexual Violence, and Feministička 94. Through their multilayered political commitments, they put forward a feminist anti-war discourse, thus coming to terms with the question (and the impossibility) of turning unintelligible and unmournable forms of life and death into a translatable political form. Staša Zajović, a key figure in the history of *ŽuC* in Belgrade, explains:

> Our participation in the antiwar movement has nothing to do with a natural role or a maternal duty, but it is a political choice and commitment. We are against militarists, warmongers, and nationalists. We do not allow them to speak in our name.[10]

Coming from a family with antifascist history, Staša was always, from the days of the 'old Yugoslavia', a leftist dissident, not because she was anti-communist, as she explained persistently in conversations with me, but because she was committed to a different vision of communism: 'I was feeling I was more communist than all those male communists whose communism seemed to be not ideological but coming out of a loyalty to the president and related to personal interests.' Staša's personal history is intimately intertwined with the history of Begrade's *ŽuC*. In her words:

> Since the spring of 1991, I took part in several international caravans. I heard of Women in Black. We went to Sarajevo, with the Peace Caravan. The first action of Women in Black in the Balkans took place in Sarajevo, on the 27th of September 1991. That action offered me a very powerful sense, both bodily and psychic. Upon my return to Belgrade, I worked day and night to that direction. That's how Belgrade's Women in Black started on the 9th of October 1991.[11]

Finally, after the cessation of conflicts and the dissolution of the Socialist Federal Republic of Yugoslavia, the *ŽuC* activists, not sharing the non-governmental organisation-ised (NGO-ised) consensus of 'peace' and the widespread complacence toward the 'transition' to liberal capitalist democracy, continued their dissident, cross-border work. In the post-socialist, post-Yugoslav political and economic context that Srećko Horvat and Igor Štiks have compellingly called 'desert of transition' (2015), these activists persist in their demand for justice, in ways that exceed 'the state's monopoly on the administration of justice' (Honig 1993: 158). In a context of discourses and economies of 'dispassionate' neoliberal post-politics, this is mainly why they are constructed – and often contempted – in the public consciousness as figures of political alterity and excess. As part of their intervention in the regime of gendered foreclosures through which the affective texture of memory is produced, one of their prominent tasks is the project of Women's Court in Former Yugoslavia (more on this in Chapter 4).[12] Furthermore, in this post-Yugoslav context, feminist activism, including the *ŽuC*, assumed new and additional forms, building upon the dissident legacies of a feminist scene developed in times of conflict. Those activists, who had fought for democracy and against gendered violence in the 1990s, now become implicated in questioning neoliberal capitalism, especially in respect to gendered and racialised regimes of socio-economic precarity and enduring familialist configurations (Daskalova et al. 2012; Zaharijević 2013).

Complicating, rather than abandoning, the concern with the issues of war and nationalism, which had been a rallying point for mobilisation among feminist and queer activists in the 1990s, contemporary feminist studies of the region have turned to a problematics of gendered post-Yugoslav citizenship as a perspective through which to reconsider the legacy of multi-ethnic Yugoslav socialism, as it continues to provide a space of commonality but also differentiation between different post-Yugoslav polities. Indeed, citizenship emerged as an utterly tumultuous matter in the course of my research and in my encounters with my interlocutors, as a few of them had experienced multiple changes of citizenship regimes in the context of ethnic engineering and disintegrating federation in the 1990s, such as moving from the status of federal citizen and republic-level citizen to that of temporarily stateless, refugee, and national citizen. This history of unpredictable and often violent shifts in borders and practices of citizenship in the highly volatile context of the rise and fall of Yugoslavia has made Igor Štiks aptly invoke Yugoslavia as a 'laboratory of citizenship' (2015). Recent and ongoing rebellious struggles, resistant strategies, and left-wing movements in the former Yugoslavia give new radical meaning to political community and citizenship beyond, simultaneously, ethno-national discourses, state socialist Yugoslav nostalgia, as well as liberal and neoliberal governmentality (Horvat and Štiks 2015).

In the context of this growing scholarship and political vision of citizenship that puts in question its ethno-national, liberal and neoliberal ramifications, post-Yugoslav citizenship is theorised as a domain of new or reinstated social inequalities related to gender, sexuality, ethnicity and class, and thus a domain of ongoing contestation and mobilisation. In this regard, sexual citizenship contestations regarding queer politics, protests against political corruption, and anti-austerity protests, such as the ones that have manifested in Slovenia and Bosnia–Herzegovina but also across South East Europe, mark the terrain of citizenship as profoundly contentious (Bonfiglioli et al. 2015). It was along these lines that Staša Zajović, in talking with me once, intertwined the provisional intersections between feminism, antimilitarism, and antinationalism with the historical embeddedness of her own and her comrades' lived experiences:

When I find myself in a place dominated by machismo, I am a feminist. When I am with women who talk only about domestic violence, I bring up antimilitarism. Some women joined the movement for reasons related to pacifism and ethics, and on the way, they get to know about feminism.

And Nađia Duhaček, a young intellectual who joined *ŽuC* after the war and the disintegration of Yugoslavia, spoke to me about the 'threatening combination of feminism and antimilitarism' in terms of a potentiality of dislocating normative demarcations and creating alternative alliances: 'It is fascinating to me', Nađa remarked,

> that when you connect feminism with antimilitarism and anti-nationalism, antinationalism begins to be queered, to open up to empowering subversions. The same holds for feminism too. The fact that the group is open to men is one such practice that opens new spaces for both feminism and antimilitarism.

In Nađa's words, the intertwinement of feminism and anti-nationalism becomes a site of queering, that is, of continuous and incomplete twisting, resignifying, and dispersing in the direction of a horizon of reclaimed possibility.

Such complex interconnections and redeployments are rendered central to the terrain of feminist activist citizenship in post-Yugoslav states. As broader issues of belonging and distribution play out within the ongoing processes of Europeanisation that transform the region into what Marina Blagojević has called a 'semi-periphery' (2009), an abiding challenge feminists face is how to retain the element of activist dissent in the context of a capitalist citizenship that increasingly fosters managerial forms of gender mainstreaming. For those activist groups, which are reluctant to subscribe to the adjustments required by growing cultures of non-governmental governmentality and, at the same time, seek to remain outside the snare of the state and the ethno-national order of the successor states, this challenge also involves pressing questions of funding and often entails reliance on international donor organisations. In this sense, the space of feminist activism that arose out of the violent breakup of Yugoslavia and the nation-building processes of the 1990s seems to be caught between – but also resistant to – two versions of contemporary post-political configurations: state-centred neoliberal governmentality of managing and normalising the past, on the one side, and the legal and psychological traumatic realism of reconciliation, on the other. *ŽuC* activists seem to get in the way of these pervasive lures. They are 'still in the streets', as one of their key mottos has it, denoting an unrelenting agonism but also a persistent political commitment to the public and an independence from state and market attachments. Their enduring collective bodily presence evinces agonistic longing for a different way to inhabit and enact the political. Thus, their concerted action invests in how to attend to agonism in times of neo-conservative governmentality, when activism is hailed to slip into the pragmatic and bureaucratic cynicism of NGO-isation and become untethered from its collective, transformative and affective, passionate qualities. In the words of activist Hana Ćopić: '*ŽuC* does not comply with NGO standards, and for good reasons. The price of professionalisation would be the abolition of dissent.' But how to maintain the spirit of dissidence and survive (let alone live) both as an activist and as an activist collectivity in the midst of everyday violence remains, for Hana as well as for others, a daunting question.

In conversations with me but also in communiqués, activists have addressed the pressures imposed by the state and donors in a post-conflict, market-oriented context. Sustaining the transformative spirit of the movement and guarding against institutionalisation, demobilisation and even incorporation and co-optation have been enduring concerns for the activists with whom I interacted. As one activist asked: 'What do we do when the state and other formalised institutionalised powers, including restorative justice initiatives, appropriate and misuse our ideas?' As she admitted, there can be no programmatic answer to this question, only collective wariness of pitfalls as well as provisional and pre-emptive resistance to the snares of a neoliberal state and institutions. Perhaps we should understand the responses to such challenges, entailing both emotional pressure and political disenchantment, as a certain aspect of the traumatic but still hopeful component of activism itself in our present moment.

Towards Non-Sovereign Agonism

The *ŽuC* modes of contentious intimacy mark out a space for relational, non-sovereign agency in the wake of sovereign violence. In the contexts of nationalist conflict in the former Yugoslavia and of contestations around post-Yugoslav citizenship, this agency implicates the potential to stand critically beside the normative matrices of 'standing' as a presupposition of self-sovereign subjectivity. In this account of subjectivity, becoming a subject is a differential and differentiating effect of power, produced in conditions of susceptibility and relatability. For our purposes here, we need to ask what kind of space this mode of subjectivity opens up for a collective action that accounts for the ethical and political challenges of trauma, loss, and memory in the midst of warfare violence and in the aftermath of atrocity. We are also allowed to ask what established norms regulating relationality would such political subjectivity have to contest and remould.

Through the space opened by the *ŽuC* political commitment, then, I am led to rethink subjectivity outside the 'sovereign' hold of sovereignty, instead of and against fantasies of mastery and self-mastery, and yet not as privation of the possibility of agency and responsibility (Butler 2005). I argue that *ŽuC* political subjectivity, as a spectral plurality of non-sovereign dispositions, decentres both defining orders of sovereignty: the one of unilateral and militarised national sovereignty and the one of subjectivity based on the model of self-grounding, phallogocentric, occasionally violent but distinctly inviolate, sovereignty. As it is clearly manifested in their political work, acknowledging and enacting one's decentredness (in both national and, more widely, subjective terms) becomes a resource for becoming implicated in collective projects of deconstituting the norms that regulate, foreclose, or impede relationality. Attending to the deconstruction of sovereignty, in all its manifold and ambivalent inflections, does not have to vitiate the ethical and political value of all self-determination. It might, however, enjoin us to reinstate self-determination as determination with the other, as an interminable and indeterminate finding of oneself with/in the other. In this sense, I have been concerned in my research with how the *ŽuC* concerted political work against the nationalist and militarist banality that led to ethno-nationalist violence in what has become the former Yugoslavia yields an ek-static and transformative mode of social belonging. For *ŽuC*, *stajanje* – the activist practice of standing still in public – as standing in place and as standing beside oneself vis-à-vis the Yugoslav archives of war and post-war, entails, in ways I will unravel further, the engendering of a new sensorium of non-sovereign political subjectivity. Their standing disrupts the ways in which bodies are interpellated to engender and inhabit the nation. In *ŽuC* agonistic politics, the collective ability to persist, survive, and revolt draws on a broader, shared – albeit dismembered – sociality regulated by power relations and, specifically, the powers of war. Collective resistance rises from loss and also from enduring loss and accounting for loss through creating alternative ties of belonging; it is, ultimately, what makes survival possible – albeit not necessarily less unbearable. Indeed, as I argue throughout this book, the aporia with which we engage in the context of *ŽuC* cross-border poetics of memory and grievability, is that what is at stake is nothing other than the agonal and agonistic passion inscribed in becoming bereft from the loss of others, in being 'already given over, beyond ourselves, implicated in lives that are not our own' (Butler 2004: 28). While enacting such non-normative intensities of grief and relationality gained through activism, the collectivity created a new and renewed space of political agonism.

Chantal Mouffe deploys the concepts of agonism and agonistic pluralism to offer a framework of thinking about democracy in a way that differs from deliberative liberal paradigms of democracy as a negotiation between interests and a consensual resolution of conflicts. In this formulation, rather than rational consensus, which is the effect of hegemonic sedimentation and ends up closing down the *agon*, agonistic passion and struggle is the definitive condition of democracy. 'A pluralist democracy', Mouffe summarises, 'needs to make room for dissent' (1999: 756). Drawing on a non-essentialist conception of the subject, she poses the question of political identity as a form of identification – a foundational element in her radical democratic project. Such configuration of acknowledging the ever-present possibility of difference and disagreement unsettles the epistemological foundations upon which the body politic is conceived in instrumentalist accounts of aggregative democracy but also in nationalist contexts of self-enclosed community. Expanding on Mouffe's perspective, my aim here is to engage a radical political project that provides the conditions of an open-ended possibility for making room for dissent rather than deliberative consensus, moral harmony, and juridical reconciliation. I draw attention to the passionate attachments at the heart of this political engagement, which works beyond and against the deliberative paradigm and actively mobilises the possibility of contestation. If Mouffe casts citizenship as a 'form of identification that enables the establishment of a common political identity among diverse democratic struggles' (1993: 6), the challenge for political subjects is to question the congealed norms and totalisations that determine what is 'common' about popular sovereignty and political identity in times of national emergency and in the face of nationally disavowed political loss. They do so not in order to prescribe a definitive answer but rather to performatively introduce an open-ended agonistic contestation at the very level of the established matrix of intelligibility. The horizon of their agonistic politics is not confined to deliberative genres, democratic constitutionalism or even democracy as a juridical doctrine. Their agonistic politics cannot be reduced to moral(istic) outrage either. Rather, it is about an embodied performativity of becoming other, as a political call to respond to what most needs a response: the exclusionary processes upon which identification is premised. In that respect, these political subjects are constituted through a performative dis-identification vis-à-vis the sedimented power structures that have authorised the norms of identification, articulation, and belonging. Their loss is a condition of self-estranging, becoming other to themselves:

> When we lose some of these ties by which we are constituted, we do not know who we are or what to do. On one level, I think I have lost 'you' only to discover that 'I' have gone missing as well. (Butler 2004: 22)

But what other ties emerge out of the affective intensities associated with the activist performativity of accounting for uncommon loss?

In reckoning with the enforced effacements that render political space a space for appearing bodies, these activists perform the spectral potentiality of displaced and disconcerted memory: one that incalculably complicates the way in which people 'come together' in the *polis*, particularly in contexts afflicted by state violence that remains disavowed by this state. In spectralising the conventional friend/enemy distinction and in occupying the disturbing subject position of the designated 'internal enemy', which has been conferred upon them as a status of abjection, they depart from where they (un)belong in order to relate and respond to those estranged as external enemies. They become their phantom residues; they occupy the space created by those absent. By positioning their bodies at the centre of the city to signal those turned into enemies by dominant ordinances of appearing and assembling, they actualise the multilayered modalities of stasis as a means of embodying their own and others' dissident belonging. As I unravel later, stasis, in this context, involves an embodied practice of inhabiting the *polis* through contestation and dissent, but also the desire to stand critically beside the conceits of self-sovereign subjectivity. These political subjects' standing in public bespeaks the inter-implicated traumas and potentials of standing for loss and standing against the will of the *polis*. Thus, camaraderie outside the ordained matrix of belonging becomes an inscription not only of imposed estrangement but also of agonistic ek-stasis.

Notes

1 For a perspicacious discussion of the nexus of law, sovereignty, governmentality, and the question of life with regard to Butler's work, see Loizidou 2014.

2 In this reading, 'sovereignty' and 'governmentality' do not designate successive moments in a linear diagram of power but rather different political technologies of ordering the political body. Although I take into consideration Foucault's conceptual distinction between the political rationalities of

sovereignty and governmentality, I am more interested in exploring their articulation and coextensiveness.

3 Derrida writes: 'In speaking of an ontotheology of sovereignty, I am referring here, under the name of God, this One and Only God, to the determination of a sovereign, and thus indivisible, omnipotence.' Derrida, *Rogues*, 157.

4 However, Arendt's approach to sovereignty is not absolutely and homogeneously dismissive. At certain moments of her oeuvre, which bespeak a rather ambiguous and ambivalent attitude towards sovereignty, she seems to concede that sovereignty is rather inevitable in modern political life (see for example, *On Revolution*, 1990).

5 Derrida writes in *Specters of Marx*: 'That is why we always propose to speak of a democracy *to come*, not of a *future* democracy in the future present, not even of a regulating idea, in the Kantian sense, or of a utopia – at least to the extent that their inaccessibility would still retain the temporal form of *a future present*, of a future modality of the *living present*' (1994: 80–1).

6 Derrida's ambivalence with regards to sovereignty is consonant with his reservations about the term 'democracy' as well. His hesitation has to do with the figuration of democracy in the tradition of Western modernity through the notion of 'fraternity', which is saturated with the monotheistic tradition of women's subjugation. For an excellent discussion of the gender underpinnings of Derrida's democracy-to-come and his critique of 'fraternity' and fraternal democracy, see Pulkkinen 2009.

7 James Martel (2012) has notably argued that even Arendt and Derrida, who are very critical of sovereignty, have not avoided falling into the eschatological trap of a false choice between anarchy and sovereignty. The political theology and negative messianicity offered by Walter Benjamin would help, according to Martel, to avoid this trap and dislocate the mythological function of sovereignty that dominates our world today in interfering with popular power.

8 In this regard, I concur with, and build on, Eng and Kazanjian 2003; Cvetkovich 2003.

9 On the affects of activism, see Eirini Avramopoulou's account of feminist–queer–religious activist coalitions in Istanbul, Turkey (2012).

10 Zajović, from the meeting 'Always disobedient – The 15th anniversary of the founding of Women in Black: 9 October 1991–9 October 2006', co-ordinators: Lina Vušković and Jelena Marković. The event was held on 9 October 2006, in Belgrade's Center for Cultural Decontamination (CZKD), an independent and transnational foundation that was established

in 1993 on the initiative of artists and political activists, upon the ruins of what had been the first museum of European art in the Balkans, and is now a co-owned property of private owners and the municipality of Belgrade. When I visited the Centre together with the friends from the *ŽuC* group, they explained to me that the name of the centre refers to the mission of 'cleansing' the cultural residues of Milošević's regime. In the anniversary event 'Always disobedient', celebrating the fifteen years since the founding of Belgrade's *ŽuC* (7 October 2006), nearly eighty women participated in the panels and nearly 100 individuals attended it. *ŽuC*'s leaflets for the event referred to those who participated and attended as a 'community of disobedience and resistance'.

11 Zajović, from the meeting 'Always disobedient', ibid.

12 The organisational board of the *Ženski sud* project includes activist groups from all former republics. Serbia is represented by the Centre for Women's Studies and Women in Black (*ŽuC*). According to the rationale of the project, the task of the Women's Court in Former Yugoslavia is to create 'different paradigms of justice'. Based on women's testimonies, the Women's Court seeks to 'enable women to transform the pain they have experienced into yet another form of resistance' (<http://www.zenskisud.org/en/Metodologija.html> last accessed 21 April 2014). It encourages women 'to testify about all kinds of structural injustice: poverty, exploitation at the workplace and everywhere, uncontrolled rule of market laws, social and health threats, and abuse of religion for political purposes' (<http://www.zenskisud.org/en/index.html> last accessed 21 April 2014).

1

Mourning Otherwise

Feminism at War

In order to be able to grasp the agonistic commitments, claims, and life-worlds of the *ŽuC* activists I worked with, we need to take note of what this movement calls into play as well as what it calls upon. The question of how to recall the late twentieth-century history of the former Yugoslavia, a central aspect of the *ŽuC* labour of memory, requires a return to the discursive conditions that made ethno-nationalist ideologies and armed conflicts of the 1990s possible and probable. To address this question, I believe it is necessary to think through the complex operations of power that haunt this genealogy from the outset, especially those related to scenes of subjectification and de-subjectification, psychic economy, affective circuits, chains of signification, corporeal dispositions and conditions of dispos-ability, but also, quite importantly, the polymorphous vicissitudes of imaginary geographies and Balkanist metaphorisation (Bjelić and Savić 2002; Green 2005; Todorova 1997; Woodward 1995, 2000).

After Tito's death in 1980, the system of Yugoslav federal government was faced with severe political and economic chal-lenges. In the course of the 1980s, the economy of the country, especially its welfare institutions, began to dismantle. An austerity programme was signed with the International Monetary Fund to service the debt. A policy of cutting public expenditures and transferring the burden to the constituent republics instigated public discontent, scapegoating, and accusations of ethno-national discrimination with regard to employment, housing, and citizen rights (Woodward 2000: 26–7). In 1981, widespread protests by Kosovo Albanians, demanding the reinstatement of their autonomy and a separate republic within the Yugoslav federation, were suppressed by violent police intervention and the declaration of a state of emergency in the capital Pristina. After a period of political upheavals and economic crisis in 1980s, paramilitary groups and right-wing political parties began emerging in the republics. The Constitution of 1974 had provided for a collective leadership in the party among the six republics and two provinces. Under conditions of harsh austerity and economic inequality, however, an escalating tension among the party branches of the constituent republics in the Yugoslav Communist Party (League of Communists of Yugoslavia) led to the composite party's dissolution along federal lines at its 14th Congress convened in January 1990.[1] The Slovene and Croatian delegations left the congress, protesting the Serbian delegation's policy of 'one person, one vote' in the party membership, which would favour the largest ethnic group (the Serbs) in the party and in the State. After that event, the communist party effectively broke up into different parties, renamed into Socialist or Social-Democratic, for each republic. Meanwhile, the Serbian Academy of Sciences and Arts (*Srpska akademija nauka i umetnosti*, SANU) drafted the SANU Memorandum in 1986, denouncing the weakening of the Serbian central govern-ment. Slobodan Milošević, a communist who up to that point had decried nationalism, became president of the Communist League of Serbia in 1987 and began deploying an aggressive nationalist ideology. Breaking the communist tradition of neutrality on the issue of Kosovo, the new leadership yielded to demands by Serb minority groups in Kosovo, who claimed that they were discriminated against by the Albanian majority government (Woodward 2000: 26). On 28 September 1990, the (still one-party) Serbian assembly adopted a new constitution, which declared 'the sovereignty, independence and territorial integrity of the Republic of Serbia' and abolished almost completely the autonomous status of the provinces of Vojvodina and Kosovo within the Serbian republic, although the Serbian assembly had already terminated the Kosovo assembly in June 1990. On the same day, the Slovenian assembly adopted amendments to Slovenia's constitution asserting the republic's jurisdiction over the Slovene territorial defence force. During the 1990s, communist parties lost power to nationalist ones in the first multi-party elections held in Yugoslavia. In Serbia and Montenegro, Milošević and his Socialist Party of Serbia (*Socijalistička Partija Srbije*, SPS) won the elections in 1990 (with a narrow majority) and formed a coalition with nationalist politicians on the basis of a legitimising rhetoric of self-victimisation and a promise for protection of all Serbs throughout Yugoslavia. So Milošević's rising to power in a nationalist coalition signalled his pursuit to rebuild Serb-dominated, pre-war and pre-socialist Yugoslavia. As the SPS programme had appealed to those critical of Tito's purported devaluing of Serb interests in Yugoslavia in the 1980s, the Yugoslav principle of 'Brotherhood and Unity' providing for the federation of equal constituent states with full sovereignty, was jettisoned by the new regime in favour of an 'all Serbs in one state' vision (Gordy 1999). In the pre-election period, the SPS presented itself as the only force able to safeguard the interests of the Serbian people: 'with us there is no uncertainty' (*s nama nema neizvesnosti*), was one of the slogans used in the pre-election campaign. In short, conflicting discourses of 'national interests' and 'national sovereignty' had begun to ensnare the public life of Yugoslav republics, opening the way for the ensuing violent breakup. Thus, the republics headed for secession and Yugoslavia for disintegration.

The dissolution of Yugoslavia, especially the normalisation of nationalist military violence in the mid-1990s, has manifested the crucial role of gendered norms as constitutive of nationalist discourses. Since the late 1980s, as the discursive conditions of the ensuing military conflict were being established, various grassroots feminist and women's groups across the region were involved in raising antimilitarist and antinationalist awareness. During the war years, feminist groups engaged in solidarity activities with victims of war violence and refugee women in the major cities of the former republics (Cockburn 1998). When the news about the war rapes in Bosnia emerged in August 1992, these groups responded immediately and consistently, setting up solidarity networks and organising numerous protest actions, struggling to demystify and denaturalise the issue of sexualised war violence against women, and attempting to put it onto the agenda of international institutions (Djuric-Kuzmanović et al. 2008). At the same time, feminist groups active in Belgrade, such as the Women's Studies Center, the Centre of Antiwar Action, the Autonomous Women's Centre, the SOS Hotline, and Feministička 94, sought to forge a feminist critical perspective on militarism, alternative to the mainstream glorification of war culture (Mladjenović and Hughes 2001). Among them, the Belgrade Women's Studies Center was initiated by the group Women and Society (*Zena I Drustvo*) and in the beginning under the coordination of Daša Duhaček and Sonja Drljević.[2] From its inception in 1992, the Center maintained a feminist and antinationalist political stance. During its first decade of history, it operated against the backdrop – and against the logic – of the wars of the 1990s. Many of those founders and members of the first Academic Board of the Center, such as Neda Božinović,

Sonja Drljević, Daša Duhaček, Slavica Stojanović, Žarana Papić, Lepa Mlađenović, and Jasmina Tešanović, actively participated in the formation of the first *ŽuC* group. The principal initiator of *ŽuC* was the feminist activist Staša Zajović, a long-time member of feminist collectivities, including Women and Society.[3]

The critical perspective offered over the course of this book is signalled by the 'partial perspective' (Haraway 1988) of local feminist anti-war activism, which was situated as a counter-position to militarised, gendered, and sexualised sovereignty. Amidst tropes of essentialised 'cultural difference', aggressive claims of ethno-national sovereignty, and mutual invocations of 'international conspiracies' against Serbia or Croatia, local feminist anti-war groups developed alternative conceptualisations of Yugoslavia's collapse, by focusing on the gendered and sexualised operations of power that remade ethno-national ideologies into war violence. Importantly, though, those contexts of gendered and sexualised sovereignty, which feminist antinationalist epistemologies of situatedness and positionality contested, were founded upon a discursive field marked by the authoritative primacy of ethnicity. Gender discourse was eclipsed by militaristic patriarchy and ethnic nationalism, or rather, as Vesna Kesić puts it, was 'subordinated to ethnicity' (2002: 314). Dubravka Žarkov rightly asserts that the 'wars' – the 'media war' and the 'ethnic war' – in the former Yugoslavia were about the *production* of ethnicity: 'these two wars aimed to make ethnicity the only mode of being, to obliterate and obscure everything that could cast a shadow on its omnipotence' (2007: 3). As Žarkov elaborates, notions of masculinity and femininity and norms of (hetero)sexuality played a crucial role in the production of a regime of ethnicity as the only possible regime of intelligibility. In this context, pronatalist demographic discourses reducing women to reproducers of the nation gained particular salience (Drezgić 2010). This newly dominant ethnicisation was performed through the objectification of women's bodies in accordance with the ideology of patriotic motherhood. Thus the space had opened for using women's bodies – the bodies of one's 'own' women and women of 'other' ethnicities – as a conduit for negotiating, consolidating, or encroaching on boundaries of ethno-national belonging and non-belonging during the wars of succession (Papić 2002).

By the end of the 1980s the political categories of citizenship and 'the people' were already subsumed under a fixed, undivided, and instrumental definition of the ethno-national (Zaharijević 2013). In this context of transformation 'from state socialism to state nationalism' (Papić 1994), the regulation of 'sex' became the point at which ethnicity constituted a realm of intelligibility signalled by what lay beyond it. The disciplinary device of 'sex' emerged as a constitutive aspect of nationalisms in the former Yugoslavia but also of representational schemes that played out in the terrain of the war.

Sociologist Žarana Papić, a long-time feminist activist and theorist of ŽuC and co-founder of the Belgrade Women's Studies Center, has addressed the socio-political context of Serbia during the 1990s as one of nationalist and patriarchal authoritarianism, which involved the forces of 'retraditionalization, instrumentalization, and naturalization of women's identities, social roles, and their symbolic representations' (2002: 128). During the decade of the 1990s, the politics of ethno-national sovereignty, international policy of redefining Europe after the Cold War, and the interrelated politics of signification developed into a dense web within and about the regions of the former Yugoslavia. The totalising logic that undergirds stereotypes of 'cultural difference' so often operative in representations of the Balkans and Balkan identities gained new currency. The mainstream Western media representations of violent nationalisms and the disassemblage of the former Yugoslavia in terms of 'sectarian violence' rehearsed and further solidified culturalising systems of knowledge and power that cast 'violence' as an inherent property of particular cultures, groups, or regions. Complex historical contingencies and discursive geographies were reduced to spectacularised commodities through voyeuristic culturalist tropes of eternal ethnic hatred and irrational passions, which worked to exonerate Western imperialism and to occlude the historical and political determinacies of the war.

Such essentialising regimes of knowledge production were deployed by representational apparatuses of 'Western' liberal democracies to reaffirm the regulatory discursive formation of 'civilised Europe', and to make the Balkan romance of atavistic tendencies and sexualised primitivity available for consumption in the global public sphere. Outsiders' perceptions of the conditions that led to the wars of Yugoslav succession depicted the Balkans as a 'violence-prone area' (Woodward 2000). This culturalist explanatory schema was rehearsed to legitimise the politics of imperialist intervention, including, crucially, the massive bombing campaign against Serbian targets undertaken by NATO (the North Atlantic Treaty Organization) as a purportedly inevitable response to local violence. That imperialist intervention, in violation of international law, would have been impossible if it were not for the ideological construction of 'helpless victims, robbed of all political identity and reduced to their naked suffering' (Žižek 1999).

Widespread tropes of depoliticising and ethnically essentialising 'cultural difference', which oscillated between demonisation and idealisation, were also a crucial aspect of local war propaganda and its gendered and sexualised technologies of othering. 'Cultural difference', with all its implications of 'uncivilised' and 'backwards', is typically evoked in terms of gender and sexuality. In the context of Yugoslavia's dissolution, such externally and internally devised tropes became the basis for a massive deployment of 'sex', either in the form of pejorative stereotypes about Balkan irrationality, unregulated libido, and propensity to violence or in the form of glorified representations and self-stereotypes of unconventional and eroticised temperament. This representational war was instantiated by emblematic figurations that acquired salience within the imagination of the nation, such as the sensational demonisation of the Serbs as a people through their representation as a metonym for mass rape, or, on the other hand, the proud self-appropriation of essentialised ethnic hetero-masculinity. Furthermore, the possibility of accounting for widespread violence against women, as well as for their practices of resilience and resistance during the breakup of Yugoslavia, was already foreclosed by the discursive and epistemic violences of ethnicisation, postcolonial nationalism, orientalism, and imperialism; it became foreclosed by these subjectifying representational regimes that turned women's bodies into victims and passive witnesses. Mainstream depictions of wartime sexual violence allowed it to enter the arenas of common intelligibility only as common propaganda (Hayden 2000: 29). The depiction of the wartime rapes through the frame of 'genocidal rape' conducted by one ethnic group against opponent ethnic groups was developed and extensively deployed by the nationalist governments and their controlled media, as well as by some Western feminist scholars (Kesić 2002). In various idioms of ethno-national rhetoric and iconography, women were attributed a particular form of subjectivity as victims by virtue of their construal as territorial markers and procreative bearers of 'ethnic blood'. Hence the violations they had to endure were recognisable as relevant only for re-establishing the potency and honour of their nation or ethnic group. At the same time, sexualised war violence was portrayed in ways that rendered female victims, paradigmatically Bosniac women, as 'only victims', in accordance with Orientalised images of women as wretched victims of

Muslim patriarchy (Engle 2005; Helms 2013: 27; Žarkov 2007; also Mertus 1994). Such iconic figures and ready-made essentialist representations were forged largely outside and, to be sure, against the subjectivity of women themselves, but they were noticeable in the realm of women's activism too (Helms, ibid.).

In this embattled context of literal and figurative injunctions and violations operative within the scheme of intelligibility that Veena Das has aptly called 'desire for nationalism' (1997: 68), the conflation of ethnic and gender signifying practices was at the heart of the 'sexualisation' of war violence (Kesić 2002). Clearly, at issue here is the enmeshment of nationalism, especially Serbian nationalism of blood and soil in the context of *ŽuC*, and discursive processes of sexualisation in a period of intense social discord in the former Yugoslavia. As Bjelić and Cole have convincingly demonstrated, if discursive formations of 'sex' were central to the history of the violent breakup of Yugoslavia, these are intimately linked to disciplinary power/knowledge regimes of modernity and, more specifically, to the history of heterosexual pleasure within them, and should not be interpreted, in accordance with the widespread tendency in Western liberalism, as relapses into 'pre-modern' impulses and attachments (2002: 303).

This gendered and sexualised imagery that rendered war violence intelligible (Žarkov 2007) was a primary site of awareness of and action by several feminist collectivities in all republics or newly founded nation-states of what became the former Yugoslavia. Not all feminists and feminist collectivities, however, were critical of the emergent ethno-national definition of citizenship. There were certainly patriotic feminists who subscribed to ethno-national regimes of identification and citizenship that denied recognition to 'those branded as traitors or collaborators' (Zaharijević 2013: 14; see also Miškovska Kajevska 2014).

ŽuC, by contrast, assumed unbelonging (to a national identity) as a political space for feminist critique to the politics of nationalism and its gendered underpinnings. Although it condemned the crimes of 'all sides' and acknowledged 'all victims', *ŽuC*, as a firmly antinationalist feminist group based in Serbia, became concerned primarily (albeit not exclusively) with Serbian nationalism and, more specifically, with the nationalist mobilisation and military aggression initiated under the banner of Greater Serbia by Serbian and Bosnian Serb military and paramilitary forces against Muslim and Croat civilians. Hana Ćopić unsettled the apparatus of representing *ŽuC* as internal enemies and national traitors: '*ŽuC* activists were the ones who also talked about Croatian operations against Serbs. Nevertheless, this is overlooked by those committed to representing *ŽuC* as traitors.' These activists opposed vehemently local and international representations and ideological constructions that reduced the war to a civil war between various 'ethnic groups'. Instead, as they considered Serbian nationalism to be the cause of secessionism that led to the collapse of Tito's legacy, they first focused their critique on Serbian aggression against Bosnia in 1992. *ŽuC* activists sought to bring to the awareness of a public heavily siding with the pervasive war regime the ethnic cleansing in Srebrenica, the terrorisation of non-Serb civilians, the siege of Sarajevo and the shelling attacks on its citizens, the sexual violence, and the incarceration of civilians in detention camps.

Although feminist groups from different regions of the former Yugoslavia were concerned with the differential ways war affected men and women, and set up solidarity networks to support those who had undergone sexualised violence, nevertheless an intense political disagreement arose over the question of whether wartime rape was a crime of gender or nation (Helms 2013). This disagreement eventually led to a split among feminist groups in the former Yugoslavia, which accounted for the tensions between Serbian antinationalist feminists and one camp of Croatian feminists (Miškovska Kajevska 2014). By contrast, the Croatian antinationalist feminists firmly supported solidarity with Serbian feminists. In October 1992, the *ŽuC* group issued a report stating that: 'The high percentage of Muslim women raped in the war in Bosnia is not a reason to forget the suffering of women of other nationalities and religions, atheists, or those claiming no particular nationality' (Women in Black 1993: 92). In December 1992, the Zagreb weekly newspaper *Globus* published an unsigned article with a list of 'women to be eliminated', which included the names and personal information of prominent Zagreb intellectuals, such as Rada Iveković, Vesna Kesić, and other members of the Zagreb Women's Lobby, labelling them as 'witches' and accusing them, among other misdeeds such as of communism-profiteering,[4] of having covered up the rapes of Muslim and Croatian women by Serbs in Bosnia and Herzegovina. Their critical stance vis-à-vis the ruling party and their insistence on the gendered aspect of the war was clearly depicted as antinational and anti-Croat, but also as sexually 'deviant': the article's anonymous author associated their political and national unruliness with their 'failure' to marry (fellow Croats) and have children.[5] In their response, the members of the aforementioned feminist collectivity noted that although rape was a war strategy used in a more systematic and widespread way by the Serbian and Montenegrin Army, the Croat public should be aware of 'the deplorable fact that "our boys" also do it'.[6] The polarisation of women's collectives within the territory of the Yugoslav successor states over wartime rapes became manifest in two international meetings held in Zagreb, in 1992 and 1993, amidst a reigning nationalist imagery of women as either loyal members – sanctified mothers, wives, and sisters – of their national community or internal enemies and national traitors.

Thus, since the late 1980s, while the discursive conditions of the ensuing military conflict were being established, various grassroots feminist and women's groups across the region were involved in antimilitarist and antinationalist political work. Feminist groups engaged in solidarity activities with victims of war violence and refugee women, in the major cities of the former republics from the beginning of the war (Cockburn 1998; Cockburn et al. 2001). As Tanja Djuric-Kuzmanović, Rada Drezgić, and Dubravka Žarkov wrote: '*Women in Black*, an openly feminist group that most persistently opposed the politics of the regime of Slobodan Milošević in Serbia, used the image of mourning women in order to critique the militarist politics' (2008: 276). Elissa Helms (2003) has suggested that women's anti-war activism resorted to gender essentialisms: that is, representations of victimised, nurturing and peacemaking femininity. Helms has offered a critical look at the ways in which women's NGO initiatives by and for Bosnian women in the aftermath of the 1992–5 war in Bosnia–Herzegovina became involved in reproducing – while complicating – gendered affirmative essentialisms and ethno-national narratives of victim-hood (2013). Indeed, the logic of gender profoundly pervades and structures the relationship between victimhood and nation. Without doubt Helms' insightful contribution to an understand-ing of this interrelation has relevance for my work. However, my vantage point, marked as it is by an engagement with another kind of feminist movement from the ones that inform her study, differs in its emphasis, as it focuses more directly on the embodied, affective work of an antinationalist feminist col-lectivity that is ambivalently positioned within and against the field of 'their own' successor state of Yugoslavia. My research with antinationalist feminists in Serbia has made clear to me that ŽuC's agency centres on condemning militarist ideology and demanding justice from an antinationalist feminist perspective rather than on promoting ethnic reconciliation or celebrating women's peaceful nature.

In my enquiry, I have been particularly interested in the ways *ŽuC* deploys the idiom of 'mourning woman' in order to dismantle the militarist and hetero-familialist discursive matrix that has historically lent the stereotype of female mourning its normativity. In this sense, the question of 'essentialism' has been among the concerns that initially shaped my enquiry, as it pertained to the performative possibilities and perils implicit in the relation of the politics of mourning to its constitutive history. I seek to provide an alternative framework for engaging with the complicated ways in which *ŽuC* anti-war activism works to dismantle the repertoire of gendered assumptions underlying the reified, essentialised matrix of feminine-maternal peace-loving ethics of care. Although the trope of mourning might never be 'purged' completely of the familial and national logic it harbours within it, this activist mourning does not merely reiterate a humanitarian biopolitics of suffering but rather it enacts a critical affectivity that undermines the intelligibility of women's proper place of victimhood vis-à-vis the phallocentric logic of nationalism. Indeed, the ambiguities produced by this process of destabilisation proved to be among the most crucial stakes of this work. It is precisely through such a deconstructive-performative approach that I seek here to show how these activists' non-essentialist performative politics disputes the interpellating calls of gender categories and, especially, their investment in the powers of nationalism and militarism. In the midst of their mourning, by becoming radically implicated in disavowed losses and identifications, they situate themselves within the inscriptional space of existing norms and designations in ways that confound their regulatory claims of properness turning them into an agonistic occasion for antinationalist and antifascist feminism. In this sense, the self-reflective mourning of the activists with whom I worked resonates with Gillian Rose's claim that the work of mourning involves 'relinquishing *and taking up again* of activity which requires the fullest acknowledgement of active complicity' (1996: 122, emphasis in original).

Emergencies and Emergences

The feminist antimilitarist organisation Women in Black emerged in Jerusalem in January 1988, one month after the beginning of the first intifada, when a small group of Israeli Jewish women on the left, actively supported by Palestinian women, started marching into the West Bank to protest against the occupation. They also initially organised vigils in Jerusalem and later on in various other places around the country. Dressed in black, they would stand every Friday, usually for an hour in the afternoon, at some prominent place, such as a major intersection. The hallmark of those gatherings would be their wearing of placards with the phrase 'End the occupation', accompanied by a raised black hand. Gradually, the movement spread from Israel/Palestine to become a worldwide feminist movement opposing militarism, racism, social and economic injustice, 'humanitarian wars' and the 'war on terror' (Cockburn 2007). Since its inception, Women in Black has become an international movement of women who hold vigils, usually at rush hour in central public squares, at busy intersections or in front of major buildings and monuments, to protest against ethno-nationalist violence, militarism, imperialist power, capitalist injustices, racism, sexism, and homophobia.

In the vein of feminist dissent and patriotic disloyalty signalled by Women in Black in Israel, *Žene u Crnom Protiv Rata* (Women in Black against War) emerged in 1991 in Belgrade, as part of the resistance movement against the regime of Slobodan Milošević, and, more specifically, as a feminist critique to nationalism and militarism. They held their first vigil on 9 October 1991, after the outbreak of war in Croatia, in front of the Student Cultural Center in Belgrade's city centre. That first gathering of feminists in the city's centre marked one of the first public protests in Serbia to denounce the destruction of multi-ethnic Yugoslavia by the authoritarian and militarist regime of Slobodan Milošević. Ever since the inception of the movement, the main aspects of their politics have included: attempts to introduce the gender perspective into the mainstream anti-war movement in Serbia and in other Yugoslav republics; initiatives for solidarity among the states of the former Yugoslavia, with a particular emphasis on divided communities, such as Mostar, Bihac, and Prijedor; struggle against the use of rape as a means of war making and ethnic confrontation;[7] the organisation of actions of commemoration at the points where atrocities were committed in the name of the nation: Srebrenica, Vukovar, Sjeverin, Prijedor, Omarska, Tuzla, Visegrad, Štrpci, Bratunac, Zvornik; and to call the Serbian public to account for the massive extermination of Bosnian Muslim civilians in Srebrenica, in July 1995.[8]

Supported by and allying with other antimilitarist groups – such as the movement of conscientious objectors – and Belgrade's opposition intelligentsia, the first group of *ŽuC* consisted of feminists, leftists, war objectors and war deserters, refugees, people politically excluded from civic belonging by virtue of ethnicity and sexuality, as well as foreign allies and comrades. The latter helped significantly in mediating the communication among feminist groups in different regions of Yugoslavia during the war, at a time of closed borders and blocked communication. Within a context of intensified war fever and nationalist mobilisations, when the nation demanded the resolute and unambiguous loyalty of its gendered subjects, this collectivity, along with feminist groups in Croatia and Slovenia, protested against compulsory mobilisation and opposed growing nationalist fervour with all its gendered implications. As phrased in their first public statement:

> The work of women in peace groups is presupposed; it is invisible, trying, women's work; it is part of 'our' role; to care for others, to comfort, aid, tend wounds, and feed. The painful realization that the peace movement would, to some extent, also follow a patriarchal model caused a serious dilemma for feminist-pacifists. We wanted our presence to be visible, not to be seen as something 'natural', as part of a woman's role. We wanted it to be clearly understood that what we were doing was our political choice, a radical criticism of the patriarchal, militarist regime and a nonviolent act of resistance to policies that destroy cities, kill people, and annihilate human relations. (Women in Black statement, 1993, cited in Mladjenović and Hughes 2001)

Note that this was a time of widespread popular fascination with the leader, Slobodan Milošević, and a time in which the majority of Serbian women sided with 'Slobo' as he overtly shifted from a leader of socialist Yugoslavia to a nationalist politician aggressively promoting Serb sovereignty (Papić 2002). Anti-war feminists were those who did not become *seduced* by the interpellating orderliness of nationalism. As the *ŽuC* slogan puts it: 'We will not be seduced (or deceived) by our own' (*Ne dajmo se od svojih prevariti*).[9]

Despite and against the increasing national homogenisa-tion of the body politic in Serbia around a war regime, *ŽuC* organised weekly anti-war public actions from October 1991 through October 1995 at the Republic Square in Belgrade. Since then, their street actions have been continuing on specific-ally scheduled dates with varying frequency depending on the intensity of political exigencies. The silence of the standing women has been accentuated by slogans written on placards: 'Women, traitors of war, protest for peace' or 'We are disloyal'. When they did not meet with the public's apathy or overt contempt, these actions often ignited enraged attacks, such as those launched by the extreme right-wing militarist group *Beli Orlovi* ('White Eagles') in 1993. During the war in Bosnia, these activists denounced both the official Serbian policy and the paramilitary policies of ethnic supremacy, ethnic cleansing and ethnic rapes, while after the war they asked for an official assumption of responsibility on behalf of Serbia for its political and military nationalist activity. In 1995, *ŽuC* was prohibited from conducting solidarity work in a refugee camp. The activists continued to organise vigils until October of 1998, on the verge of NATO air strikes. After the overthrowing of the regime in 2000, they persisted in mobilising against nationalism and its concomitant sexism, but also economic injustice and neoliberal corporatisation, by organising actions of solidarity counter-memory in places where crimes were committed 'in the name of the nation'.

ŽuC activism should be contextualised within a heterogeneous and malleable realm of dissent in the context of 1990s Serbia (Erdei 1997; Jansen 2000; Lazić 1997; Spasić and Pavićević 1997; Torov 2000). Clearly, given the backdrop of a peculiar mixture of Yugoslav federalism and Serbian populist nationalism fabricated by the Milošević regime, one should take into consideration not only the internal heterogeneities of discourses of dissent (ranging from anti-communism to reformism, left-wing Yugoslav dissidence, and antinationalism), but also the political tensions and hierarchical distinctions within antinationalist discourse itself (ranging from 'elite' liberal cosmopolitanism to alter-globalism, pacifism, feminism and queer activism) (Jansen 2008). The political collectivity of *ŽuC* formed yet another polyvalent network of resistant and dissident solidarities within an already multilayered landscape of anti-war and anti-regime civil opposition during the 1990s (Fridman 2006).

Activism of Loss, Loss of Activism

It is in this context that I am looking at the historical conditions of possibility for the emergence of *ŽuC* as a form of grassroots political subjectivity engaging with displaced and dissident mourning. This feminist and antinationalist movement stemmed from a tradition of radical feminist and antinationalist thought and politics in the 1980s, mobilised against nationalism and its gendered/sexualised constituents in the 1990s, and formulated a critique of politics of 'transition' in the 2000s while struggling not to be absorbed by the depoliticised routine of post-conflict, post-Yugoslav NGO-isation. The *ŽuC* network became known in the public sphere mainly through its weekly vigils in the centre of Belgrade and in different places in Serbia and also in the former Yugoslavia. They were active in the massive demonstrations against Milošević in March 1991 in Belgrade before the war broke out, as well as in the massive demonstrations in Belgrade against the shelling of Sarajevo in 1992, often in cooperation with other dissident groups, such as the 1992-founded association of intellectuals 'Belgrade Circle', as well as the 1996–7 Winter Protest against the Milošević regime.[10] Their politics, openly feminist and firmly antinationalist within a wider landscape of an anti-Milošević coalition that was not always and univocally antinationalist (and also not always feminist), was signposted by two suggestive mottos: 'Not in our name' ('*Ne u naše ime*') and 'We will not be seduced by our own' ('*Ne dajmo se od svojih prevariti*').

In addressing the hopes and the strictures implicit in the *ŽuC* desire for the political, I have been asking how it is positioned vis-à-vis the currently forceful trend of elite humanitarianism, especially in an era of complacent diplomacy of healing and forgiveness. To what extent do these activists find themselves today under pressure – by their donors and others – to relinquish dissent and to assimilate into the corporative typology of non-governmental administration? How do they wield the dominant donor representations that typically cast women as 'natural' agents of ethnic reconciliation (Helms 2003)? How do they deal with interpellations to the managerial rationality of the post-political administrative order with its gendered underpinnings? Are they called to disavow and depoliticise the traumatic element and to reduce it to a spectacle of rationally administered order? Ultimately, is there also a lost or abandoned activism to be mourned, so to speak, in this era of euphoric non-governmental governmentality?

This last question regarding activism and its losses, or activism marked by loss, is crucially relevant in the context at hand. Rosalind Morris, in exploring the 1997 repatriation of the corpse of an exiled Thai revolutionary and its public depiction as the final interment of communism, has compellingly identified 'the loss of a commitment to revolutionary historical transformation' as 'the most significant loss of our age' (2003: 30). So, echoing Morris's perceptive claim, *ŽuC* activism reckons with this loss akin to the current dispassionate post-political hegemony by re-marking dissent with recurrent, experimental, and ex-centric meanings, despite the firmly entrenched lures of conformity. For these political subjects, the agonistic element in (accounting for) loss and otherness is a vehicle for performing a history of the present. Still, their ethics and politics of impossible mourning are imbued with the agonistic and generative intensity of loss. In other words, this is not so much about lamenting the loss of revolution but rather about prompting the revolutionary effects of loss.

Might we say that *ŽuC* activism, in addition to bringing into public view disavowed losses of the ethnic other – friend, kin, neighbour or complete stranger – also 'mourns', even implicitly, the 'lost ideals' of Yugoslav feminism or even the Socialist Federal Republic of Yugoslavia? For *ŽuC*, lost ideality, if any, is much more complicated and, in fact, forward-looking than a nostalgic longing for the remains of the 'East' – a sort of *Ostalgie*.[11] On the contrary, as I was able to trace from my engagement with the *ŽuC* activists, if there was some sense – albeit ambiguous and volatile – of 'lost ideality' to be 'mourned', that was not the 'existing socialist' regime itself that had been lethally marred by the upsurge of nationalism in the country's recent history, but rather the antifascist history and unrealised potential of multicultural conviviality, beyond and outside ethno-national purity and fixity. In this respect, these activists' attachment is to a 'Yugoslavia' as a site of resistance to be sustained from within the confines of loss and not as a lost origin to be recovered.

Slavica Stojanović, *ŽuC* activist, one of the first members of Belgrade Women's Studies, and the first Director of Reconstruction Women Fund, explained how she had to transfigure her love of Yugoslavia as an affective site of antifascist political and personal history into 'giving up' that once-unified country:

In the early 1990s, I was disturbed because I loved the former Yugoslavia very much. My grandmother was an Austro-Hungarian emancipated woman and when Yugoslavia was formed – first the kingdom and then the Yugoslav federation – she was very enthusiastic. Having lived as a minority, she was fed up with nationalism. So, I was raised in an antifascist atmosphere. My mother was a member of antifascist youth. Having this kind of background, I was confronted with a situation in which I loved Yugoslavia – with a love grounded in the political history of my family, my grandmother and my mother – but eventually I had to give up the Yugoslavia that was leading us to a war. As Yugoslavia was on the verge of breakup, I had to resolve this conflict in myself. I had to give up Yugoslavia.

Although some of my interlocutors would easily acknowledge the 'positive effects' the former socialist state had on women's lives, others argued that state-sponsored women's emancipation and gender equality worked to legitimise a persistent patriarchal ideology and entailed the diminishment of the space of women's political subjectivity. Daša Duhaček has offered an astute account of this 'loss' in the realm of women's political subjectivity: 'The women in Yugoslavia did not learn the lesson in citizenship as a way of constructing political subjectivity. Instead, a thin layer of ideologically based egalitarianism was superimposed on a stable patriarchy' (1993: 135). Rather than a kind of nostalgia for a burdened socialist Yugoslav past itself or a desire to restore it, the affect of lost ideality figured, for those of my interlocutors who were veterans of Yugoslav dissidence and of 'ambivalently Yugoslav feminism' (Zaharijević 2013: 14), a certain space for imagining an unattained ideal and motivating what is yet to come – an alternative to both ethno-national demarcations and the multiple violences and injustices generated by our globalised contemporaneity.

Above all, however, their enduring commitment is to losses unrecognised as such by official master narratives: those singular and disparate losses of people, communities, affective bonds, and the possibility of co-habitation and relationality that was denounced and attenuated by pervasive nationalism and militarism. So, there was something especially intimate that these activists had 'lost' in those disavowed affective and political losses, and it is this deeply complicated sense of loss that, in moving and motivating them, became the touchstone for their political subjectivity. As some of my Serb informants intimated to me, if they felt Yugoslavs (*Jugoslovenke*) before the wars of succession, the Serb politics of expropriating the Yugoslav identity for ethno-nationalist use had rendered it impossible for them to identify as Yugoslav any longer. Serb identity, on the other hand, had been equated, for them, with the nationalist and militarist ideology of the 'aggressor state', and thus, they renounced it vehemently by taking up feminism as a space of enforced – albeit paradoxically enabling – homelessness and contentious citizenship (Zaharijević 2013).

Coming from Serbian and various ethnically mixed backgrounds, the women (and a few men) from the *ŽuC* movement with whom I worked have lived through the events of Serbian nationalist projects, ethno-nationalist ideologies, war, and disintegration in 1990s. Those events have affected their life-worlds in ways painfully transformative of their subjectivities, dispositions, relations, and desires. The lives of my friends in *ŽuC*, as well as the lives of their kin members and friends, were devastated when 'their' ethnic communities, having coexisted for a long time, entered into armed conflict with 'other' communities. So, it was also a certain possibility of intimacy and social proximity that *they* have lost in these disavowed losses. Their loss is political and social as well as profoundly personal. As such, this intensely felt sense of embodied dispossession has been, and continues to be, a formative – and affirmative – aspect of their political subjectivity. My friends have experienced, witnessed, and related to displacement, imprisonment, extermination, violation, international sanctions, and bombardment. They have undergone, endured, and resisted the multiple violences of the Milošević regime and the innumerable ungrievable losses precipitated by the breakup of Yugoslavia. The fabric of their sociality and political subjectivity has been shattered in many ways. In and through this shattering, they have deployed and reoriented strategies of survival, solidarity, and alternative co-habitation while passionately contesting the regimes of banalised ungrieavability.

Contemplating the lived intensities of such operations of survival, mourning, and testimony might prompt one to pursue the questions: Why do these activists insist on holding on to the irrevocable remains of this painful past? Why do they refuse to let this past vanish? Why do they resist concurring with the assignment of its management to post-war juridical rationalities? What sort of critical potentiality do they seek to activate in refusing 'institutional' closures, in recollecting and retelling these injurious stories, and in attending to a persistent claim of accountability for the dispossession of the other?[12] Arguably, there is an ethical and political stake in their persistent and restless commitment to continuously inscribing, and transcribing, themselves into the events of the 1990s. As Slavica commented, in talking with me: 'The dominant discourse nowadays looks at the future. Talking about the past is not considered an appropriate thing to do. For us, however, it is important to insist.' The *ŽuC* gesture of inhabiting the same space of injury assumes a special significance in a context where ruling elites seem all too inclined to forge a historical continuity that brackets off the recent burdened past or relegates it to the formal repertoires of post-socialist and post-conflict jurisdiction.

ŽuC activists contest the prevailing truth regimes, including those of post-nationalist exaltation, which command that, when it comes to the history of the breakup of Yugoslavia, there is nothing left to fight over – there is nothing worth fighting over. Theirs is not a 'normal' or introjective mourning, as described by Freud in 'Mourning and melancholia'. Instead of getting over the loss, they maintain its structural possibility as another affirmation of the political, from which to resist sovereignty. In reflecting the complexities and subtleties that underlie the above question of why these activists insist on recalling an ineluctable, painful past, I came across, again and again, manifestations of their exilic, post-nationalist feminist sensibility as an agonistic means to replot and re-member the political. Resisting the loss of activism emerges as constitutive dimension of their dissident and transformative mourning. Conversely, they resist and defer assuasive impulses of an immediately available psychic, symbolic, and political closure. In this respect, their radical performative stance on memory cannot be reduced to a moral or juridical governmentality of retribution and atonement. Hence it does not fit in a matrix of forgiveness versus resentment. Their demand is not absorbed by grand narratives and grand gestures taking place on the level of 'official' discursivity. In times when the fraught link between politics and the commemoration of wartime atrocities and injustices has drawn post-Yugoslav public attention through spectacularised media events such as the trial of Ratko Mladić at The Hague, their demand has involved intervening in the fabric of everyday and insidious sociality, that is, where normativity acquires its structural determinacy and naturalised intimacy. So, my anthropological attention was captured by the ways in which these political subjects inscribed their protest within, despite, and against the spatial and temporal forms of power that make up 'the scene of the ordinary' (Das 2007: 218). The activist work of antinationalist feminists in Serbia at a time of intensified ethno-nationalist violence resonates with Veena Das's perceptive remark in reference to the embeddedness of subjects' experiences into events of violence as lived at the level of the 'ordinary': 'Thus, just as I think of the event as attached to the everyday, I think of the everyday itself as eventful' (2007: 8).

Indeed, it is through these eventful intersections of political trauma and traumatic political, in their varying hues, that the work of *ŽuC* in Belgrade and in other sites of post-Yugoslavia propels unexpected futures for a (desire of the) political yet to come. The justice that this political collectivity puts into practice does not imply a retributive or legalistic sense of justice. It rather chimes with the Benjaminian idea of solidarity with the annihilated victims of injustice (1969). As *ŽuC* activist Miloš Urošević put it in a conversation with me:

> In our vigils, we are in the place of the victims of nationalism, those who have no way to speak, and, at the same time, in the place of those who are alive but commonly viewed as lives not to be lived.

And another activist, Slavica Stojanović, articulated the *ŽuC* demand as one of 'political accountability' rather than one that would prescribe 'the moralism of guilt'. In my friends' perspective, a critical engagement with a politics of accountability would involve mobilising the possibility for justice without and beyond moralised forms of vengeance or reprieve.

Counter-Memory, Living On

Through the concepts of 'subjugated knowledges' and 'counter-memory', Foucault has put practices of remembering and forgetting in the context of power relations. The point of critical genealogies is to trace the epistemic frictions and subjugations that have produced sedimented histories and memories. Thus, critical genealogies disrupt monumental history with a sense of counter-memory: they transform 'history into a totally different form of time' (1977: 160). During its own history, *ŽuC* has been performing a politics of counter-memory that undoes the banalisation of disposability incurred by ethnocentric and heteronormative national cultures. Contrary to exercises in discourses of blame but also of moralistic testimonial truth-declaring, the activist work of *ŽuC* is geared toward bearing witness as an arduous engagement in the political action of counter-memory. Their mnemonic and commemorative affective politics of social dissent puts into play – rather than leaving in abeyance or pretending to fix – the constitutive tension between the normative and the counter-normative forces historically at work in the registers of mourning and bearing witness.

Since the emergence of the movement, *ŽuC* has been interweaving feminism with antinationalism in order to embody a politics that reimagines old and new contingencies from the standpoint of gendered stories of destitution, loss, forbearance, and resistance. In acutely combating official and formalised disavowal, and in publicly acknowledging the dead of the 'rival side' (officially construed as inhabiting the space of death anyway), these activists have been undermining the prescriptive associations of mourning with the feminine, the familial, and the patriotic, while, at the same time, exposing the silences shrouding injurious national and gendered histories. Indeed, as I argue throughout this book, the poetics and politics of dissent, as it is performed by *ŽuC*, dismantles nationalist and phallocentric discourses, while, at the same time, recalling the meaning of critique as an eventful practice of reiterating that also reclaims and redirects the object of contestation, be it memory, mourning, gender or national affiliation.

So these activists' performative politics of counter-memory does not aim to increase or expand memory in a context and a world that have too much of it. Rather than a concern with managing too much or too little memory, they focus on the conditions that make possible a 'common sense' of what is worth remembering. My enquiry over the last decade has made me increasingly aware that *ŽuC* deploys, dismantles, and inverts the master narratives of national memory and mourning in order to demand accountability from those who author, or master, these master narratives. Given that the cultural idiom of mourning

– in the former Yugoslavia, as elsewhere – is imbued with the nationalistic and heterosexist fantasy of the 'mother of the nation', the weeping mother who has honourably sacrificed her sons to the nation's military pursuits, *ŽuC* undermines the normative role assigned to women by nationalism and kinship normativity by re-embodying the sign of mourning outside the sanctioned boundaries of proper femininity and national allegiance. The sexually and nationally marked idiom of mourning, predicated upon the relegation of the female to the maternal as a means of honouring the nation's reproductive aims, is catachrestically appropriated by *ŽuC*: mourning is enacted beyond and against the proper meanings and places of *oikos* (as home and homeland, both conventionally construed as topoi of the heteronormative imperative).

This performative work of reflective and agonistic mourning turns a 'common place' of national memory into a disturbing heterotopia that de-normalises the way in which the nation *takes place* as the exclusive sharing of a common space and time (including a common space and time for proper mourning). As the national commonplace in its reassuring orderliness is displaced and reoriented onto the ones with no liveable place in the common affectivity of the national archive, another sense of reflective sharedness is emerging from this ongoing remembering of trauma and loss. These agonistic – rather than consolatory and accommodational – modes of memory are not meant merely to remember in the sense of recuperating historical truth in order to make an archival corpus complete (a task ultimately impossible but also susceptible to authoritative conceits of fullness). In other words, their efforts are not directed toward 'mastering' the past (*Vergangenheitsbewältigung*).[13] Instead, they address and politically reactivate the master narratives of remembering in ways that account for their ellipses, stratifications, and dismemberments. The very putting into play of these norms of mnemonic intelligibility, without anticipation, is a crucial part of the *ŽuC* political vision. In this sense, this agonistic politics involves deploying the actuality of counter-memory as a history *in* and *of* the present: that is, not as a mere affirmation of the present as it is, but rather as a critical performative engagement with the established matrix of memorability that produces and sustains presentness and the present.

As I further unravel later, these political subjects do not only expose their bodies to the *polis*'s regime of intelligible appearance (Arendt 1998; Butler 2011). They also expose this regime as exclusive and differential through their embodied engagement with the spectrality of appearing and disappearing, assembling and dissembling. In appearing out of place in the *polis*'s space of appearance/apparitions, their memory for those who cannot appear is not enacted as recovery but rather as trace: that is, as the mark of loss and testimony, which always entails and affects the survivor – the one who becomes dispossessed after the other's death. From the perspective of my interlocutors, counter-memory is the survival of memory: a survival that 'carries within itself the trace of an ineffaceable incision' (Derrida 2004: 7). The subjects with whom I worked are bearers of this iterable 'trace', or incision, that denotes memory, testimony, trauma, and disruption. They carry on a survival with an incision. They are marked by, and bear witness to, the trace of the other's loss, which they transform into a performative power that leaves traces in the body of politics. Inspired by Derrida's analytics of survival (*survival*, *survivre*) as both more life and more than life (1985), Bonnie Honig explores the relevance of this double meaning of survival for democratic theory: 'in their agonistic partnership, these two aspects of survival – mere life and more life – set the parameters of democratic life and emergency politics and invite us to deliver on their promise' (2009: xviii). From this perspective, living on – as always conditioned by unequal structures of 'living together' and 'falling apart' — is not an exercise of indivisible sovereignty, but rather bears on the most intimate and intense traces of democracy. Thus understood, the struggles and agonies of survival give rise to a new understanding of the effects and affects of agonistic mourning.

Critical Agency and Political Catachresis

This book concerns laying claim to mourning rites for the other and with the other, as an unsettling mode of *parler-femme* (Irigaray 1985b), or of speaking (as) woman, which has the potential to hold grids of intelligibility open to the disruptive performative. This line of enquiry resounds in the questions that Luce Irigaray has posed with respect to Antigone's pathos: 'Is mourning itself her *jouissance*? . . . Does she anticipate the decree of death formulated by those in power? Does she duplicate it? Has she given in? Or is she still in revolt?' (1985a: 219). While Irigaray is right to invoke Antigone as a figure of ambivalent and fractious complexity, the rigid disjunction between *either* reiterating *or* subverting, inverting or perverting can only be taken as a heuristic device. It is precisely through taking up and re-enacting the inextricable link between injured engagement with regulatory norms and a passion for their transformation that the bodily intensity of *ŽuC* intimate assemblies disturbs the configurations of power within which it is inscribed. To ask such questions in the context that concerns me here is to pursue the question of critical agency through the perspective of what Judith Butler, apropos of her work on Antigone's claim, calls 'political catachresis': 'Antigone is the occasion for a new field of the human, achieved through political catachresis, the one that happens when the less than human speaks as human' (2000: 82). In contrast to readings that take Antigone as a universal figure of exemplary lamentation and her lamentation as a model for liberal dissidence, I draw from Butler's argument in order to tackle the problematic of mourning as a layered figure of political catachresis critically engaging with the hierarchies of grievability (2000).[14]

I concur with Bonnie Honig's cogent critique when she takes issue with an extrapolitical ethics of 'mortalist humanism' that is currently being developed often in the name of Antigone. In seeking an alternative to treatments of Antigone as a universalised figure of anti- or post-political mortalist humanism, she argues that Antigone's dirge and eventual death are political acts pointing 'in the direction of an agonistic, not a mortalist, humanism' (2010: 26). There is no doubt that agonism draws not only on suffering, vulnerability, and finitude but also, and perhaps simultaneously, on desire, pleasure, hope, and mutuality (ibid.). Honig rightly remarks that the mortalist humanist idea 'informs the recent move away from a justice of accountability in (post)conflictual politics and toward truth and reconciliation commissions that focus, rather, on forgiveness . . .' (2013: 26). In challenging understandings of Antigone as outside the political, she evokes an array of political enactments of protest — from the Argentinean Madres de Plaza de Mayo to the 'anti-war mom' Cindy Sheehan — that are grounded in maternal mourning. Expanding Honig's worry that a politics of lamentation determined by a paradigm of mortalist humanism might have depoliticising effects (and turn into a 'lamentation of politics'), I am most interested in extracting the political implications of calling into question the humanist distinction between 'agonism' and 'mortalism', which undergirds the gesture to pit an agonistic against a mortalist or lamentational humanism.

In departing from humanist frameworks of theorising agonism, I would like to ask whether the analytics of agonistic democratic politics is doomed to re-inscribing and perpetuating foundationalist binaries such as those between pleasure and finitude, courage and vulnerability, or between natality and susceptibility to suffering and death. More provocatively, (why) would one need to move away *from* mortality *to* natality in order to argue for agonism or engage with agonistic politics? And why would one seek to analytically remove agony or agonal politics from the register of agonistic commitment? In what follows, I would like to delineate an account of agonism as an occasion for displacing the moral and juridical foundations of the 'human' that often underpin approaches of agonism. In this account, I attempt to render such foundations and reified dichotomies contingent and contentious. To do so, I suggest that it is important to address, again and again, how politically consequential it might be to invoke the trope of natality – in all its religious and reproductive undertones that bespeak an *arché* – in order to make sense of, and foster, a political praxis of 'bringing something into being', as though this is purely inaugural and free of determination. Furthermore, by evoking natality as a theme that underpins the notion of human action, we might risk remaining by and large within the biopolitical bounds of maternal logics, which has been scripted as an absolutely universal synecdoche of newness, and a paradigmatic signpost of self-negating relationality. As I further discuss in the last section of the book, Honig usefully disallows a mere reduction of natality to maternity (2013). I am interested, however, in countering the recalcitrant surfeits of humanist thinking that the natality paradigm carries, even inadvertently. In this regard, I would like here to displace the certainty of the structural opposition between an alleged positivity of natality and negativity of mourning, and, instead, explore their mutual and undecidable imbrications.

The political mourning of *ŽuC*, which might be termed 'mourning' only by virtue of an agonistic catachresis, has de-authorising effects in the national and feminine, universalised matrix of grief. I would contend, then, that catachresis in this context implies both incompleteness and impropriety; it is understood not merely as a figure of speech but rather as the act of 'reversing, displacing, and seizing the apparatus of value-coding' (Spivak 1990: 228). What makes the poetics and politics of *ŽuC* mourning catachrestic in and of itself is that it dismantles 'the apparatus of value-coding', particularly the one related to the politics of grievability. At the same time as they repeat and differ, as their difference unfixes the 'loyalty' of ritualistic repetition, these political subjects break through conventional loyalties and ascribed identities of gender, sexuality, and nation. Disloyalty is construed in this context both as performative interruption of established and familiar chains of reiteration and as non-compliance to the ordinances of national intimacy.

The transformative plasticity of political signifiers – albeit contextually constrained by the sedimentation of prior conventions that Butler calls 'condensed historicity' (1997b: 3) – is central to the texture of performativity understood in terms of citationality. Butler has rethought agency as 'the hiatus in iterability' (1993: 220). What is called agency, then, consists in

> a repetition that fails to repeat loyally, a reciting of the signifier that must commit a disloyalty against identity – a catachresis – in order to secure its future, a disloyalty that works the iterability of the signifier for what remains non-self-identical in any invocation of identity, namely, the iterable or temporal conditions of its own possibility. (1993: 220)

Drawing from this account of performativity, this project seeks to explore the differential nuances and political possibilities of catachresis, as they take place in the realm of antinationalist feminist re-inscription of grievability.

I would like to argue in favour of breaking through the literalist, universalist, moralist, and humanist scripts of mourning and easing the grip of the binary between affirmative militancy and regressive grief, a binary often conventionally inscribed in terms of political, proactive, or emancipatory natalism versus reactive, depoliticising mortalism. Drawing on the material presented within this book, my suggestion is that once we challenge such configurations, we might be able to begin to make sense of the incalculably complicated and politically enabling ways in which these activists stage mourning as a site of agonistic resignification in order to interrogate the hierarchies, injustices, and foreclosures upon which the dominant regime of grievability is sustained. In embodying the spectral potentiality of displaced memory, they performatively bring forth an alternative public, however suffused with friction and precariousness, which redefines the ways in which people come together and go to pieces in public.

If being hardwired into the citationality of violences of grievability is inevitable, I ask what agonistic demands and possibilities would emerge from this complicity; what possibilities of agonism that would rework and deconstitute established structures of violence and complicity. For sure, the embodied practices of the activists with whom I worked are, in many inevitable and intractable ways, embedded within and interpellated by the injurious effects of nationalist, militarist, and heteronormative discourses. Their practices, like all possibility of agency, are immanent to these sedimented terms of power and modes of subjectivation. It is through and despite such terms of power and subjectivation that these subjects come to enact their desire for the political. Their working on the register of grievability implicitly reinvokes a broad discursive genealogy of 'care for others' as a morally and socially ordained virtue, and a mode of subjectivation, historically associated with the privatised, liberal morality of middle-class white femininity. However, what is most pertinent to the purposes of my argument is how the ŽuC movement is enacted as a non-sovereign intersubjectivity, at once formed by normative matrices and acting upon them, beyond the binary between affirmation and negation. This performative politics 'queers' mourning by exposing and decentring its categorical schemes of identification and incorporation, be they related to the nation's friend/enemy distinctions or to patriarchal and maternalist kinship structures. Activist Nađia Duhaček talked about the *ŽuC* entanglement of feminism and antinationalism in terms of mutual 'queering'. Indeed, *ŽuC* agonistic mourning signals performative processes of collective contestation vis-à-vis matrices of gender, kinship, and national normativity. In their own different and distinct ways, non-normative affiliations emerging out of this agonistic politics of mourning echo the Mothers of Plaza de Mayo in Argentina, who, as Cecilia Sosa has shown, enact a queer form of kinship with their children, as their emblematic claims 'One child, all the children' and 'Our children gave birth to us' displace the familialist temporal pre-conditions of grief and render loss collective (Sosa 2014).

As I noted earlier, the question of whether or 'to what degree' the abjectified queering of affective affiliations emerging out of the performativity of mourning might come, despite itself, to re-entrench the essentialised ordinances of normativity cannot simply be answered in a programmatic fashion. This uncertainty holds in all queer moments. Although there is no doubt that relations of power can be further secured through processes of destabilization and transgression (Ahmed 2000), and although there might be always a need to ask this question anew, a kind of programmatic 'assessment' would subsume the contingent performative temporalities and corporealities involved in the specific field of power relations. There is arguably no act that could be labelled intrinsically subversive or transgressive in and of itself, out of the structural determinacy and contingency of its context; and no critical agency could be ever considered to elude regulatory inscriptions or to be immune to the perils of being renormalised by the terms that it repudiates. In this sense, more relevant to my approach would be to trace the thick performative texture of critical agency in all its infinite malleability and incalculability. My perspective, guided by the desires, losses, and visions of my interlocutors, seeks to gesture toward such openness. Holding on to openness is not to be conflated here with disregarding the multiple closures and foreclosures operating in the field of power relations. Rather, it is to seek to find the critical tools to attend to the ways in which people, under strained circumstances, are prompted to act within and against fields of power, through engaging with differential, differentiating, and self-differentiated political eventualities.

In theorising critical agency, I follow Lila Abu-Lughod who, taking up Michel Foucault's well-known formulation that 'resistance is never in a position of exteriority to power' (Foucault 1981: 95), has suggestively alerted us against reductionist conceptualisations of power and resistance. She importantly proposes that instead of perceiving acts of resistance as transgressions of structures of power, they should be read within (rather than outside) complex interworkings of formative power configurations, as a 'diagnostic of power' (1990). Even more relevantly to our purposes here, Talal Asad has focused on pain in order to think critically about agency – one of the conceptual bulwarks of Western liberalism – beyond triumphalist accounts and their reliance upon embedded and celebrated assumptions of self-empowerment, individualism, and voluntary history-making. Such paradigmatic model of 'agency', Asad remarks, 'presupposes a teleological history and an essentialised human subject' (2000: 29). In this context of liberal ethics, agency is premised upon the idea of a subject's capacity and desire to author its own history by moving 'in a singular historical direction: that of increasing self-empowerment and decreasing pain' (2003: 79). Arguing against the tendency to romanticise agency as the self-ownership of an individual threatened by an external injurious power, Asad asks 'whether pain is not simply a *cause* of action, but can also itself be a *kind* of action' (2003: 69, emphasis in original).

In the vein of this immensely instructive critique, as I seek to rethink the performative condition of becoming and unbecoming a political subject as shaped (albeit not exhaustively) by social norms and in relationality to others, I am indebted to Judith Butler's theorisation of subjectivity, agency, vulnerability, desire, and ethical responsibility, as they are formed within – and occasionally against – matrices of normative intelligibility (1997a, 2004, 2005). Drawing on Foucault's insights on the notion of critique as located within the field of self-formation and de-subjugation (*désassujettissement*) (1997: 47), Butler writes:

> But if that selfforming is done in disobedience to the principles by which one is formed, then virtue becomes the practice by which the self forms itself in desubjugation, which is to say that it risks its deformation as a subject, occupying that ontologically insecure position which poses the question anew: who will be a subject here, and what will count as a life, a moment of ethical questioning which requires that we break the habits of judgment in favor of a riskier practice that seeks to yield artistry from constraint. (2001)

To echo this perceptive formulation, I would like to argue that what is at stake in my study is precisely a contested domain where subjects 'risk their deformation as subjects', 'occupy ontologically insecure positions', and, at the same time, 'yield artistry from constraint'. In this text, I explore activist agency as it performatively takes place within delimited and intractable assemblages of power, embodiment, subjectivity, and de-subjugation.

From this perspective, the eventness of the *ŽuC* critical agency encompasses diverse affective processes of subjectivation and de-subjugation involved in lived experiences of trauma and loss. Affective responses to loss and banalised disposability are performed through moving and being moved: through mutual exposure of bodies in movement and in proximity of others. In this regard, we might think of entwined movement and proximity along Sarah Ahmed's lines: 'Hence movement does not cut the body off from the "where" of its inhabitance, but connects bodies to other bodies – indeed, attachment takes place through movement, through being moved by the proximity of others' (2005: 100). Such performative textures of the connection of bodies to other bodies – afflicted bodies and bodies in distress but no less in transformation and agency – are central to the constitution of the feminist activist collective subject that concerns me here. The mode of 'being moved by the proximity of others' describes the *ŽuC* critical agency as a mode of situated and restless sociability that moves away from the *polis*, and, at the same time, returns to it, thus embodying a relationality, much as this may be traumatic and broken.

'Anamnestic Solidarity' and 'Wounded Attachments'

The affective register of becoming 'beside oneself' and 'being moved by the proximity of others', as it is performed by the *ŽuC* activists, cannot be reduced to the kinship and sexual contract that assigns women as maternal or sisterly self-negating 'caretakers' of their own nation's honour. Perhaps it can never immunise itself against re-inscription in it either. Nonetheless, the modality of simultaneous moving and being moved by others, in this context, describes a political agency that passionately relies on relationality to those cast as unworthy of relation, in order to transfigure such violent legacies of disposability. Hence, relationality transforms itself into a question of the political and its foreclosures, thus giving rise to concern about how to forge a grammar of solidarity with others in the aftermath of violence, without resorting to the reifying categories of universal moralism and without repeating the ethical violence at the heart of humanitarian attempts to appropriate and idealise the other as an object of solidarity.

As the material explored in this book illustrates, all collective political mobilisation of the Nietzschean sense of a wounded attachment, especially in critical modes that no longer rely on liberal legalistic discourse, does not necessarily amount to depoliticising, injury-based, and blame-forming identity claims. Exploring a crucial aspect of contemporary liberal American politics, Wendy Brown is right to alert us against 'legal "protection" for a certain injury-forming identity' (1995: 21). Sharing this critical perspective on identity politics and the liberal state, but propelled by a different context from the one informing Brown's reflections, I seek to address woundedness more in terms of solidarity, relationality, subjectification, and collective freedom than in terms of protection, individual rights, identity politics, and state policies. Thus, I pursue the question of whether such re-articulation of collective and collectively mobilised vulnerability would be a gesture that occasions (rather than finalises) political action.

In this sense, I strive here to offer an alternative to ordinary binary schemes such as victimhood versus agency, or vulnerability versus resistance. The challenge, at once theoretical and political, is how to address political injury and related solidarity projects without perpetuating essentialised narratives of victimhood, in all their gendered and ethnicised ramifications. At the same time, however, another related challenge is how not to withdraw from addressing such injuries in the name of their inextricable associations with entrenched essentialisms of victimhood (which, to be sure, abound in the context of this study).

To respond to such conundrums requires breaking through both celebration of resistance as impervious and invulnerable and deploration of injury as inactive and depleted of agency.

So, both the notion of 'victim' and the notion of 'solidarity' are at issue in this context, as they are both given a potential for conceptual and political reorientation for the purposes of capturing the malleabilities and ambivalences implicit in acts of collectively contesting injustice. What is at stake here is what Christian Lenhardt, in an essay on Marx and Benjamin, called 'anamnestic solidarity' (1975: 151). Indeed, Walter Benjamin, in his 'Theses on the Philosophy of History', refers to solidarity with the victims of historical justice (1969). At the same time, he has defied the culture of commemoration as a mode of closure – that is, as an 'affirmative' process of healing the wounds caused by the war. His resistance to conventional cultures of commemoration is undoubtedly related to his own trauma inflicted by the anti-war suicides of his friends, and his fear that mourning would put a closure on the cause for which they had died (Jay 1998). Benjamin's solidarity of remembering, which gives primacy to the victims' perspective, is at odds with modes of conventional mourning (as closure) but also of conventional solidarity (as objectified enclosed community). In a similarly critical view on conventional solidarity, Jodi Dean has elaborated on the concept of 'reflective solidarity' as openness to difference which 'provides a form of consideration of the other' (1996: 30) beyond identity politics and in opposition to exclusionary demarcations. In the affective economy of alternative engagements with grievability that is at issue here, the 'anamnestic' and 'reflective' textures of solidarity are enacted to mobilise political responsiveness and collective protest.

The *ŽuC* critical engagement with impossible mourning does not indicate a kind of mourning that would eventually 'work through' the wound in a linear process of moralistic self-recovery.

Rather, in building alliance with those cast as expendable and dispensable, it claims a political life based on responsive relationality in light of these disavowed losses. This event of being-with, which is performed by marked gendered bodies against the logic of the nationalised and masculinised border, might work to counter the conventional idea of 'community', which hinges on the principles of fraternity, victimhood, ethno-national affinity, and exclusionary nationalism. Instead of essentialised self-enclosed and delimited sovereign entity, community is here construed as by definition liminal and inoperative, always coming to the limit of its own working. Rendering the proper logic of community inoperative is indispensable to how community is possible (Nancy 2004). In Nancy's words: 'Community without community is *to come*, in the sense that it is always *coming*, endlessly, at the heart of every collectivity (because it never stops coming, it ceaselessly resists collectivity itself as much as it resists the individual' (2004: 71). When Nancy gives this sharing the name of 'fraternity' (1994), however, even not in the sense of a unified common family but rather as a relation of those who become brothers 'in the sharing of [the dead father's] dismembered body' (1994: 72), he tacitly partakes in a long tradition of familialist, indeed fraternal, and phallogocentric construals of community (Pateman 1988). Following Derrida (2005c), Tuija Pulkkinen (2009) has usefully registered doubts about the use of fraternity as a privileged trope for democratic belonging and sharing. Indeed, unsettling the proper logic of community – that is, common origin – requires the questioning of the concept of 'fraternity' and its violent determination of who belongs to the community and who does not. It requires thwarting the tendency to neutralise difference, namely the other of the brother: the sister, the stranger, the non-affiliated.

In this troubled terrain of producing political subjectivities involved in an ambivalent moral economy of solidarity, community-without-community is put into practice, without identity and without finality, by means of addressing the injunctions and injuries through which being-in-common is established in the first place. This does not mean that solidarity can ever (easily, entirely) escape partaking in, and being inadvertently complicit with, the violence of appropriating the other. And yet, it should never stop coming. Arguably, this troubled entanglement at the heart of relating to otherness is one of the daunting questions that mobilise this study.

Notes

1 The party, then called 'Socialist Labor Party of Yugoslavia (Communists)', was founded as an opposition party in the Kingdom of Serbs, Croats and Slovenes in 1919. Under the leadership of Josip Broz Tito from 1937 to 1980, it became the first communist party in power that opposed the directives of the Soviet Union and thus was expelled from the Cominform in 1948.

2 See <http://www.zenskestudie.edu.rs/en/about-us/center-s-history> (last accessed 23 October 2016).

3 The formation of the group was inspired by the feminist conference 'The Woman's Question: A New Approach', which was held in 1978 at the Student Cultural Centre in Belgrade. The purpose of the meeting was to challenge socialist patriarchy and the reduction of women's struggle to class struggle (Papić 1995). As a result of that meeting, Women and Society discussion groups formed in 1979 in Zagreb and Belgrade with similar ones founded in subsequent years in Novi Sad, Sarajevo, and Ljubljana (Hughes et al. 1995). The official Yugoslav state women's organisation, Plenary for Women's Social Activities, had condemned the feminist group Women and Society as an 'enemy of the state', 'capitalist' and 'friendly/ leaning towards feminism' (Papić 1995). In 1990, feminists formed the Women's Lobby to campaign against militarisation, nationalist politics, and national-demographic pressures exerted on women to reproduce more for a Great Serbia. After the first multi-party elections in Yugoslavia, in 1990, which resulted in a Serbian Parliament with minimal women's representation, they formed the Women's Parliament, on 8 March 1991, in order to

monitor new legislature pertaining to women (Mladjenović and Hughes 2001).

4 One of the habitual anti-communist and anti-feminist representational strategies used in the 1990s was to depict women as 'collaborators' with former communist regimes (Slapšak 2002: 150).

5 *Globus*, 11 December 1992, pp. 33–4.

6 <http://www.women-war-memory.org/index.php/en/povijest/vjestice-iz-ria/41-liste-zena-za-odstrel> (last accessed 2 April 2014).

7 The camps of ethnic rape in the former Yugoslavia realised in the most painfully emblematic manner the biopolitical project of regulating the body politic according to the norms of ethnic and patrilinear reproduction. The military prevalence over the rival ethnic community was consolidated through the rape of the enemy's women and their use as reproductive means of demographic predominance. In the notorious Serbian camp of Omarska (established in a former quarry close to the city of Prijedor), in Bosnia–Herzegovina, Bosnian Muslim women and Croatian women were held captive, sexually harassed, made pregnant by force and detained until the eighth month of their pregnancy so as to deny them access to an artificial termination of pregnancy. Thanks to the struggle of survivors of the rape camps, on 18 December 1992, the United Nations (UN) Security Council condemned the 'massive, organized and systematic detention and rape of women, in particular Muslim women, in Bosnia and Herzegovina' and declared it an international crime that must be addressed (UN Security Council Resolution 798). An account of the history of the 20,000 women raped during the war in Yugoslavia is offered in the movie *Grbavica* by Jasmila Žbanić (2005). Moreover, the documentary *Calling the Ghosts* (1996) by Mandy Jacobson and Karmen Jelincić registers the testimonies of two women, Jadranka Cigelj and Nusreta Sivać, who survived the repeated rapes they were subjected to in the Omarska camp.

8 In the small Bosnian town of Srebrenica, in July 1995, Serbian paramilitary groups gathered Muslim families in sports fields, schools, and factories and exterminated, in five days, 8,000 boys and men. Ratko Mladić's aim was to eliminate the enclave of Srebrenica, the sole exclusively Muslim town that existed in 1995 in the region of eastern Bosnia. Pleading guilty to the charge and assuming the responsibility for the fact that the Dutch peacemakers, the Blue Helmets who had been assigned by the UN and NATO the mission of protecting the enclave, left the enclaved civilians to be prey for Mladić's men, the entire Dutch government resigned in 2002. The question of the participation of nearly 100 Greek volunteers

in the occupation of the town on the side of the Serbian troops remains unexplored; once the massive massacre of Muslim civilians had started, they paraded through the town centre and planted the Greek flag amidst the ruins of an Orthodox temple. Although mass graves have been found, some claim even today that the ethnic cleansing operation has never taken place.

According to the verdict of the International Court in The Hague, in February 2007, Serbo-Bosnian forces were responsible for the Srebrenica massacre. According to the ruling, there is no evidence that the Serbian government bears direct responsibility for the organisation of the commitment of genocide in Bosnia–Herzegovina, except for its failure to prevent the commitment of such acts. In the summer of 2007 the Serbian government acknowledged and apologised publicly for the massacre of Bosnian civilians in Srebrenica by Serbian forces. This acknowledgement on the part of the government marks a dramatic shift away from the former official Serbian position, which covered over or understated the size of the disaster.

9 Adriana Zaharijević mentions that Žarana Papić (1949–2002), feminist theorist and activist and founding member of *ŽuC* and the Belgrade Center for Women Studies, in one of her lectures delivered in late 1990s, explicated the distinct political potential of feminism in the former Yugoslavia by insisting that 'it was only feminists who had not been seduced – or willing to be seduced – by nationalism' (2013: 16).

10 Marina Blagojević has characterised the 1990s in Serbia as a 'history of protests', whereby students' and citizens' protests led to the formation of a culture of civil resistance against the Milošević nationalist regime and against militarism (2006: 147).

11 The German term *Ostalgie*, derived from the words *Ost* (East) and *nostalgie* (nostalgia), is used to commonly refer to nostalgia for life under the socialist system of East Germany (German Democratic Republic, GDR). It refers to a nostalgia industry in the former East Germany that has entailed social practices of reviving and commercialising GDR everyday life and products, in ways that, as Daphne Berdahl (1999) has suggested, both contest and affirm a new order. Post-communist nostalgia is not unique to the GDR, however, and pertains to other post-socialist contexts in Eastern Europe.

12 This is not to imply that the *ŽuC* non-governmental activism disparages the 'institutional'; on the contrary, they attend to it as a terrain for political action. Their intense struggle has occasionally had remarkable results on an institutional-juridical level, as in the case of successful feminist campaigns undertaken in collaboration with other women's groups and

non-governmental organisations (such as Medica Zenica in Bosnia–Herzegovina, in their 2006 campaign) for the prosecution of rape as a war crime and crime against humanity, as well as for the official recognition of war rape survivors as civilian war victims.

13 The German word *Vergangenheitsbewältigung* (mastering, working through, or coming to terms with the past) relates specifically to the ways of remembering and commemorating the atrocities committed under the rule of the Third Reich, and in particular the Holocaust. The term also implies the question of the German state and the German people's responsibility for the Nazi atrocities. The question of thinking (of) 'after Auschwitz' marks Theodor Adorno's writings and in particular the 1959 lecture 'Was bedeutet die Aufarbeitung der Vergangenheit?' ('What does working through the past mean?'; Adorno 1963). Attempts to reconfigure how the communist past is remembered in former socialist republics in Eastern Europe are often cast as a post-socialist *Vergangenheitsbewältigung*.

14 Veena Das (2007) invokes the figure of Antigone as witness in the context of her reflection on the gendered division of speech and silence in mourning during the Partition of the British Indian Empire. Nichanian (2003) also raises the spectre of Antigone in the context of Armenian genocide to indicate the practice of bearing witness to a past event for the political work of present. Similarly, Mark Sanders (2003) invokes Antigone in investigating the testimony of an executed guerrilla's mother before the South African Truth and Reconciliation Commission.

2

Gendered Intimacies of the
Nationalist Archive

Ours is a cruel mourning. It is mourning without sentimentality. (Slavica Stojanović, interview with the author)

Remembering is never a quiet act of introspection or retrospection. It is a painful re-membering, a putting together of the dismembered past to make sense of the trauma of the present. (Homi Bhabha 1987: 123)

Restaging the Archive

On 8 March 2012, the year of the twentieth anniversary of *ŽuC*, a street demonstration stopped at 49 Jovanova Street, and a commemorative plaque was placed at the house where Ksenija Atanasijević once lived from 1940 to 1981. The plaque described Atanasijević as a 'philosopher, feminist, and anti-fascist'. In contrast to the solemn formality of commemorative public rituals that habitually exalt national identity, this public performance installed a different, hitherto unclaimed, memory at the centre of the city's topography. Through such dissident acts of performing irreconcilable memories in the city, *ŽuC* activists seek to trouble the sedimented intimacies of the nationalist archive. Ksenija Atanasijević (1894–1981) was a major Serbian

89

Vesna Pavlović, *Forming a Vigil. The fifth anniversary of Women in Black, Republic Square, Belgrade, October 1996*. Gelatin silver print.

philosopher and feminist thinker, who in 1924 became the first female university professor to be appointed to the Arts Faculty of the Department of Philosophy at the University of Belgrade, where she taught classics, philosophy, and aesthetics for twelve years. In 1936, due to her resistance to engaging with academic cliques, she was removed from her university position, a position that was never restored to her. Atanasijević was a member of the Serbian Women's League for Peace and Freedom, as well as of the Women's Movement Alliance. She was also editor of the first feminist journal in the country, *The Women's Movement* (*Ženski Pokret*), published from 1920 to 1938. In 1942, her articles against anti-Semitism and Nazi ideology led to her arrest by the Gestapo. After the war, she was accused of spreading controversial political ideas and was arrested by Tito's regime. She was released from prison in 1946, after which time she was only able to work as a clerk in the National Library of Serbia (Nenic 2006; Novakov 2011).[1]

How did this public event of restaging the archive by attending to the 'internal enemy' play out in *ŽuC*'s overall politics of counter-memory? Clearly, the *ŽuC* modes of non-conventional mourning question the ways in which the idealised propriety of public memory is archived – in the sense of preserved, deposited, sheltered, put away, become history of the present. They do so by embodying the figure of 'gender enemy' as a means to intervene in the ways gendered and national norms regulate what counts as memorable in the wake of fractured communities of memory. Improper public mourning exposes the limits of cultural intelligibility in ways typically akin to a 'woman', the perennial dissenter or internal enemy. In meditating on the figure of the female mourner outside the boundary wall of the *polis*, Gillian Rose writes: 'In these delegitimate acts of tending the dead, these acts of justice, against the current will of the city, women reinvent the political life of the community' (1996: 35).

That particular intervention in the political life of the *polis* by means of commemorating Ksenija Atanasijević was one of numerous *ŽuC* public performances of embodied contested memory that I encountered during my field research in Belgrade. Activist Saša Kovačević recalled her own experience with *ŽuC* as a story of camaraderie by summoning the biographies of other feminists, such as the extraordinary Neda Božinović, a doyenne of the Antifascist Front of Women:

> I have given my best to *ŽuC*. Even when I grow old, I will keep going there [the office of *ŽuC*] for a coffee, just the way I was making coffee for a lot of older women, the first ones, from whom I learned so many things, such as Neda Božinović, whom I adore and respect deeply. We always visit her grave and afterwards we drink coffee to her memory. But we do this feeling joy, and joy is a way to commemorate one's loved ones.

Neda Božinović (1917–2001), who had joined the partisans and fought against fascism during World War II, later became a supreme-court judge and secretary of the state in communist Yugoslavia. In October 1991, she was among the first feminists to start demonstrating silently against the war and the Serbian government. In her words:

> I have been an antifascist and women's human rights defender since 1936, and I fight for peace, tolerance, coexistence, and equality. I survived the dismantling of my country, the former Yugoslavia; in order to survive it, I chose to be a Woman in Black, in order to save the values that represent my life. (In Tešanović 2001: 12)

Indeed, as various activists' comments evinced, Neda's picture, hanging on the most prominent wall of *ŽuC* headquarters, transmitted an alternative, agonistic lineage of affiliation. Neda's commemoration was one more performative instance of

counter-memory: one that resonated with *ŽuC*'s acts of responsiveness to the other bodies of the archived memory.

In her work on intergenerational projected memory,
Marianne Hirsch has notably asked how familial identification

> can extend to the identification among children of different
> generations and circumstances and also perhaps to other, less
> proximate groups. And how, more important, identification
> can resist appropriation and incorporation, resist annihilating
> the distance between self and other, the otherness of the other.
> (1999: 9)

Indeed, identification as disidentification, but also belonging and
unbelonging, in all their multilayered and incalculable intensities,
are at stake in the liminal figures that haunt the body politic from
within and from without. The question of how memorability
can extend to 'other, less proximate groups' assumes a crucial
urgency in the *ŽuC* practices of self-estrangement from the law
of self-other demarcation that regulates nationalised memory
politics. Engaging with irreconcilable and inappropriate/d
remains, and doing so from a gender-enemy perspective, works
to delegitimise the monological bereavement mandated by the
epistemic violence of national archiving.

What has emerged from my anthropological explorations of
anti-nationalist memory is that the former-Yugoslav context of
the 1990s nationalist power, in its impact on performing and
regulating gendered and nationalised subjectivities, involved an
intense politics of the archive. The notion of the 'archive' is used
here to designate a historically and politically qualified constellation of the spectral remains —including cultural imaginaries,
written and unwritten artefacts, epistemic genres and structures,
technologies of monumentality, everyday snippets, discursive
formations and affective states — that sustained the temporalities of the war and its related acts of sovereignty. Rather than

being a mere repository of historical data, the archive actively regulates the possibility of memory-work within prevailing matrices of power and knowledge. Derrida has reminded us of the archive's constitutive relationship with the sovereignty of the law – as the *arkhē* of the commandment and the history or the autobiography of the *archons*, the magistrates. The 'archic, in truth patriarchic, function' through which the archive comes into play is co-implicated with a certain law of the house: the residence ('domicile, family, lineage, or institution') of those who commanded and held the political power of guardianship, interpretation, and consignation (gathering together) (1998: 3). It is in domiciliation, writes Derrida, that the archive 'takes place': 'in house arrest' (ibid., p. 2). Far from being a mere storehouse of retrieved records of the past, then, the archive is a site where the power of the present is actively managed, confirmed, and contested. 'There is no political power without control of the archive, if not of memory', Derrida argues, elaborating the notion of 'archivisation' as a constellation of powers, knowledges, methods, and technologies that determine what can be archived.

To what extent, however, is archivisation domicilable by the principle of the *archon*? The notion of archivisation as a dynamic and incomplete process of conjuring power/knowledge loci, in all their durability and contingency, has also interested Foucault, who theorised the archive as a 'system of discursivity', what he notably called 'the law of what can be said' (1972: 129). Meltem Ahiska, in her work on the politics of archives in Turkey, has raised the question of the archive as it stands at the interstices of bureaucracy, history, and memory, and as it directly relates to questions of publicising and publically authenticating the past (2006). This chapter is about the ways in which the performative practices of the *ŽuC* movement come to inhabit and trouble such sovereign accounts of archival discursivity as a vehicle for authenticating and accommodating an incomplete past. If these activists *keep* something about the archive, this is what is 'not yet', in Derrida's terms: namely, the event of an 'other' archive.

Antinationalist feminist activism against the war in the former Yugoslavia has been implicated in a performative poetics that interrogates and reworks the fundamental categories that uphold this 'system of discursivity' – namely, the witness, the event, and the archive (Papailias 2005; Stoler 2010; Taylor 2003). Through their genres of unsettling memory, *ŽuC* activists make political claims by transmitting traumatic memory within, despite, and beside 'the law of what can be said'; by performing what remains unaccounted for in the sanctioned processes of archivisation. In a context where public recollection, in all its partiality and complicity with forgetting, was instituted through a complex repertoire of authoritative authentication, *ŽuC* responded to the structural forgetting in the 'transitional' 2000s by carving out a space within public memory for minor and minoritarian events. In their disquieting embodiment of archival silences and secrets related to those displaced as 'enemies', *ŽuC* activists bring into productive crisis the common sensibility of anamnesis.[2] While exposing the internal dissonances of national memorability and memorialisation, they reorder the inflections of what is publicly and nationally authorised as audible, sensible, and memorable. Thus, in resonating with what Dimitris Papanikolaou has astutely described as the embattled cultural politics and poetics of 'archive trouble' (2011), these activists expand realms of possibility within the very structure of the archival drive – its troubles and passions, as well as its omissions, spectres, and promises.

Papanikolaou's concept of 'archive trouble' names the trouble that one has establishing, or 'archiving', the concept of the archive, as Jacques Derrida has argued in *Archive Fever* (1996). The notion of the archive cannot be reduced to the authorised metaphysical assumptions of past versus future or conserving versus innovating. Rather, the question of the archive furnishes for him, for us, a way of tracing the implications of Yerushalmi's words 'Is it possible that the antonym of "forgetting" is not "remembering", but "justice"?' (2005, p. 117). As Derrida argues, the archive's complicity with the force of law – with *archon*, or the superior magistrate, and with *arkheion*, his domicile and ancestral lineage – renders all history into an autobiography of the publicly recognised authority. But if all history is a history of sovereign power, this entanglement is open to the spectral appearances of counter-memory. Although the archive is a public apparatus of distributing significance with violent effects, it nevertheless works as a phantasmatic reservoir of what is left publicly unsaid and unaddressed, reduced to abjected knowledge, or uncontrollable by the monumental powers of official memory. It is these subjugated intimacies of the unarchivable that keep the archive from its relentless return to the absolute *arkhē*, which names both the commencement and the commandment: in other words, the institutional authority (*arkhē*) of the archivist to determine the beginning (*arkhē*). This is about an interminable process of depositing, indexing, memorising, and archiving indeed, whereby authority and its future (and, concurrently, future and its authority) are at stake rather than origins and the past. As Derrida writes: 'The archivist produces more archive, and that is why the archive is never closed. It opens out of the future' (1996: 68). In its relationship with power and knowledge, the performance of archivisation simultaneously records and produces the future of the event, by means of at once preserving and effacing memory, and at once enabling and thwarting access to public traumas and secrets. Therein lies the trouble that regulates the tenuous and deferred processes of archiving as producing both the archivable and the non-archivable. The order of the archive can never be assured, then. It is 'at once *institutive* and *conservative*. Revolutionary and traditional' (Derrida 1996: 7, emphasis in original). The affective disquietude that threatens the certainties of every archival desire is captured by Derrida's definition of 'archive fever':

> We are *en mal d'archive:* in need of archives. Listening to the French idiom, and in it the attribute *en mal de,* to be *en mal d'archive* can mean something else than to suffer from a sickness, from a trouble or from what the noun *mal* might name. It is to burn with a passion. It is never to rest, interminably, from searching for the archive right where it slips away. It is to run after the archive, even if there's too much of it, right where something in it anarchives itself. (1996: 91)

The archive exposes and, at the same time, covers over the patriarchal authority 'of the house' (Derrida 1996: 7). There is something in it that undercuts the order of memorisation. What is, however, this 'we' that 'desires for the archive' and 'runs after' it? What genres of 'we' are activated and undone through the passions – or agonies – at play in *mal d'archive*? And what about the performativity of counter-archival passions that take place outside the confines of domiciliation and toward more dispersed and nomadic directions? Rosi Braidotti deploys counter-memory to define a contingent nomadic modality that resists assimilation into established matrices of representing the feminine. Feminist memory, she posits, is a 'rebellion of subjugated knowledges' (2011: 60). In the context of *ŽuC* feminist and antifascist recuperation of Ksenija Atanasijević's memory, for instance, the possibility of an alternative *mal d'archive* arises: one that does not shore up ontological, pre-discursive alterity but rather invokes subjugated knowledges to show how archival exclusion is figured as feminine. In enacting how 'women', and in particular those deemed as women-out-of-place, become susceptible to being abjected within a community during periods of ethnic conflict (Iveković 1993; Menon 2004), these activists

perform an alternative epistemology of memory and accountability, which moves through unpredictable lines of becoming.

What motivates my reflections on counter-archival performativity here is the passionate commitment of *ŽuC* to
inscribing disruptive moments of affective disquietude in the
unifying domains and claims of national archivability. Diana
Taylor has explored how the written archive and the repertoire of embodied memory and transient immaterial traces are
brought together and work in tandem in transmitting traumatic
memory and making political claims. Taylor fruitfully warns
against a comprehension of the relationship between the archive
and the repertoire as sequential or as reduced to 'true' versus
'false' and mediated versus unmediated. She importantly adds
that this relationship should not be reduced to a binary between
the archival representing hegemonic power and the repertoire
signalling the anti-hegemonic challenge (2003). In light of these
caveats, it is not to be reduced to a distinction between successful mourning (archive) and incomplete mourning (repertoire).
In the *ŽuC* uncomfortable memory-work, the 'repertoire'
and the 'archive' sustain and punctuate each other in ways that
reconfigure both, rendering them decentred and indeterminate.
They do so not to 'speak the truth' or to produce an accurate
record of 'lost histories' but to open up to echoes and silences
that subtend the scene of exposure and response to others. In
this sense, these activists produce the archive as performative,
or as a performative repertoire. At the same time, they enact a
repertoire as inevitably embedded in, and haunted (albeit not
predetermined) by, the archival.

Involving a performative reclaiming of the agency of remembering and transmitting memory, the archive re-emerges as the
affective repertoire of unclaimed loss. But although loss can be
said to be one of the normative aspects of the archive, the loss
that these activists address is the one that remains lost in the

authoritative apparatuses of commemoration. In the context of *ŽuC*, affectivity is about being affected by, and responding to, such claims. Yael Navaro-Yashin's work on war debris in Northern Cyprus in the aftermath of the partition of the island in 1974, whereby refugees were allocated houses and land left behind by the 'other' community during the war, has brought to the fore such conflicted realms of affect. Using the metaphor of 'ruination', Navaro-Yashin has suggested that what is left of former social interaction between communities is the displaced community's abandoned spaces, leftover objects and, most notably, the border itself, which retain memories and evoke special affects among the people left behind (2009, 2012). This study of affect and abjection in a post-war polity conceives of the intricate connections of affect and politics in a new light, and in ways that pertain to the *ŽuC* affective engagements and dis-engagements. *ŽuC* puts to work the indeterminate archival play of 'what remains' in the memory of an abandoned and abjected sociality: what is elevated to the status of a memorable 'event' and what is deemed disqualified in the aftermath of devastation. What is at stake in the work of these activists is not a 'nostalgic desire for the archive', however, but rather a desire to trouble the normalising drive to 'return to the origin'. If the conventional notion of homesickness, with which Derrida has associated archive fever, denotes a melancholia caused by prolonged distan-tiation from one's identified home and a compulsion to return to it, their 'homesickness' is actualised in a reverse fashion, as a suggestive arena for de-forming identifications of home and forming nomadic affiliations. Home – including the domicile that the archive stands for – is construed as a conflicted field of moving beyond oneself and resignifying one's own 'passionate attachments' (Butler 1997a).[3] It is relocated within the possibil-ity of decentring the origin and the supposedly 'original' that underlie the sensual and consensual modes of commemoration.

Enacting dissonant possibilities of passion (or agony) and trouble (*mal*), this alternative modality of *mal d'archive* recounts that which does not count, and thus forges a political grammar of feminist memory. This grammar contravenes the archival violence to which the dead and survivors of the war, as well as of the wars that take place in contexts of peace, have been submitted. Either in recuperating the memory of Ksenija Atanasijević, or in recollecting others construed as enemies, the *ŽuC* precarious genres of mourning and commemoration pose challenges to archivability. They upset the injurious terms of monumental and patrilineal *archē* that render the archive univocal by determining what is proper and what improper in collective memory.

Proper Memories, Proper Names, Proper Victims

In 1986, influential members of the 'nationally conscious' intelligentsia centred around the Serbian Academy of Sciences and Arts (SANU), a respectable institution in Serbian society, issued a 'Memorandum' that formulated the tenets of Serbian nationalism and alerted the Serbs, especially those living in other Yugoslav republics (mainly Kosovo and Croatia), to their alleged discrimination by Yugoslavia's constitutional structure. The document specifically deplored the discrimination of Serbs by Albanians in Kosovo and denounced the autonomous status of Kosovo and Vojvodina. Most significantly, it stated that Serbia 'sacrificed' 2,500,000 victims for Yugoslavia in World Wars I and II but had become a 'victim' of the Yugoslav federation. Although widely denounced by government officials, albeit not by Milošević himself, the SANU Memorandum and its disciplinary invocation of the theme of national origin captured the attention of the general public and political figures as well.

Despite official denouncements, nationalist politicians would later form connections with authors of the Memorandum. Among them, prominent philosopher Mihailo Marković became the vice-president of the Milošević's party from 1990 to 1992, and Dobrica Ćosić, known as the 'father of the nation' due to his theoretical contribution to the formulation of modern Serbian national politics in the late 1980s, was appointed the first President of the new Federal Republic of Yugoslavia (which consisted of Serbia and Montenegro) in 1992. Svetlana Slapšak, an academic among those who did not heed the nationalist appeals, described the Memorandum as a project designed to foster 'preventive' nationalist aggressiveness (1992).[4]

What is most relevant to our purposes here is that archival anxieties over (un)buried collective traumas, drawing heavily on ethno-national but also gendered discursive regimes, opened the way for a reinvention of Serbian memory and the preparation for a military campaign. In this process of national self-fashioning, the past would be brought back to political life in order to orient a post-socialist present. For several years, well before the wars started, a process of naturalising nationalist self-assertiveness was well underway within public discourse and everyday life, not only in Serbia but also in other ex-Yugoslav republics. As the 1986 'Memorandum' manifests, but also a few other public spectacles of national archiving that are unravelled in later pages, wars in the former Yugoslavia were heralded and presaged, in insinuating and insistent ways, long before 1991. Various speech acts of recollecting, reinventing, and reviving the past had already opened the way for the normalisation of violence. Before and during the wars that led to the dissolution of Yugoslavia, nationalist elites extensively rehearsed the power of archivisation and spectralisation through the mobilisation of what Robert Hayden has called 'secret or hidden histories' (1994: 167). Nationalist common sense was structured by a 'duty to remember', in all its mystical intimacy and, to be sure, irrevocable partiality. As Susan Woodward put it: 'historical memories were recalled (or invented) by political leaders to justify the claims they were making against the federal government or each other' (2000: 24).

Normative remembrance was deployed as an apparatus of what Lauren Berlant calls 'national sentimentality', in order to produce dehumanised others, to formulate discourses of retribution and, ultimately, to justify war. In an interview with me, *ŽuC* activist Slavica Stojanović recounted the beginning of the war through the prism of the intimate relationship between nationalism and sentimentality:

> War comes with sentimentality. The nationalistic and militaristic ambiance was imbued with an overwhelming current of sentimentality. Its main vehicle was the media. At some point I found myself reading the newspaper in the morning, crying for the whole day and then recovering in the afternoon. And I said 'I am not going into that.' The constant message was: 'We love Serbia, we love Slovenia, etc.', propelling a kind of self-victimising sentimentality. So, I stopped reading newspapers. And then there was the ritual of TV news, at 7.30 every evening. We were on the verge of war, we wanted to learn what is going on. But, of course, the news was completely fabricated. An hour-long commentary following the news was sheer propaganda featuring horror, skulls, killed children. I remember being in my room once, watching the news in the dark. I had a guest at home, and she simply grabbed the door to enter my room. I jumped like a beast from my bed, terrified – so taken I was by the news. And I said 'not again'. I switched the TV off and it stayed off for ten years.

As public affectivity was formulated through the routine calculus of endangered intimates and dangerous intruders, rituals of national commemoration were established as a crucial component of the discursive formation of national sentimentality. Such ritualisation of 'archive fever' in the public cultures of nationalism in the former Yugoslavia during the 1990s encompassed divergent enactments 'between admissible and inadmissible memory' (Feldman 2004: 166). Through various cultural artefacts and technologies of history–effects, such as public celebrations, monuments, printed matter, and mediatised spectacles, national memory came to be fixed as a discursive scene for sensing national bravery and redemption. Commemorative events, public monuments and other forms and objects of history culture became a public site of 'banal nationalism', whereby conflicts over national memory permeated the fabric of habitual, everyday life practices (Billig 1995; Gordy 1999; Torsti 2004). Official documents and oral cultures, media and modes of visualisation, as well as tropes of making claims about history, all emerged as a multilayered assemblage of techniques for the social production of a heroic, traumatic, and stratified memory. These commemorative scripts and rituals of national indexicality deserve our critical attention. Thus, in what follows, I seek to illuminate the passionate and affective energies operative in the social production of the memorable in the twilight years of the former Yugoslavia and onward. Indeed, for the period with which this book is concerned, the 1990s to 2000s, the nationalist archive has been writ large in the processes of moulding present regimes of truth. And yet, as the *ŽuC* agonistic poetics of counter-memory evinces, the archive can also serve as a staging ground where structural failures and critical strategies can emerge.

In her study on 'archival poetics', Penelope Papailias (2005) has considered how blurred genres and social practices of 'recollecting', which are involved in the production of local historiographies, become potential sites for cultural performatives and counterhistories. By drawing attention to the vernacular ways in which traumatic events of twentieth-century modern

Greek history are documented and narrated, her study sheds light on how narrative structures of historical (self-)knowledge are fused to the poetics of archive as history-in-the-making. As in Papailias's study, the genres of archive – including recollection and mourning – in the case of the breakup of Yugoslavia reveal an authorised figuration of traumatic remembrance within the bounds of public discourse, but not necessarily inside predictable and established standards of archival formation. In this vein, then, I attempt here to address the way archival production works as a discursive terrain of authentication but also unavoidably as a field of differential appropriations, contested narrations, and dissonant recurrences.

As I will develop below, nationalist structures of ethno-historical memory, particularly through the gendered modalities of the male national hero and the mother of the nation, sustained a public culture of intimate knowledge that helped to turn the former Yugoslavia into a zone of political emergency. During the time of my fieldwork in Belgrade, fragments of this archive kept surfacing, often within unexpected chains of citation. The *ŽuC* work of memory, inscribed within and against the archival totality of war and nationalism, also undercut its claims of completeness. As these political subjects introduce differential marks – such as residues of improper memories and bodies – in the corpus of national imaginaries, they mobilise the archive as a performative occasion for making subversive memory work. It is to the iterability of these complex intimacies between gendered bodies and the body-archive of nationalism that I now turn.

Claiming the Dead Body of the National Hero

Under the sway of ethnic nationalism and its memory cultures in the former Yugoslavia, the dead body of the national hero, in its figural and spectral persistence, was entreated to consolidate the normative ideal of the death-defying national body politic. In war propaganda myths that were circulating in the warring parts of the former Yugoslavia, the sublime figure of the dead warrior (*mrtav ratnik*) of past wars was imbued with an affective and sexualised aura. *Mrtav ratnik* was one of the recurrent tropes in public spectacles that formed the ether that my interlocutor Slavica Stojanović described as 'war sentimentality'. It figures, in Stathis Gourgouris's suggestive formulation, 'the archive of (self-)representation, the sacred inventory of idols that make a national history possible' (1996: 45).

One of the moments that most emblematically embodied the nationalist desire for a return to the 'place of absolute commencement' (Derrida 1996: 91) through the nationalist worship of the dead soldier was the grandiose 'historical speech' given by Slobodan Milošević, then President of Serbia, at Kosovo Polje (Field of Blackbirds) in Gazimestan of Central Kosovo, on 28 June 1989, three years after the SANU 'Memorandum' was issued. The speech was the lynchpin of a day-long ceremonial event to mark the 600th anniversary of the Battle of Kosovo Field, an event that signalled the defeat of the medieval Serbian kingdom by the invading army of the Ottoman Empire under the leadership of Sultan Murad I. In symbolising the nineteenth-century rise of Serbian nationalism under Ottoman rule, the story of the Battle of Kosovo carries a high charge of national intimacy and maintains a profound hold on the Serbian imaginary (Živković 2011).

In the context of the leader's national address, past battles of pre-war, Serb-dominated Yugoslavia were conjured to mobilise for future ones. As Diana Taylor remarks in reference to military parades in Argentina under dictatorship: 'Staging order, as in ritual, would make order happen. The iterability of the performance contributed to the dictatorship's legitimacy. The "restored" nature of the performance suggested that order itself had been restored' (1997: 67). In the Gazimestan reanimation of the foundational event of the tragic but heroic Serbian defeat against the Ottoman Empire, national subjects were hailed to redeem the nation by securing the collective immortality that Benedict Anderson (1991) has written about, especially when, as it was claimed at that particular moment, the nation teetered on the edge of dissolution. This idiom of genealogical intimacy between the menaced nation and its redeeming subjects, an idiom endowed with the compelling performative force of public rituals and speech acts, had come to be integral to the biopolitical economy of the nationalist state and its reliance on gendered intimacies such as the figure of *mrtav ratnik*.

Heavily invested with national sentimentality, the Kosovo Polje-staged event was attuned to the spirit of those days and years in Serbia. In the late 1980s, Milošević permitted the actions of Serb nationalist organisations and restored the legitimacy of the Serbian Orthodox Church in Serbia. A few months before the Gazimestan commemoration, on 23 March 1989, the Kosovo assembly, surrounded by tanks and police, had voted for constitutional amendments that drastically reduced the autonomy of Kosovo, and many Albanians were killed when demonstrations against the new constitution were suppressed by Serbian security forces. Amidst tension between ethnic Serbs and Albanians in Kosovo, as well as between Serbia and the other constituent republics of the then Socialist Federal Republic of Yugoslavia (especially Croatia and Slovenia), Milošević rehearsed the heroic Kosovo past as a repository of sentiments of common origins and traumatic national memory. He did so before an estimated million Serb men and women gathered at the charged place where the battle had been fought in 1389. Milošević's oratorical performance was intended to interpellate the audience into a shared and fetishised trauma. This return to a primal scene of national suffering for Serbs was expected to create a common sensorium through which to turn a scene of defeat into an idealised object of origin and redemption. At stake was the staged citation of a sacred site as the moral foundation of the nation's common memory, for the purposes of the present. In the Gazimestan 'theater of memory' (Feldman 2004), where remains of past wars were summoned by the leader and uncovered bodies were brought to the proscenium of national discourse, the politics of memory was tied to a territorial imagination.

The economy of sublimation enacted in the Kosovo Polje event was made possible not only by the leader's paternal vitalism but also by the figure of the dead hero's bodily remains. The *mise en scène* of national self-affection involved the spectacularised bodily remains of the fallen warrior hero, as the arch-trope of nationalist bereavement that so often sustains the biopolitical economy of militarised nationalism. Thus, the proper place of the nation's emblematic battlefield, Kosovo Polje, was coupled with the proper name of the warrior, Miloš. These concurrent idioms of propriety illustrated a metonymic relationship between the battlefield qua the nation's birthplace and the warrior's dying body. At the beginning of his speech, Milošević invited the audience to ask themselves 'how to face Miloš'. Miloš Obilić was the legendary hero who assassinated the Sultan at the Battle of Kosovo, and was consequently slain by the sultan's bodyguards.

In the leader's rhetoric, 'Miloš', evoked in the first name of intimacy, embodied the brave but wounded ethnic nation of the past to which present national intimates are accountable. The fallen warrior's proper name was deployed by Milošević to confirm what ought to be authenticated as proper rememb-rance. The force of naming entails a politics of historical truth claiming or, better, a politics of bringing into existence a historical ontology (Hacking 2002: 26). Following Ian Hacking, in another context, Ann Laura Stoler has argued that tracing historical ontologies requires the study of shifting 'assignments of essence' (2010: 4). In Stoler's perspective, colonial ontologies, being predicated upon such 'essences', are subject to constant reactivation, 'both productive and responsive, expectant and late' (ibid.). Indeed, the call to 'face Miloš', in the leader's words, worked as an interpellatory call to a nationalist historical ontology as an 'assignment of essence'. The mythopoetic figure of the fallen hero thereby gave a name and a body to the discursive force of the leader's ceremonial speech. The latter did not merely recall a past event but rather intimated a knowledge of the past to form a present interpellatory event. From the leader's perspective in the Gazimestan event, the rhetorical question 'how to face Miloš' condensed the task contemporary Serbs had to take up with revitalised promise: to make themselves worthy of their dead ancestors. Living up to this task entailed a certain incorporation of the body of the dead hero. Through the spectrality of the dead warrior's intimate corporeality, the nation emerged as an organic community whose life was under threat from national others, but also potentially reactivated by national intimates eager to 'make history'.

The commemoration of the 600th anniversary of the battle was also a major religious event. For a few months before the Gazimestan event, the remains of Prince Lazar of Serbia, who had also fallen in the Battle of Kosovo, were carried in an Orthodox ritual procession around the Serb-inhabited territories of Yugoslavia (Milošević 2000). Prince Lazar, according to the founding myth, was said to have had a dream the day before the battle in which a falcon offered him the choice of gaining either a heavenly or an earthy kingdom; he chose the former and thus lost the battle. According to this tale, etched in the Serbian collective memory, Prince Lazar asserted: 'It is better to die a heroic death than live in shame. I would rather die of sword in battle than bow to the enemy.' The interconnected figures of Miloš and Lazar, their heroic deeds and deaths, thus became an integral part of Serbian archival impulses surrounding the Battle of Kosovo. The assembled crowd's identification with the glorified national male warrior and state father – enhanced by a metonymic conflation of the proper names Lazar, Miloš, and, notably, Milošević – would very soon prove crucial to the project of emboldening a collectivity of warriors in post-Yugoslav Serbia. The pilgrimage tour around Serbia, which began on 28 June 1988 and ended in September of the following year, was an attempt to instil a sense of affirmative, commemorative collectivity. At the invitation of the Serbian Orthodox Church, attendees had arrived from all the Serb-inhabited parts of Yugoslavia and even from overseas to pay their respects to the holy relics after queuing for hours.

Milošević's invocations of pre-war mythologised narratives were strategically connected to the ways in which Tito had constructed the Yugoslav federation in opposition to that pre-war Yugoslavia, 'which was based on the hegemony of the Serbs as the "founders of unity"' (Žižek 1999). However, it was not only the medieval national trauma of 1389 in Kosovo Polje that was unearthed in Milošević's commemorative speech to animate the pre-war national sentiments of collective victimisation and pride, but also the Serb World War II trauma of 1941–5. As the Serbian leadership in the 1980s appealed to revisionism of the history of Yugoslavia in World War II, the previous Tito-era tradition of remembering all battlefield casualties of Yugoslavs in World War II was abolished and replaced with the Milošević government's policy of commemorating the Serb casualties of World War II as victims of the Croatian Ustashe.[5] And just as the spectre of the dead male national hero was summoned in the religious tour of his relics, an archival fever unfolded at the local and national level through the systematic media coverage of the exhumation of skeletal remains from World War II.

Since 1989, contested images of exhumed relics conjuring old wounds of Yugoslavia had infiltrated into highly publicised debates. In 1991, Serbian television broadcast the exhumation of the remains of thousands of Serb victims of the Ustashe in caves and mass graves found in Herzegovina. A series of public commemorative events followed to create an ethnically exclusive community of memory (Hayden 1994; Papić 2002; Verdery 1999; Wagner 2008). As Katherine Verdery writes about the turbulent conditions in which the reburials of the late 1980s and early 1990s took place in post-communist Eastern Europe: 'Burials bring people together, reminding them of the reason of their collective presence – relatedness – but that relatedness has now become ethnically exclusive' (1999: 108). The pivotal role of death in the nation's collective memory and public discourse has been also brought to the fore by Benedict Anderson, who talks about the 'accumulating cemeteries' from which the nation's biography draws exemplary deaths to be remembered as 'our own' (1991: 210). This remembering of past national traumas as 'our own', however, is typically coupled, in national-ist narratives, with denying other communities' traumas.

The ideological emplotment of nationalised and ethnically exclusive remembrance of death and trauma differed signifi-cantly from the Yugoslav politics of commemoration, which, after Tito's break with Stalin in 1948, was premised upon multi-ethnic solidarity, according to the model of the movement of the non-aligned countries. Communist commemoration and narratives of World War II, which were signalled by the Yugoslav principle of 'Brotherhood and Unity' (*Bratstvo i Jedinstvo*),[6] had been replaced by a nationalist war memory which sought to redress the alleged Titoist 'de-ethnicization' of World War II events and casualties (Bougarel et al. 2007). This shift in the official politics of memory became manifest in the reopening of mass graves but also, later, in the depreciation and even destruction of monuments commemorating the Partisans (Bougarel 2007).

So before and during the war in the former Yugoslavia, the social memory of World War II Yugoslavia became an arena of displaced re-enactments of ethno-national trauma. In the wake of mass ethnicisation and militarisation, the country's history was recast by nationalist and religious elites into tales of collective suffering and betrayal (Jansen 2000). If ethno-national trauma was the pervasive trope of this veritable 'archival fever', however, narrational attention to traumatic events and allocation of responsibility were differentially layered and strategically shifted, in a process akin to what Žarana Papić described as 'peregrination of the trauma' (2000). Thus, although a great deal of attention was focused on the Croat Ustasha[7] crimes by state media policy in early 1990s, Serb Chetniks' crimes were set aside.[8] The insistent representation of the Ustasha side – iconised by the unearthed bones from 1941 – as an exclusive agent of war crimes responsibility and Serbian collective injury was deployed in the project of radicalising Serbian nationalism through instilling a sense of pre-emptive legitimisation of the aggression that was to come (Papić 2002). As with the incitation to selective remembrance signalled in the context of the Gazimestan event, within the format of the exposed ghosts of Serbian casualties of the 1940s, a spectral historiography of typified national trauma was conjured to claim a collective truth of suffering. The revised memory of war heroism was meant to present the Serbian national struggle in the 1990s as an immediate successor of the partisan struggle in World War II. Under the banner of the 'political lives of dead bodies' (Verdery 1999), national victimisation and martyrology was manipulated by authorities and nationalist elites to alienate all those burdensome 'others' – former neighbours, friends, and relatives. Robert Hayden had predicted that this violence would have an adverse impact not only on non-Serbian victims but also on the Serbian people. Ironically, in light of the violence in post-communist Yugoslavia, the memory of the suffering of the Serbian people during World War II would be eventually forgotten (Hayden 1994: 182).

The dramaturgy of national anamnesis scripts the ethnic nation as a past trauma that is always experienced after. In Cathy Caruth's account, trauma is located in 'the way that its very unassimilated nature – the way it was precisely *not known* in the first instance – returns to haunt the survivor later on' (1996: 4). The affective life of the nation-form lies precisely in this phantasmatic return and its concomitant anxieties. As Gourgouris has cogently suggested, the nation 'can only "exist" as a phantasmatic projection *retroactively* posed once the desire has been articulated' (1996: 127). In this regard, 'the Nation is both there *and* elsewhere *all the time* . . . both past and present, or to paraphrase Anderson, both irredeemable memory and limitless future' (1996: 45, emphasis in original). In these terms, nationalism relies on a phantasmatic logic, which produces and affirms, again and again, exclusionary figurations of attachment and reparation, intimacy and enmity. One-sided attachment to violations by an other is a constitutive aspect of this logic. And so nationalism is imagined, mythologised, desired, and lived through the profoundly affective work of traumatic memory – always recursive and returning, emergent and enduring.[9]

George Mosse (1990) has famously drawn our attention to the mix of feelings of pride and mourning that have dominated the cultures of war memory since World War I. The cult of the fallen soldier became the centrepiece of what Mosse called 'the myth of the war experience', referring to processes of refashioning the memory of war into a sacred experience (which, in his account, declined after 1945). After World War I, the scale of mass death but also the fact that the soldiers were no longer mercenaries but volunteers – that is, national citizens – signalled changes in warfare that led to the naturalisation and justification of war through the sublime myth of war death as a noble sacrifice for the nation. Joanna Bourke (2000) has compellingly explored the layered temporalities inherent in the 'intimate history' of wartime violence as embedded within cultural, social, affective and imaginary apparatuses in the twentieth century. She has addressed the ordinary, intimate, gendered and sexualised processes involved in the production of 'citizen soldiers' who can be made to seek pleasure in killing. War death becomes an occasion where the production of the hierarchical sacredness and sacrificiality of death (and life) constitutes the political space of the nation's sovereignty, purification, and timeless continuance. The sacredness of war victims is invoked as a way in which not only 'human life is included in the sovereign nation-state' (Edkins 2003: 101), but also the nation is brought to life as a self-generating political body.

Michel Foucault has argued that from the nineteenth century onwards a technology of regulatory power centred on life was deployed to make processes of normalisation acceptable: 'It is no longer a matter of bringing death into play in the field of sovereignty, but of distributing the living in the domain of value and utility' (1980: 144). This does not mean, however, that sovereign power is rendered obsolete. Rather, it persists in redirecting tactics of government as government of population (2007: 107–8). The sovereign right 'to take life and let live' is complemented and permeated – but not replaced – by the right 'to make live and let die' (2003b: 241). In this respect, biopower – as power that fosters and preserves life – manages human beings-as-species through establishing and engineering 'biological-type caesuras' (2003b: 255) within a population. Operating within the biopolitical domain, at the levels of both centralised and aleatory modes of power, racism introduces a break between what must live and what must die. Even if Foucault claims that racism functions through 'not a military or warlike relationship of confrontation, but a biological-type relationship' (ibid., p. 255), and especially in light of intersections of sovereign and regulatory power in the context at hand, it seems imperative to expand Foucault's scope of analysis and lay out an account of war as a modality of power exercised through the relationship between sovereignty and biopower; in other words, through both the right to kill and the right to make live. Therein lies the formidable power of the cult of the fallen soldier.

A suggestive aspect of the change that Mosse had called 'domestication of modern war' (1990: 11) was the different social status of these new soldiers, who had relatives and other community members to care about them. Thus, in practices of war commemoration, personal and familial bereavement intersected with, and eventually was superimposed by, national grief for the combatants' sacrifice. The cult of the war dead as sacrificial victims who bring the nation into being has been at the core of the creation of nationalist founding myths of war through commemorative ceremonies and war memorials, as well as through the separation of the dead into cemeteries according to nationality. Most importantly for our purposes here, the figure of the fallen soldier bears clear overtones of class, nation, and gender categorisation. Discourses of noble and heroic masculinity produce and are themselves produced by the national founding myths of war memory and war memorials. Through the theme of the vitality of the national body, a theme instantiated on the level of 'living and dying', 'power spoke *of* sexuality and *to* sexuality' (Foucault 1980: 147). Thus, gender, sexuality, and the body arise as primary idioms of power and knowledge through which nationalist discourse is articulated in a performative ensemble akin to what Etienne Balibar has called 'secret affinity' between nationalism and sexism (1991: 102).

Dissonant Masculinities: 'This Is Not Our War!'

Miloš Urošević, twenty-seven years old at the time of my research, became a *ŽuC* activist in 2003. He had escaped military service after having been designated as unfit through official procedures of psychological evaluation. During our first conversation, he actually mentioned the exact date he first joined the group, 'April 8, 2003', to ask for help to avoid mandatory military service. 'One day', he recounts,

> the military came at 3 o'clock in the morning to take me. I had been prepared what to do when they would come. My mother said: 'Now they are going to beat you up.' I responded quietly to her: 'Don't worry, they cannot do anything to me.' I followed them to the police station, where I was interrogated. They asked me for details. I told them I was an activist, although I was not yet one, that I support peace and that I am gay. I volunteered to do civil service. They said I was incompetent (*nesposoban*) even for that. I replied: 'I agree, I am incompetent for this.' They said: 'We will put you down, then, according to the law 81, as psychiatrically incompetent for military service.' And I replied: 'Yes, I am emotionally incapable of killing other people (*emotivno nezreo da ubijam druge*).'

As my friend's narrative manifests, the figure of the fallen soldier, through which the ethnic nation is allegorised as simultaneous loss and longing, is estranged by those who are abjected by the modes of intimacy that define the national ideal. To be sure, if militarised nationalism wielded the power to constitute gendered subjectivities whose physical bodies would perform the national body politic, the premises of masculine heroism and military euphoria were imbued with internal ambivalence and instability, as well as contested by lived actualities of dissent. The women and men I engaged in the field were involved in such actualities, against all odds and to unpredictable effect, by enacting an alternative poetics of gendered embodiment.

The dissonant voices included, significantly, the war resisters and conscientious objectors: those men of draft age who avoided conscription into the armed forces. Indeed, a high percentage of young men under military obligation resisted official compulsory mobilisation in Serbia (Aleksov 1994, 2012). Besides opposition to the war that was based on antimilitarist political convictions, the unpopularity of the war mobilisation was also linked to the accumulated frustrations related to the harsh economic conditions that had afflicted great segments of the population; especially after the UN Security Council imposed economic sanctions against Serbia and Montenegro in May 1992, which added to the impoverishment resulting from Milošević's policies, people faced severe shortages of food, fuel, and medicines (Sagall 1995). Those avoiding 'military duties' faced strict punishment, such as loss of civil rights, prison sentence for up to twenty years and, according to the 1995 Law on Inheritance Unworthiness, deprivation of inheritance rights for those conscripts who had escaped abroad to avoid being drafted (Aleksov 1996; Zajović 2013b). In addition, objectors and deserters were exposed to the everyday perils of stigmatisation in the wake of the society's intense militarised impulses:

> In some cities, the names of deserters were being written on lampposts and notice boards (in places obituaries are customarily displayed), therefore symbolically proclaiming them 'dead', and in reality, they were being sentenced to social death. . . . Many physical assaults and acts of retribution against the mothers of deserters were also recorded. (Zajović 2013b: 93)

As my interlocutors narrated to me, the resistance of the conscientious objectors formed a powerful antimilitarist movement within the adverse circumstances of escalating militarisation and divisions of 'traitors' and 'patriots' that swept Serbia's everyday public discourse. Amidst reports on growing numbers of warrants for desertion, war resisters, deserters and conscientious objectors were imprisoned, tortured, forced to sign statements of confession, and subjected to violence and hate speech. As Ivan Vejvoda (1994), a journalist and founder member of the Belgrade Circle, reported, thousands of conscripts had to go underground, into 'internal exile', hiding at friends' and relatives' houses, while others left the country.

From the outbreak of the war in 1991, anti-war gatherings in Serbia, such as marches, concerts, and occupations of the city centre, sought to mobilise against the war and to voice solidarity to all those resisting it (Erdei 1997; Jansen 2000). Those anti-war events were at the same time anti-Milošević political manifestations. In September 1991, the Belgrade-based Center for Antiwar Action (CAWA) organised the Peace Caravan that gathered peace movements from all over Europe into a convoy that travelled throughout Yugoslavia. After the emergence of ŽuC in 1991, which openly supported draft resisters, the Association of Independent Intellectuals Belgrade Circle (*Beogradski Krug*) was founded in January 1992, which organised weekly gatherings promoting anti-war ideas and cooperation among the successor states of Yugoslavia. Members of the Belgrade Circle also went out into areas of tension out of Serbia, like Mostar, to network and express solidarity with anti-war collectivities. During the winter of 1991–2, candlelit vigils were held every evening in memory of those being killed in the war and in solidarity with those resisting it. The anti-regime, anti-war student demonstrations that took place in March 1992 in Terazije Square gave rise to the Terazije Parliament Forum (*Forum Terazijskog Parliamenta*, FTP). In April 1992, when the war had spread to Bosnia, an anti-war concert was held in Belgrade's main square and was attended by as many as 50,000 people under the central motto 'Don't count on us', a message addressed in opposition to the nationalist mobilisation. A few months later, thousands of people took to the streets of Belgrade wearing black ribbons, in an event called 'The Black Ribbon mourning for Sarajevo', held in solidarity with the inhabitants of the besieged Sarajevo. The summer of 1992 was marked by massive anti-war demonstrations, which were brutally crushed by regime armed forces. A major wave of street demonstrations against the government were also held in 1996–7, labelled as the 'Winter Protest' and organised by university students, opposition parties (notably, the coalition *Zajedno* (Together)), and antinationalist groups such as *ŽuC* and Belgrade Circle (Jansen 2000, 2001). Peace actions in Serbia during the war included also the founding of various collectivities, such as: CAWA in Belgrade in July 1991 as coordinator of war resistance and which also offered legal help to draft resisters; the party Civic Alliance for Serbia, under the leadership of Vesna Pesic, the founder of CAWA; the Center for Cultural Decontamination, which promoted an alternative anti-war culture; Otpor in 1998; the independent trade union Independence; and, on a less formal level, a vibrant underground anti-war youth culture (Erdei 1997; Jansen 2000). Attuned to the belligerent impulse of the ruling party and segments of the opposition, the regime's propaganda machine portrayed the antinationalist and anti-war protesters as 'traitors' and 'pawns of the West'.[10]

Since October 1991, *ŽuC* had expressed solidarity and worked closely with the movement of war resisters and conscientious objectors. In the 1998 *ŽuC* 'manifesto' titled 'I am a conscientious objector' (Women in Black 1998), the group made clear that for them feminist solidarity with conscientious objection is a matter of 'disobedience to militarization and armed patriarchy' and 'not part of the woman's role as caregiver'. The 2006 street action 'In memory of the deserter', whereby *ŽuC* activists performed a live monument in solidarity with the deserters and conscientious objectors, was another artistic–activist occasion for forging a political alliance of memory premised upon the modality of becoming-enemy. One joint action of *ŽuC* and Art Klinika, an artist collective from Novi Sad, addressed the act of Vladimir Živković, a coercively drafted reserve trooper from Valjevo, who, in the fall of 1991, took an armed transport vehicle and drove it in front of the Assembly building of the Socialist Federal Republic of Yugoslavia, as a sign of protest against war. That manifestation posed the question of which sentiments, stories, and events become admissible and which become inadmissible to the registers of nationalised history. Amid militarisation of the state and society at large, that was a scandalous question: 'Are the participants of that event heroes or deserters? Patriots or traitors? . . . Is there a history outside history? How does an event become part of history and how is it deleted from it?' (Art Klinika 2010, Zajović 2013b). In posing the question of 'history outside history', the activists displaced the archive by introducing a ghostly temporality embodied by the ones whose memory was expropriated and occluded.

Public opposition to military service and participation in *ŽuC* public actions have made Boban Stojanović, queer and conscientious objection rights advocate, a popular target of mass media derision and public harassment. In his words:

Together with Women in Black, we held a vigil in Republic Square on July 10, holding placards bearing the words Responsibility and Solidarity, at the same time presenting to the citizens of Belgrade the film *Women of Srebrenica Speak* by Milica Tomić (produced by *ŽuC* in 2008). It was surreal – the Square was in the dark, the women of Srebrenica were addressing Serbia, Belgrade was silent, only from time to time someone would come forward and spit on us. (Stojanović 2009: 65)

Indeed, the reconfiguration of the apparatus of 'enemy' is at the core of ŽuC politics, as it is manifested in its emblematic mode of self-enunciation: 'As women we are traitors'. In reoccupying the position of the internal enemy, which has been conferred upon them as a status of derision, these activists forge a link of responsiveness to those estranged as external enemies. It is by virtue of this shared self-estrangement from the production of militarist normativity that supporting – and organising joint actions with – conscientious objectors and war deserters has been a constitutive hallmark of feminist anti-war activism during the years of the war.

ŽuC activism interrogates war as a matrix of gender interpellation. It does so by making the signifier 'women' part of its political strategy, especially in light of the sedimented orderliness of nationalist masculinism. Calling into question gender purities and polarities, ŽuC puts to work this signifier as a critical political project of resignification and cross-identification beyond fixed, phallogocentrically induced gender and sexual categories. Dragan Protić, also known as Prota among his friends, shared with me once his feelings and thoughts about being a man among women in activism.

> For me, it was never important to count women or men, nor to count as woman or man. I do not wish to be located in my standard and predictable place. I like being in search all the time, and what is so important about ŽuC is that you are allowed to search. It is this making allowance for difference that characterizes ŽuC.

In a similar vein, Goran Lazin stressed his appreciation for the ŽuC 'openness to all genders and sexualities'. As he reported to me, his mother fears that he might get attacked because he is a ŽuC activist and not so much because of his queerness. And he added: 'Being a ŽuC is more provocative than being queer.' Indeed, for Prota and Goran, as well as for other activists, engaging in cross-border antinationalist and feminist political subjectivity entails not only crossing in spatial terms but also performing a lived experience of gender exile; a constant state of transforming and becoming, akin to what Rosi Braidotti has referred to as the positionality of 'as-if': 'the affirmation of fluid boundaries, a practice of the intervals, of the interfaces, and the interstices' (1994: 7).

I have talked with my friend and informant Miloš Urošević a few times about what it means for him to performatively occupy the position of 'woman' in being a *ŽuC* activist. 'As a gay man, I am not a man', he said bluntly, once. And he added: 'Remember what Monique Wittig had written, that lesbians are not women.' For Miloš, neither 'man' nor 'woman' can be perceived as *one*. During *ŽuC* street actions, onlookers have often attacked him. He has talked to me about his experience of taking part in demonstrations as an experience of love and camaraderie rather than trauma, however:

> I love feeling my body to be a creative medium of protest. In the demonstrations, my body matters, in contrast to social perceptions of bodies like mine as valueless and polluted. I become a medium of all the bodies that have been expelled and banished as worthless.

Miloš has often referred to the work of Adriana Cavarero, a thinker that he admires a lot, to explain his take on the links between activism, mourning, and public exposure of the inappropriate (and inappropriated) body. As Miloš was talking to me about activism of mourning and activism as mourning in terms of 'everyday responsibility', our conversations made me aware of the ways Cavarero's ideas of how embodiment entails an ethics of responsiveness (2000) can be especially pertinent to queer masculinities in times of war.

The dislodging of mourning from masculinist, hetero-normative, and nationalist imaginings was powerfully portrayed in Lepa Mlađenović's obituary for her close friend and comrade Dejan Nebrigić, another queer *ŽuC* activist: 'He was not the territory of Serbia, he refused to be the body of Serbian politics, rejected the Serbian army. . . . He refused to be buried in a Serbian graveyard' (Women in Black 2001a: 352). In remembering her comrade's life, the author recalls the daunting dilemma that the two of them faced during the years of the war: how to fight for gay and lesbian rights amidst nationalist killings and prison camps, when no available political language of public belonging was left for queer existence.[11] And yet, Dejan, Lepa, and many others were not put into place by the disciplinary technologies of shame but rather devised non-authorised and anti-authoritative performative forms of resistance to open up spaces for queer subjugated knowledge and archive-making. As Lepa recounts:

> During the winter of 1992, in the first flat of *Women in Black*, in Marko Kraljevic Street, below the market, in a corner near window, Dejan Nebrigić was working at his typewriter. Above his desk hung a poster with a photograph of two young men whose faces were touching in a moment of tenderness. This picture conveyed the tenderness of love between two men, never seen before in a public place in the history of my town. Dejan Nebrigić walked into *Women in Black* organisation saying: I am one of you! (Urošević and Mlađenović 2013: 296)

But also the lifelong activist history of Lepa herself, as a lesbian *ŽuC*, is connected to the contested affective textures of the former Yugoslavia's breakup as they have been marked by injurious interpellations but also by the abiding resilience of various foreign and non-assimilable bodies. The opening of the 'Lepa Mlađenović Lesbian Reading Room' in Novi Sad by the

Novi Sad Lesbian Organization in 2011 was, indeed, not only an expression of gratitude and comradeship but also a gesture of creating a critical archive of counter-stories that are rendered invisible and inaudible in official national narratives.

Desiring the Nation, Worshipping the Leader

As exemplified in the emblematic Gazimestan phantasmagoria, the performative effect of mass-cultural commemorative rituals was to foment nationalist sentiments of intimacy through an affirmative identification with the male hero's body. The common themes of betrayal and heroic redemption were mobilised to unite the nation in the honourable mission of fighting for the nation's survival against its enemies. As Achille Mbembe has put it: 'Such is the logic of heroism as classically understood: to execute others while holding one's own death at a distance' (2003: 37).

Embedded within a heteronormative regime, the ritualistic reverence of heroic figures from the glorious past functioned as an affective matrix where participants were initiated into a cult of military sensationalism. The warrior's body emerged as a potent idiom for desiring the nation and sensing its losses through the invocation of sexual metaphors and images (Mostov 2000). Yet, the eroticising of the nation required not only sexual potency but also the desexualising of individual national subjects as depicted in the young recruits' ascetic and purified bodies (Mostov 2000). In a process that Julie Mostov aptly described as simultaneous sexing the nation and desexing the physical body (2000), the warrior was depicted by recruitment propaganda as a sexually innocent son of the nation, whose libidinal energy was directly translated into the fetishised sensuality of military vigour.

Sensing the nation requires, above all, the eroticised body of the leader. The allure of the leader, 'Slobo' (nickname for Slobodan), who was seen as an icon of national resilience, was strikingly manifest in the epic aura of the Gazimestan staged event, where hundreds of thousands of people had gathered to collectively identify with, and recognise themselves in, the 'national spirit':

> not in order to hear the leader, not in order to send a political message to the others, but simply in order to close the circle of a delusional order, to give support to themselves for the war/s, to recognize themselves. (Arsić 2002: 259)

The passionate cry of the crowd 'Slobodan, we love you' and the leader's affirmative reply 'I love you too' spoke of the euphoric intimacy between the leader and his subjects against encroaching foreign bodies.

In his speech, Milošević deployed the mythologised narrative of the Kosovo battle in order to harbinger and legitimise in advance the possibility of an upcoming war (Papić 2002):

> Six centuries later, now, we are being again engaged in battles and are facing battles. They are not armed battles, although such things cannot be excluded yet. However, regardless of what kind of battles they are, they cannot be won without resolve, bravery, and sacrifice, without the noble qualities that were present here in the field of Kosovo in the days past.[12]

Milošević's speech at the Gazimestan commemoration reiterated the message he had already articulated a few months before, at a rally in Belgrade: 'Every nation has one love that warms its heart. For Serbia it is Kosovo.' The theme of Kosovo as the 'sanctuary' of Serbia appeared later, in the form of a protest slogan 'Belgrade is the world, Kosovo is sacred' (*Beograd je svet, Kosovo je svetinje*), in the 1999 anti-NATO demonstrations (Jansen 2000: 401).[13] The 600th anniversary of the legendary Kosovo battle was abundantly publicised by the Serbian popular media that during Milošević's era was known to espouse Serb nationalism. The state-controlled Belgrade daily newspaper *Politika* reprinted Milošević's Gazimestan speech and asserted in an editorial:

> We are once more living in the times of Kosovo, as it is in Kosovo and around Kosovo that the destiny of Yugoslavia and the destiny of socialism are being determined. They want to take away from us the Serbian and the Yugoslav Kosovo, yes, they want to, but they will not be allowed. (Zirojević 2000: 207–8)

Proponents, mainly the increasingly invigorated national elites in Serbia in the mid- and late 1980s, insisted that the Gazimestan event was simply the celebration of a historic anniversary, which transmitted the message of multinational 'brotherhood and unity' amongst peoples. Oppositional commentators, however, read in Milošević's speech a repudiation of the Titoist antinationalist legacy and an unyielding commitment to the project of creating a Greater Serbia (*Velika Srbija*). Those critical commentators saw the Gazimestan festivities as harbingering the Yugoslav wars and the collapse of Yugoslavia.

As manifested in the festive euphoria staged in the Gazimestan event, fostering a narcissistic common sense centring on the Kosovo myth was a key authoritative response to the insecurities that had begun to dominate political life after 1989. What Allen Feldman has called, in the context of his work on the South African Truth and Reconciliation Commission, 'theaters of memory' (2004), emerged in this context as apparatuses of authentication that crucially encompassed rituals of gendered intimacy. Theatres of memory were constructed as monumentalised scenes of national imagining and national desiring through gender interpellation.

Making 'Women' Appropriate to the Nation: Fairies, Witches, and Mothers

The pervasive form and norm of national commemorative celebration served as a staging ground not only for bolstering male warrior culture but also for female-maternal sublimation. Nationalism, especially at times of violent conflict, is marked by an increased visibility of women's bodies as boundary markers between different national and ethnic communities (Kandyoti 1991; McClintock 1995). The nation's honour depends on devoted female bodies, as epitomised in the national image of desexualised mother and wife whose reproductive practices serve the ethnically pure and heteronormative reproduction of the nation (Helms 2007; Mosse 1985). In the context of the violent breakup of Yugoslavia, the idealisation of the male warrior's vigour worked in tandem with the impulse to regulate women's bodies as a way of affirming national fighters' sense of manliness. Accordingly, fixed and disjunctive 'masculine' and 'feminine' identities were summoned to safeguard the life and identity of the nation (Mayer 2000; McClintock 1995; Parker et al. 1992; Yuval-Davis 1997). To be sure, women were not only opponents of militarisation but often were themselves militarised. Women were summoned as desexed warriors in war propaganda. Occasionally, however, recruit images depicted female volunteers dressed in fatigues but still looking 'feminine' and 'sexy' (Mostov 2000: 95). The Movement of Women for Yugoslavia, which emerged in the beginning of 1991 to support JNA (Yugoslav

National Army), was actively involved in propaganda against war deserters, representing desertion as a 'shameful act' at a time of widespread draft dodging (Zajović 2013b).[14]

In her ethnographic study of practices and self-representations of Bosnian women involved in local NGOs and political parties, Elissa Helms (2007) has examined the ways in which during and after the war women were depicted as symbolising the victimisation of their respective ethno-national groups. Against the backdrop of a representation of politics through the trope of a demonised sexualised female figure ('politics is a whore'), women who were engaged in public sphere activities adopted discursive strategies that insisted on their status as civilian victims of the war. The status of wartime victim, associated with the morality of proper womanhood, would grant these gendered subjects the permission to enter the realm of politics, which was deemed to be a typically male activity. In the Yugoslav context of armed conflict, gender essentialist presumptions about military men and victim women structured not only mainstream accounts of the war but also the possibilities and the perils of women's anti-war activism (Helms 2013).

Figures and fabulations of devoted females whose motherly bodies ensure the appropriate reproduction of the nation has been foundational to discursive regimes that sustained the rise of nationalisms in the 1980s. Indeed the bodies of women became the foundation of the nation – the cornerstone of its walls and its borders. Branka Arsić has reflected on the Serbian myth about the sacrifice of a woman in the foundation of the nation-city (2002). Three noblemen brothers were building the city but their endeavour somehow always failed: they built during the day and the edifice got ruined at night. The building had upset a fairy, who would eventually allow the building of the city only if one of the builders' wives was sacrificed by getting built into the walls of the city. By demanding the masterbuilder's wife, the woman-fairy, Arsić remarks, functioned as the lesbian supplement that critically mimes and upsets the privileged signifier of the symbolic order. In this mythic theme, which is pervasive in Balkan folklore, the woman, as the eternal stranger, ought to be entombed in the foundations of the *polis*. Live confinement in foundations, crypts, and other subterranean spaces is a typical way to punish women who have stepped out of the proper provinces of their gender. The plethora of mythological fairies and witches embody the uncanny reappearance of the encrypted women, the foreign inside the house, and, above all, the inner enemy of the *polis*.[15] This didactic myth of foundation is embedded in a 'foundational fiction' – according to Doris Sommer's phrase (1991) – of nationhood, whereby the fantasy of encrypted women becomes the naturalised ground (literally and figuratively) on which cities rise up and national traditions are formulated.[16] The legendary accounts of women buried alive in the foundations of city-nations speak of discursive associations of the feminine with national territories: the latter are typically feminised and thus rendered vulnerable to enemy invasion and rape (Helms 2013).

The gendered intimacies of nationalism were enabled by sexual and bodily politics that involved stereotypical fantasies associated with 'women' in ethno-heteronormativity: seduction, submissiveness, susceptibility to violation. Putting women's bodies in their designated place, and making them appropriate to the nation, was a strategic biopolitical aspect of the conditions that made the wars in the former Yugoslavia possible. Anxieties about women's bodies – both those ethnically intimate and those abjected as ethnic enemies – served as the grounds for marking the boundaries of the nation as a body-archive.

The systematic use of gender-motivated and sexualised violence against enemy women as a tactic of war and ethnic cleansing during the wars in Croatia and Bosnia–Herzegovina had already been made possible and pre-emptively amnestied by an intense propaganda campaign. The Serbian media had already accused Albanians of raping Serbian and Montenegrin women, in 1986–7 (Kesić 2002; Žarkov 2007), while the shift 'from respect to rape' (*od štovanja do silovanja*) and from venerable motherland to the 'fallen woman' was inscribed in Croatian public discourses and popular press (Kesić 1994). It was in this context of marking women's place in the nation as dangerously ambiguous that, at the outbreak of war with Yugoslavia, President Tudjman of Croatia spoke of abortion as the nation's 'tragedy', calling women who have abortions 'mortal enemies of the nation' (Salecl 1992: 59; Mostov 2000). Following keen presidential involvement in the pronatalist project, in 1992 the Croatian government established the Ministry for Renewal with a special Department for Demographic Renewal, which was directed by a fervent opponent of abortion, contraception, and feminism (Mostov 2000).[17] In various nationscapes of the former Yugoslavia in the 1990s, idioms of national survival appeared to play a prominent role in the discourses of demographic anxiety that had taken on intensity within a context of growing ethnicisation.

Demographic Anxieties, Gendered Epidemics

Although the state in the Federal Republic of Yugoslavia had encouraged women's participation in the workforce and guaranteed rights to free birth control, in post-socialist societies the rise of nationalism resulted in a shift to a normative idealisation of women's reproductive role. Although abortion had been legal in Yugoslavia since 1951, the constitution of 1992 abolished article 191 that guaranteed access to abortion as a human right. In this context, nationalist discourses referred to women who had abortions as traitors, while presenting alarmist reports comparing the number of abortions to the number of soldiers killed in the war (Mladjenović and Hughes 2001). The cult of Mother Jugović, a mother of nine sons who, according to a local legend, gave their lives in the battlefield of Kosovo Polje, was invoked when, in June 1993, amidst intense national-demographic rhetoric focusing on the 'natural' and 'national' mission of women as mothers, the Church in Serbia inaugurated the 'Majka Jugović' awards to mothers with four or more children, commemorating the Battle of Kosovo in 1389 (Rajic 1993, cited in Mostov 2000: 106).

In the first years of post-socialist transition, reproduction was cast in the wake of various neo-conservative trends as a women's patriotic duty. In 1991, under the sway of the Catholic Church's anti-abortion pressures, abortion was outlawed in Croatia, even for women raped in campaigns of ethnic cleansing. In 1993, legislation was proposed to ensure the 'renewal' of the Republic of Croatia by confronting late marriage and ensuing childlessness, what had come to be called 'non-womanhood' (Enloe 1993: 242). In Slovenia, the first post-socialist elected government, a right-wing conservative administration, pledged to abolish the constitutionally guaranteed legality of abortion in 1990; the draft of the new constitution referred to the 'sanctity of life'. Women reacted spontaneously by massive demonstrations which encircled the parliament in Ljubljana. All women Members of Parliament (MPs), including even the conservative ones, joined the rally (Bahovec 1991; Slapšak 2002). The controversial phrase was removed from the text of the constitution and the Constitutional Court eventually passed a decision according to which the right to abortion on demand would be upheld and abortion would continue to be available during the first ten weeks of pregnancy as it had been since 1974. In late 1980s Kosovo, Serb nationalist discourses, conveying demographic concerns over the high fertility rate among Albanians, also prodded Serbian women to have more children. A Serbian MP was reported as stating in 1993: 'I call upon all Serbian women to give birth to one more son in order to carry out their national debt' (Korac 1996: 137).

The pronatalist campaigns that were launched in various former Yugoslav republics during the 1990s condemned not only abortion and contraception but also 'ethnically mixed marriages', which, under the sway of militarisation, emerged as a categorical trouble surrounding the question of national belonging. In the wake of escalating anxieties related to keeping community boundaries intact, allegiances were to be realigned and improper attachments to be forsaken. In their activist work, my *ŽuC* interlocutors have criticised extensively the ways in which national demography offered the discursive space for crafting proper national and gendered selves who desired the nation's enduring self-presence in space and time. As Vesna Kesić, a prominent Croatian feminist and anti-war activist, put it: 'When nationalist politicians came to power throughout Yugoslavia in the 1990 elections, women's bodies became everybody's business' (2002: 315). As she elaborated, the participation of women in national parliaments dropped drastically, and women's rights, including the right to legal and safe abortion, were threatened (ibid.). In the 1990s, anxious national scripts of demographic decline, which rendered population 'the subject of needs, of aspirations, but also [as] the object in the hands of the government' (Foucault 1991: 100), were making the rounds from Serbia to Croatia, and from Slovenia to Bosnia and Kosovo.

Milošević's rise to power was, to a great extent, the result of a national-demographic campaign about the fate of Serbs in Kosovo. Amidst public agitation incited by nationalist allegations about inter-ethnic rape in the late 1980s in Kosovo, Serbs were portrayed as a threatened minority. At a time when relations between Serbia and Kosovo were already troubled, the 1986 turmoil over rapes of Serbian women by Albanian men in Kosovo added to the ethnic tension. Those accounts did not seem willing to take into consideration the official records according to which the sexual attacks that took place in Kosovo in the last years of the 1980s were not ethnically motivated (Kesić 2002).

In Serbia, since the late 1980s, the consolidation of nationalism as the state ideology was marked by pervasive demographic discourses about declining Serbian birth rates and increasing non-Serbian population, in particular ethnic Albanians in Kosovo. Concerns about proliferating Albanians, Muslims and Roma, construed as demographically unregulated, were framed in terms of an insidious war against the Serbian people. Various parliamentary bills and resolutions in 1990 suggested a demographic policy predicated upon a double standard: pro-natalism for Serbia and Vojvodina and population control for Kosovo. Official documents, such as one titled 'The Warning' (*Upozorenje*), which was issued in 1992 and was adopted by the ruling party, were deployed to incite women's desire to bear children for 'their' nation (Zajović 1995). Nationalist pronatalism has spurred ardent protests among feminists. In her article 'Birth, nationalism and war', Staša Zajović, a prominent figure in *ŽuC* of Belgrade, probed the relationships between maternalism and nationalism, and denounced the pronatalist propaganda (1995). On another occasion, the same author noted that the Serbian nationalist demographic discourse was organised around the normative reduction of the feminine to the maternal through the instrumental perception of maternity as a means 'to defend the territorial integrity' of the Serbian nation (2004).

Early in 1999, right after the crisis of 1998 in Kosovo, Vojislav Seselj, leader of the right-wing Serbian Radical Party and a deputy prime minister in the government of the Federal

Republic of Yugoslavia (composed of Serbia and Montenegro), suggested that a special tax should be imposed on couples who did not have children on the grounds that not having children is anti-Serbian.[18] Seselj's party had called for the expulsion of all Albanian immigrants and their descendants and the abolition of all social assistance to ethnic Albanians, particularly those who have 'too high a birth rate'. In the wake of new forms of racialised anxiety over threatened national integrity, contested boundaries between differently marked bodies across different ethnic backgrounds in the area of the former Yugoslavia were constituted in accordance with the embattled matrices of gender and sexual normativity.

In this conflicted context, SANU organised conferences on population policies, and the Serbian Orthodox Patriarch broadcast a Christmas message in 1995 referring to the 'epidemic' of low birth rate among Serbs (Mostov 1995: 518–19). The nationalist concern about natality was colloquially described as the 'white plague' (*bela kuga*), an appellation with suggestive connotations of (non-reproductive) femininity as pollution (Drezgić 2004: 132). Denoting an epidemic of low birth rate, the 'white plague' became a prominent theme in the Serbian public discourses and popular media (Blagojević 2000; Drezgić 1999, 2004, 2010; Jansen and Helms 2009; Zajović 1994).

In a context of enormously intensifying ethnicisation (Jansen and Helms 2009), intra-national reproduction was politicised and militarised. In Croatia, the concern with *bijela kuga* was also salient among nationalist and religious elites. Both Serbian and Croatian pronatalist campaigns warned of the rapid population increase of local Muslims and Albanians, drawing on depictions of Muslim women as over-reproducing 'others' (Milić 1993: 112–13). In Bosnia–Herzegovina, in ways less pronounced than those documented in Serbian and Croatian pronatalist campaigns, a pronatalist discourse was produced by Bosnian secular and Muslim nationalists during and after the war (Jansen and Helms 2009). An edict issued by Islamic leader Mustafa Cerić, one of the founders of the Bosniak Academy of Sciences and Arts, called on Muslim women to have five children (Latić 1993). In the Serbian context, in particular, the 'white plague' was deployed as one more allegory of national loss. As with the rituals of archiving stories of suffering through worshipping the body of the male warrior, the idioms of demographic anxiety and intra-national pronatalism, in their persistent reifying of women's bodies, also implied a desire for the nation's survival.

At a moment when authoritative discourses wavered dramatically between national exaltation and anxieties of isolation, tropes of epidemics and therapeutics worked to enhance sentiments of intimacy among national subjects. In its modality of nationalist regulation of natality, biopower, as an ensemble of discursive practices, affective dispositions and imaginative investments wherein 'national culture meets intimacy forms like sex' (Berlant 1998), operated pre-eminently in the intimate registers of the subjects' ways of living and dying. In that national-demographic regime, nationalist concerns about fertility rates have been integral to a wider post-socialist politicisation of reproduction and reconstitution of gendered subjects (Gal and Kligman 2000). As Rada Drezgić has elaborated, the blame for the 'epidemic' of declining birth rate was clearly gender-specific in Serbia, as it was overwhelmingly laid on women's selfishness and careerism brought on by socialism or imitation of 'Western modern' lifestyles (2004). Within a context of embattled gendered citizenship in nationalism, women's bodies came to signal the very principle of mixture (Iveković 1993): namely, the potential for diluting and polluting the 'purity' of national community. Women, enfleshed and sexualised in accordance with the national heteronormative matrix, were cast as territorial markers (Mostov 1995): respectable, if also susceptible to trespassing. This is why they remain always in need of men's surveillance and control, as the last word of the authority to define the nation and defend it against its enemies' lies primarily with the community of male bonding – *Männerbund*, in Mosse's terms (1985). In any case, pronatalist exhortations, sustained and adroit though they may have been, failed to translate into people's actual reproductive practices in accordance with the nationalist mandates (Drezgić 2004; Jansen and Helms 2009).

Nevertheless, nationally appropriate femininity would embody not only the suffering and the courage of the motherland through conventional frames of female/maternal victimhood but also 'sexier' idioms of supporting, comforting, and entertaining the nation's men, especially members of the new Serbian ruling classes during the 1990s – from those who were finding solace in consuming pop-cultural conventionality during the years of economic hardship to those who were taking a break from their military or paramilitary actions. Women took part in ordinary circumstances of sexing (as well as rendering sexy) the nation (Mayer 2000), and they did so directly and indirectly, silently or vocally, and in various performative genres – in verse, prose, lament, and song. As I shall elaborate below, singing was one of such ways of promoting model national femininity.

Singing the 1990s

Žarana Papić, a long-time feminist activist of *ŽuC* and co-founder of the Belgrade Women's Studies Center, commented on Milošević's rhetoric at the Gazimestan event thus: 'He sent a message to the men that they were to fight "heroically" for the preservation of Yugoslavia, while women got the message to shut up' (2002: 132). Indeed, although women were silenced by nationalist discourse, they were assigned to perform, under the authority of the nation's men, the labour of embodying and sensualising the nation (Mostov 2000). Thus, singing (for) the nation was one of the gendered and sexualised idioms through which nationalism permeated the intimate folds of banal ordinariness during the turbulent 1990s. Before and during the wars in the former Yugoslavia, the national imagery of unsexual virtuous mothers of the nation was complemented by mass-mediated depictions of 'turbo-folk queens'.

The Serbian best-selling diva Svetlana Veličković, nicknamed Ceca, had an iconic relation with nationalist culture and politics. In 1995, she married the paramilitary commander of the wars on Croatia and Bosnia, Željko Ražnatović (better known by his nickname Arkan), in a wedding ceremony of traditional colour, with Ceca dressed in a folk bridal costume and Arkan in a military uniform. The glamorous political love story had started in 1993, when Ceca was invited to entertain the troops at a military camp in Erdut, where Arkan trained soldiers for his paramilitary army called the Serbian Voluntary Guard, also known as the Tigers, which was later held responsible for ethnic cleansing in Croatia, Bosnia, and Kosovo (Papić 2002).[19] Either dressed in feminine outfits or, occasionally, posing in a military uniform (Lopusina 2003: 76), Ceca embodied the patriarchal fantasy of the Serbian woman who combines the 'traditional' values of good wife and loving mother with 'modern' professional skills, such as those related to the football business and charity activities: she had presided over a soccer club since her husband, the previous president, was assassinated, and she was the president of the Third Child fund that Arkan had established in the mid-1990s to promote the increase of birth rates in Serbia by making grants in support of ethnic Serbian mothers.[20] After her husband's death in 2000, and replaying the nationalist association between motherhood and grief, Ceca went into mourning and withdrew from show business and public life for a year. In a sensational comeback concert three years later in the Belgrade soccer stadium, she told the audience, a crowd chanting the name of her late husband, that she was singing 'for my husband Željko, for Belgrade, for Serbia'. Ceca had re-emerged to substantiate the ideal figure of Serbian womanhood, this time as a mournful wife but also as a powerful player in business and politics.[21]

As a mass cultural icon that flourished under the Milošević regime, the turbo-folk queen came to embody the public sentimentality of a commercialised, heteronormative femininity. In its undertones of interconnected commodified nationalism and oversexualised femininity, the genre of turbo-folk had emerged in the early 1990s during the partitioning of the Socialist Federal Republic of Yugoslavia. In 1993, a year in which turbo-folk's popularity reached its peak, the region was beset with widespread poverty, violent conflict, and international rebuke. While the rest of the former Yugoslavia was in the maelstrom of war and Serbian nationalism was escalating into military aggression, turbo-folk was becoming a favourite popular diversion. During the forty-four-month siege of Sarajevo by the forces of the Yugoslav People's Army first and by Bosnian Serb forces of the Republika Srpska later (in total lasting from 1992 to 1996), a great part of the Serbian public was fervently consuming turbo-folk strains and related media events, such as the lavish wedding between Ceca and Arkan, which took place in an embargo-stricken Belgrade. So not only did turbo-folk not wane under those tumultuous circumstances, but rather it was scripted as a politicised lifestyle of national belonging (Cvoro 2012; Gordy 1999, 2002; Kronja 2001, 2004a, 2004b; Papić 2002; Volčič and Erjavec 2011). As the prominence of turbo-folk illustrated, the Milošević regime controlled key aspects of everyday life, including media and popular music (Gordy 1999, 2002). Nationalism leaked beyond the realm of the state and took place at the most intimate and mundane nodes of social affinity, as the regime-controlled media obsessively played strains of turbo-folk to provide a turbulent era with a lively soundtrack and a glamorous spectacle.[22] As Papić put it: 'A primary function of turbo-folk was to convey a message of normality' (2002: 141).

The massively popular and energetic music genre of neo-folk or so-called 'newly composed music' (*novokomponovana muzika*) consisted of traditional folk songs set to an overamplified techno-pop beat. Lyrics were drawn from formulaic scripts that typically included adulated bravery and unrequited love, but also motifs of patriotic sacrifice and, occasionally, royalist and anti-communist themes. For example, the popular song *Ne može nam niko ništa* (No one can touch us) by Mitar Mirić, narrating a couple's long-standing love enduring against all odds, turned into an anthem of nationalist propaganda in times of Serbia's international isolation. Similarly, the song *Kad bi bio ranjen* (If you were wounded), sung by Ceca, employed the nationalistically imbued trope of blood to praise self-sacrifice by conflating erotic love with the love for the homeland. The commonplace symbol of blood was reiterated in yet another song, *Sta je to u tvojim venama / Kukavica* (What is flowing in your veins / Coward, 1993), also by Ceca, conveyed sentiments of love for one's own ethnic identity, aversion towards other ethnic identities, and defiance of international reprehension.

The genre's popularity outlived the Milošević era but not as potently and ubiquitously as in its heyday. In the 2000s, after the wars and the subsequent fall of Milošević in the face of mass street protests, the turbo-folk scene remained a commodity and celebrity domain, incorporated not only in the extraordinary world of glamour but also in the banality of urban consumption practices. Despite its endurance, however, turbo-folk was gradually refashioned into a depoliticised genre of contemporary pop folk, surviving in post-Yugoslav commercial media spaces, in club dance culture, as well as in the body politics performed in the nightlife of boat-cafés on the Danube River. In the context of the 'transitional' Serbia's attempts to purge the mnemonic traces of the 1990s, turbo-folk, in all its associations with anti-Yugoslav nationalism, is archived back into Serbia's troubled past (Cvoro 2012). After the former-Yugoslav wars, the recrafted successor music style represented a pan–Balkan transnational regional unity rather than the 'excesses' of nationalism. Ceca emerged 'as a borderless celebrity' (Volčič and Erjavec 2011: 36), although she maintained and marketed her old explicitly nationalistic persona, as was manifested in a 2002 television advertisement for a brand of coffee, in which she appeared surrounded by tigers, in a scene clearly echoing the Tigers, the paramilitary unit commanded by her late husband. Despite its newly found appeal to the authenticity of the Balkan cultural space, turbo-folk never entirely lost its iconic standing in national Serbian politics, persisting as the favourite commercial spectacle of right-wing parties. In the 2008 presidential election campaign, for instance, the rallies of the ultra-nationalist candidate Tomislav Nikolić featured turbo-folk performances in an attempt to capture the *authentic* sentiments of the people.[23]

Turbo-folk has always been a space of contestation, however. Although its images and commodities were publically consumed on mainstream media circuits, it was detested as kitschy and even ludicrous by activists, artists, intellectuals, and other members of dissident cultures. Suggestively, Papić referred to the politically and culturally engrained normality of abjecting the other in Serbian social life of the 1990s as 'turbo-fascism' (2002: 134). For feminist anti-war activists, like Papić herself, the routinised triviality of turbo-folk iconised cultural nationalism and its reliance upon regimes of sex and power. Women whose lived experiences were not settled inside or alongside the entrenched prescriptions of proper national femininity were depicted as asexual, frigid, and unfit for reproduction. Concurrently, dissidence itself was feminised through the trope of hysteria. Thus, Vesna Pešić, founder and director of the Center for Antiwar Action, was described in an article as 'a hysterical lady who, through her political career, makes up for what she missed in her youth'.[24] My *ŽuC* interlocutors have often faced such pathologisation of their activism through stereotypical images of the hysterical woman.[25]

In a conversation with me about the social and political context of the 1990s, Saša Kovačević offered a dissonant account of the national euphoria and normality, despite and against which she and her combatants took to the streets, arousing anger in their opponents – mainly Serb nationalists:

> The atmosphere was suffocating. Everyone was living normally, as though nothing had happened. A lot of people were rejoiced at the things done in their name. And we were exhausted, unwashed, sleepless, overworked and, above all, deeply sad that we were unable to do anything to change the situation. We felt outraged that people did not react. We felt jeered. Put aside.

While pronouncing these last words, Saša took in her hands her personal archive – a collection of notes, photographs, clippings, and drawings. She pulled out a black-and-white photograph to show me: 'Notice how wretched and angry we look.' The picture was riveting, indeed. It portrayed a public vigil against the siege of Sarajevo: three women standing in the square, holding a sign 'Not in our name', looking rather isolated but determined and wholly engrossed in the exigencies of the situation. Standing in the street, especially within a very small women-only demonstration, to protest the nationalism of one's own country and hold it accountable for what is done 'in their name', was a risky pursuit at those times of national normality, when state television and radio stations played turbo-folk and refused to broadcast the siege and bombing of Sarajevo.[26] In the words of Orli Fridman: 'While the streets and the people aspire to normalization, the message of antiwar activists reminds the passers-by that not everything is normal. In this way, they pose a threat to a pleasant and beautiful Sunday evening in Belgrade' (2009: 90).

Remains and Spectres

The concern of this chapter has been with how national myths and public spectacles, which aimed to manage the conditions of appropriate commemoration, drew on imageries and imaginaries of proper gender. Diana Taylor has addressed the performative gendering of nationness through the staging of spectacles of masculinity and femininity in Argentina under dictatorship:

> Gender, then, was not simply the regulatory social system through which each sex assumed and incorporated the attributed assigned to it; it was also performative in that gender roles could be assumed or imposed, either unconsciously and apparently 'naturally' or through open or coercive acts of violence' (1997: 34)

In the wake of archival anxieties that took place in the context of the troubled 1990s in the former Yugoslavia, such gendered intimacies of the nationalist archive have been incited to define intimates and foes (Mayer 2000; Mostov 1995; Papić 2002).

In occupying the position of the internal enemy in ways that replot the gendered and ethnicised apparatus of belonging, ŽuC activists trouble these sedimented intimacies of the nationalist archive. Their memory-work is not motivated by a desire for formulaic closure and archival recognition, but rather by the performativity of abjectified unbelonging. In other words, instead of setting the archive 'straight', this dissident memory emerges as a critical mode of troubling, or queering, the prerogatives and the exclusions of a given pastness and its narrational closures, while simultaneously complicating the often normative assumptions of reconciliatory present and future. Therefore, their point is not to replace the nationalist 'archive fever' with another (i.e. a post-socialist, transitional memory politics), which could 'instigate further asymmetric subject positions, further tales left untold, further forms of cultural violence, and further inequitable regimes of truth obtained from the condition of those who have been othered by violence' (Feldman 2004: 194). After all, a drive to monumentalise the occlusions and asymmetries of the nationalist archive, that is, to seal them into another truth regime, would risk normalising even those who seek to dismantle them.

Resisting the formulae of 'becoming-archival', *ŽuC* dissident memory has not only contested the epistemic violence of national archiving. In forestalling the normative interpellations of the archive, it has also offered a possibility for mobilising critical agonism within the apparatuses of memory and responsiveness. These activists pollute ascribed archival truths with what Donna Haraway has called 'situated knowledges' (1988) and what Ann Stoler in another context coins as 'minor histories': tellings, experiences, sentiments, and counter-stories that are rendered invisible in the conventionally 'archived' order of things and 'mark a differential political temper and a critical space' (2010: 7). Engaging the affective textures of situated knowledges and memories, the political labour of *ŽuC* addresses the singularity of lives rendered unliveable. They do so, however, without monumentalising these lives, without consigning them to the conventional matrices of 'becoming-archival' (Bell 2010: 81).

Theirs is not an attempt to save missing voices and occluded stories from oblivion by ossifying them into a record of a settled past. In this respect, Vikki Bell has provided a compelling analysis of the photograph of a young man named Fernando who was kidnapped in 1979 in Argentina, which was part of the evidence submitted by the relatives of the missing during the trials of the military junta members. She suggests that as Fernando addresses a demand for justice that reaches beyond death, his picture enacts a resistance to 'becoming preserved *as past*' (2010: 81). The ghostly figure of the *desaparecidos* emerges here as a living demand for justice, and it is precisely this transformative political potential that also has been upheld by the perseverance of the Madres de Plaza de Mayo. It is because of this transformative political potential that, immediately before its demise, the junta issued the 'Law of National Pacification', which commanded that the disappeared should be considered dead.

As in Bell's reflection on Fernando's photograph as a living demand for justice, the non-sanctioned mourning of the political collective I worked with confronts us with questions concerning the ethical and political relevance of documentation and transmission to the performativity of commemorative agonism. Since 2005, Miloš Urošević has been monitoring trials on war crimes, as a representative of *ŽuC*. As he explained to me once, monitoring these trials is about constituting an act of responsiveness to the stories of people so that 'these narratives would someday become part of the official history'. Indeed, *ŽuC* memory-work calls into being the irreconcilable remains of those stories and bodies that seemingly had left no traces on the corpus of archived history and, nevertheless, returned to haunt its ordered regularity. In a conversation with me, Saša Kovačević recounted the collective project 'I Remember' (1994), which consisted in collecting and publishing women's oral and written testimonies of war displacement: 'One woman said that she had missed her cat, whom she had to leave abruptly, while she was living alone with her. Another talked about missing her girl-friend. These stories are normally obliterated in official national history.' Another activist, Prota, member of the art group 'Škart' that collaborates with *ŽuC*, talked about the collective project 'I Remember' in terms of art activism: 'Unlike other activist groups and NGOs, *ŽuC* is a kind of moving disquietude.' At the time of our conversation, Prota had already been with *ŽuC* for twenty years. His main concern as an artist/activist had to do with the question of infusing the affective energies of art into the collective praxis of the movement. In his words:

> 'I Remember' was not just a social project but also an art project, the first one to involve refugees. It was an opportunity to communicate with the other side. It was easy to be alienated from the refugee context, in Belgrade, even during wartime. Thanks to *ŽuC*, we developed the tools to break this alienation. We devised methods to create art which did not present itself simply as art. No exhibitions and presentations were involved. But that project proved that art can be alternatively deployed within the activist context.

Prota stressed to me that part of their artistic/activist method was maintaining their anonymity as artists before the mainstream mediatised discourses: 'We are invisible, we are not present; never in the media.' Instead, the emphasis of Prota and his comrades has been the construction of an alternative horizon of re-membering the public. As manifested in his words, collecting and performing testimonies of war displacement articulated a new collective imaginary for an art of counter-archiving: one which attended to the archive's inadmissible voices and thereby mobilised the possibility of responsiveness.

Saša talked also about another, more personal idiom of archive-making, which was precious to her and her political engagement:

During the war, my mother was collecting any snippets she would locate in the newspapers about us (ŽuC). She was a writer herself, and she knew how important it is to keep an archive. She was collecting everything they wrote about us, and she was adding captions: 'here Saša with her friends for this', 'there Saša with her friends for that'. As she was keeping all those clippings safe in a small purse, she used to tell me: 'You are doing right, I am proud of you.' And we were regarded back then, for a whole decade, as pariahs: as whores, traitors, homosexuals. We were demonised by the media. My mother supported my political action. She always told me that I was not a monster, that I was like my grandmother, who was a fighter with the Antifascist Front of Montenegro. While she was concerned about me, she never instilled fear or guilt in me. She gave me air to fly.

Indeed, that intimate genre of counter-archiving gave my friend 'air to fly', that is, to engage, with others, in transformative modes of survival, but also of political recollection and responsiveness.

Like Saša's mother who 'knew how important it is to keep an archive', this awareness emerged in various activists' life stories. The biography of Ljiljana Radovanović, a fifty-six-year-old married woman with two children at the time of our conversation, is linked with the history of the ŽuC archive. 'Although I had heard about ŽuC since 1992', she recalls, 'I learned more about the group in 1995-1996, through my friend Zinaida from Sarajevo who was living in Belgrade.' All those years, although she was not a member of ŽuC, she participated in the protests: 'I didn't miss even one. I sided with the students, we were sleeping at the park.' In 1999, when most ŽuC activists had to go underground, someone had to keep the movement's archive:

I started to be more actively involved right after the bombing, when Staša (Zajović) was gone in Montenegro, and someone had to keep and safeguard the archives, the computers and all the papers of the organisation. Our other friend, Dunja, was also self-exiled to avoid arrest. Because I was not marked, I did it. With Zinaida's help, I kept the archive of the organisation in the garage of my home.

In all, the *ŽuC* engagement with the haunting remains of the past has worked to delegitimise the monological and authoritative bereavement mandated by the nationalist archive. However, this genre of counter-archiving does not imply what Walter Benjamin criticises in thesis 7 of 'On the concept of history' as an attempt to reconstruct the past 'as it was' (2002). On the contrary, practicing historical materialism, as he further explains, breaks with this historicist approach and entails a 'task to brush history against its grain' (ibid., p. 392). This entails a melancholic and, at the same time, revolutionary remembrance 'wherein what has been comes together in a flash with the now to form a constellation' (*Arcades*, 462; N2a, 3).[27] The *ŽuC* dissident acts of performative archiving irreconcilable mnemonic residues during and in the aftermath of war 'brush history against its grain' and thus works to reconfigure the very texture of the political. Nevertheless, whether and to what degree this agonistic engagement with remains, as well as with what remains from the nation's stratified losses, fulfils its promise is not answerable in a once-and-for-all fashion. Disputing the sensual and consensual modes of commemoration in nationalism, which determine what is sensible, thinkable, memorable, and possible, and doing so from a gender-enemy perspective, might be, after all, an agonistic experience of the impossible. This work involves not nostalgic re-collecting but rather active and embodied rewriting the past, beyond its authorised archive drive, and toward its present and future struggles.

The legacy of women's participation in the antifascist Resistance infused contemporary feminist struggles, including pursuits of dissident memory, with a utopian affectivity. In her archival study of the Antifascist Women's Front, Lydia Sklevicky (1952–90), a leading feminist theorist of the 1980s in Yugoslavia, attends to this structural force of not-yet: 'Listening today to the voices of women from the past, one sees not only the mistaken choices which should not to be repeated, but also the unspent reserves of utopian energy' (1996: 69). She continued, citing Benjamin's thesis 5 from 'On the concept of history' (1940): 'For it is an irretrievable picture of the past, which threatens to disappear with every present, which does not recognize itself as meant in it' (cited in Bonfiglioli 2016). Hence, echoing Sklevicky's insight about the 'unspent reserves of utopian energy', feminist and queer counter-memory draws on these reserves, again and again, and becomes a contingent event that *remains*. The utopian affect of the activists with whom I worked animates their situated struggles, allowing them to grapple with the losses and complexities of the present (and) presentness while, at the same time, dialectically propelling them onward to reach for a future collectivity. Attuned to what José Esteban Muñoz has described as 'the then and there of queer futurity' (2009), their relational life-worlds, both actualised and potential, promise an enduring critical methodology of world making.

Notes

1 Atanasijević's scholarly interests expanded from philosophy and ethics to literature and aesthetics. Her books include *On Women's Emancipation in Plato* (1923), *The Ethical Base of Feminism* (1927), *The Position of Women in our Public Life* (1928), and *Philosophical Fragments* (1928–30).
2 On silences in historical narratives, see also Trouillot 1995.
3 Drawing on Freud's account of infant relation to excitation and sexuality, Judith Butler defines 'passionate attachment' as 'the formation of primary passion in dependency' (1997a: 7). Butler proceeds to reassess passionate

attachments apropos of her reflection on how the subject is formed through submission to power and dependency on reiteration of hegemonic norms. The subject emerges through the passionate attachment to the socio-symbolic order that determines which passionate attachments are and are not possible. In Butler's resignification, the subject is constituted through pre-emptive losses and foreclosed desires. Thus, attachments become a constitutive means for psychic and social survival.

4 The material that was deployed to manipulate nationalist sentiments, however, was drawn not only from political-historical tracts such as the memorandum of the Academy and political discourse, but also from other textual genres including poetry. Slavoj Žižek (2014) refers to the '*poetic-military complex*', personified in the figures of Radovan Karadžić and Ratko Mladić, who were not only political and military leaders but also poets. Poets and writers who were engaged in nationalist projects had played a crucial role in the formation of a nationalist ideological consensus in the ex-Yugoslavia of the 1970s and 1980s well before things exploded in the late 1980s.

5 This change was marked in the ordinary topography of the city of Belgrade. For instance, Marshal Tito Street (Marsala Tita) was renamed during Milošević's rule as the Street of Serbian Rulers (*Srpskih Vladara*). Along this main downtown street one of the most powerful anti-war manifestations during the war took place with protesters holding a mile-long mourning ribbon to signal the tragedy of Yugoslavia's violent breakup (Matić 1997). In May of 2007, *ŽuC* called upon authorities to take off the placards 'Ratko Mladić's Boulevard', with which unidentified persons had daubed buildings in the Boulevard of the Antifascist Council for National Liberation of Yugoslavia, in New Belgrade (Kaliterna 2013: 213).

6 'Brotherhood and Unity' was the guiding principle of Yugoslavia's post-war policy of internationalism and ethnic tolerance. The motto was introduced during the Yugoslav People's Liberation War (1941–5). The Yugoslav Communist Party promoted the principle of peaceful coexistence among Yugoslavia's 'nations' (*narodi*) and 'nationalities' (*narodnosti*) in their struggle against fascism. After the war, the 'Brotherhood and Unity' banner denoted the official policy of inter-ethnic relations in the Socialist Federal Republic of Yugoslavia.

7 The Ustasha (in Croatian, *Ustaša – Hrvatski Revolucionarni Pokret*, Croatian Revolutionary Movement) was a Croatian militant nationalist organisation that was founded in 1929–30, upon the foundation of the Serb-dominated Kingdom of Yugoslavia. Western Bosnia–Herzegovina was the birthplace

148

and centre of the movement. According to authoritative Croatian historical sources, the Ustashe movement emerged as a resistance group in response to the expansionist aspirations of the Serbs in the first decades of the twentieth century. In 1944, the units of Ustashe militia became the armed forces ('Croatian Home Guard') of the Independent State of Croatia (Nezavisna Hrvatska Drzava, NDH), which was founded in 1941, authorised and backed by the Axis powers (primarily German forces, but also Italian Fascists, as well as Hungarian and Bulgarian formations) that had invaded the Kingdom of Yugoslavia on 6 April 1941. Renowned for its brutality, the Ustashe movement is believed to have been responsible for the deaths of hundreds of thousands of citizens of Yugoslavia, particularly Serbs, during World War II.

8 The term *Četnici* (Chetniks) originally referred to the legendary and glorified Serb gangs of rebels or bandits from the era of the Early Ottoman rule, who allegedly struggled to cast off the Turkish yoke. During World War II, in occupied Yugoslavia, the Chetnik movement (officially the Yugoslav Army in the Fatherland, JVUO) was a conservative royalist and nationalist paramilitary force, aiming at the retention of the Yugoslav monarchy, the protection of ethnic Serbian populations, and the establishment of a Greater Serbia. It was formed soon after the invasion of Yugoslavia and initially resisted the occupation, although representing a monarchist concept of resistance ideologically oppositional to the communist-led revolutionary resistance movement of Yugoslav Partisans (officially the National Liberation Army and Partisan Detachments of Yugoslavia, *Narodnooslobodilačka Vojska i Partizanski Odredi Jugoslavije*). The pan-ethnic Yugoslav Partisan ideology was anti-Serbian to the Chetniks who thus turned against the Partisans as their main enemies. Eventually the Chetniks participated in the anti-communist paramilitaries collaborating with the occupation forces, and the tense relations between the two rival movements took the dimensions of a full-scale conflict. This accounts for the fact that the term 'Chetnik' was decried under the socialist Yugoslav regime. The movement of the Yugoslav Partisans, under the command of Marshal Josip Broz Tito, grew to become the largest resistance force in occupied Europe, prevailed against all of their opponents, and gained recognition from the Allies and the Yugoslavian government in exile as the official Yugoslav liberation force and as the official army of the newly founded Democratic Federal Yugoslavia (later Socialist Federal Republic of Yugoslavia). During the war of the 1990s, Serb paramilitary fighters in Bosnia and Croatia were often self-represented as Chetniks; some of them

used a style of clothing inspired by fighters in World War II and in the Balkan Wars (Rogel 1998; Torsti 2004).

9 For a rewriting of nationalism as 'spectral', see also Cheah 2003. On the notion of national fantasy, Berlant 1991. For an account of power as phantasmatic in the context of post-communist politics of nationalism in Eastern Europe, Salecl 1994. And for a study of the Serbian imaginary as a dreamwork, Živković 2011.

10 The UN sanctions had harshly affected the movements of resistance, severing them from networks of communication with friends and comrades around the world. The local mass media played a crucial role in inculcating nationalist discourses and sentiments. The regime propaganda machine was vehemently criticised by anti-regime protesters. Stef Jansen (2000) mentions that during the Winter Protest, a popular way of displaying dissent against the regime-minded media was the action called 'Noise is all the rage' (*Buka u modi*): every evening at 7:30, at the time of the main news report on state TV, hundreds of thousands of people created an outpour of clamour from their living rooms and balconies to symbolically cover the 'noise' of the TV propaganda.

11 Through his action in the Center for Antiwar Action, which was founded in July 1991, and as co-editor of the magazine *Pacifik*, Dejan Nebrigić (1970–99) has played a central role in introducing lesbian, gay, bisexual, transgender and queer (LGBTQ) voices and claims into Serbia's public sphere.

12 <http://www.slobodan-milosevic.org/spch-kosovo1989.htm> (last accessed 21 October 2016).

13 The first half of the motto was one of the central slogans during the 1996–7 anti-government demonstrations, implying a demand for ending Serbia's isolation (Jansen 2000: 401). In the context of the anti-NATO protests, however, it was resignified to assert Serbian national identity founded on a heroic Kosovan past as a repository of sentiments of common origins.

14 Other women's organisations, self-described as non-feminist, were: The Central Circle of the Serbian Sisters (*Kolo srpskih sestara*) and SSSS/Only the Serbian Women Can Save the Serbian Man (*Samo Srpkinja spašava Srbina*) (Zajović 2013b).

15 In Greek dramaturgy, confinement in a crypt is a typical threat for putting undisciplined women 'in their place'. Antigone was buried alive in a crypt as a punishment for her claiming of her brother's unburied cadaver; Aegisthos threatened he was going to have Electra buried alive if she did not learn to stay at home and behave like a proper woman (Sophocles,

Electra, 329–31, 378–85); and the Erinyes or the Furies, the group of archaic chthonic goddesses who pursue Orestes after he murdered his mother, were forced to go underground and hide themselves (Aeschylus, *Eumenides*, 937–48). The ambivalent connotations of the notion of 'crypt' should be noted here. Nicolas Abraham and Maria Torok (1978) address the figure of the 'crypt' as a live burial of the love object: an intimate recess, which the subject constructs inside her psyche, in order to conceal there the precious corpses of desires, memories, and unspeakable secrets. See Taxidou 2004 for a compelling account of ways in which tragedy and psychoanalysis can fruitfully converse with each other on the topos of mourning. In a different register, the one of modern Greek folklore, the tale of the Bridge of Arta, in northwest Greece, tells the story of a bridge's masterbuilder, who was forced to sacrifice his wife by burying her alive in the foundations of the construction – a common theme in Balkan folk songs (Leontis 1999).

16 Doris Sommer uses the term 'foundational fiction' in a different context, to situate national romances in nineteenth-century Latin American writing.

17 Under pressure from local women's groups and international agencies, the department was transformed into an NGO, the Croatian Population Movement (Mostov 2000).

18 In the parliamentary and presidential election in September 1997, Seselj's party had won the second largest contingent of seats in the Serbian National Assembly and Seselj himself had come within 1 per cent of becoming Serbia's president. In March 1998, Seselj's party received fifteen of thirty-six portfolios and Seselj was appointed as one of the five deputy prime ministers in a newly formed Serbian government where Milošević's party held the key ministerial posts.

19 A baby tiger was used as a mascot by Arkan's unit in Kraina, Croatia in 1991–2. In her 1995 concert in Belgrade, Ceca appeared in a tiger-skin bathing suit and, at the end of the event, she brought to the stage a cage containing a baby tiger (Papić 2002: 142). Once again, the scene brought forward a metaphorical fusion of wild femininity and ferocious nationalism.

20 Arkan was indicted on genocide charges by The Hague tribunal for Bosnian war crimes, although the indictment was only made public after Arkan's assassination in 2000.

21 In 2003, Ceca was arrested (and later released uncharged) on suspicion of complicity in the assassination of former Serbian Prime Minister Zoran Djindjić.

22 Turbo-folk was promoted extensively across media outlets. A striking exception was B92, a radio station that was founded in 1989 as a predominantly youth-oriented station and an anti-Milošević outlet for independent news and alternative music in the Federal Republic of Yugoslavia.

23 In 2004 and 2008, Nikolić placed second behind Boris Tadić, but in 2012 he won the runoff against Tadić to become President of Serbia. Leaders of Croatia, Bosnia and Herzegovina, Slovenia and Macedonia boycotted the inauguration in protest of Nikolić's denial of the 1995 Srebrenica massacre ('Balkan neighbours boycott Serbia's presidential inauguration', *Euronews*, 11 June 2012, <http://www.euronews.com/2012/06/11/balkan-neighbours-boycott-serbias-presidential-inauguration/> (last accessed 21 October 2016). After Nikolić was criticised during the 2012 presidential election for denying the genocide in Srebrenica, he apologised for the crimes committed in the name of Serbia and the Serbian people, on 25 April 2013. He also asked for forgiveness for Serbia for the crime committed in Srebrenica, although he stopped short of calling it genocide ('Serbia president "apologises" for massacre', *Al Jazeera*, 25 April 2013, <http://www.aljazeera.com/news/europe/2013/04/2013425102523848 273.html> (last accessed 21 October 2016).

24 *NIN*, 25 April 1997.

25 Feminist theorists such as Hélène Cixous (1976) and Jacqueline Rose (1978) have redefined the 'hysterical woman' trope through the perspective of strength and self-determined desire.

26 Ildiko Erdei has reported that a radio station in a town near Belgrade refused to broadcast a call for an anti-war gathering in the one-year anniversary of the siege and bombing of Sarajevo, 'with an explanation that no siege nor bombing exist, simply a war for the national liberation of the Serbs in Bosnia' (2008: 162).

27 For a fascinating reading of Benjamin's 'revolutionary melancholia', see Löwy 2006.

3

Spectral Spaces of Counter-Memory

Although it is not easy to find new ways and codes to express women's resistance to war, we retained the ritual of black and silence. However, the traditional symbols of black and silence are completely turned upside down. Black clothing is part of the traditional women's role; it is a historic domestic duty that women, if they were to express pain, practice only in the invisible, domestic sphere. We took black out to the square as a visible, political colour. (*ŽuC* statement)[1]

If I am getting ready to speak at length about ghosts, inheritance, and generations, generations of ghosts, which is to say about certain *others* who are not present, nor presently living, either to us, in us, or outside us, it is in the name of *justice*. (Jacques Derrida 1994: xix, emphasis in original)

Ghostly Emergences

The *polis*, writes Hannah Arendt, establishes a space where 'organized remembrance' may take place (1998: 95). Therefore, to thoroughly capture the *polis*, one must confront the way it *organises* (its) memory. And yet, what about aggrieved, displaced, and disavowed memories that haunt the *polis* and its organised remembrance? What about the violations and the desires that

153

Vesna Pavlović, *Hands and a Banner. The third anniversary of Women in Black. Republic Square, Belgrade, October 1994.* Gelatin silver print.

are embodied in this haunting and come to produce again and again the *polis* and its others? How does the political action of reclaiming a public space for remembering others and otherwise work to traverse and transfigure the *polis* and the ways in which it comes to organise its remembrance? This chapter engages with such questions, reflecting on the ways in which *ŽuC* political actors carve an expansive cartography of critical memory in the *polis*. This reflection bears on the modes of embodiment, knowledge, as well as affective intensity and density that the work of haunting the *polis*'s 'organized remembrance' renders possible.

Clearly, haunting raises anew the problem of (emerging in) the *polis*, in all its gestural and affective layers. Despite Arendt's ontological understanding of appearance, the *polis*, for her, is not a 'given'; it cannot be reduced to static physical location or surroundings. It does not materialise *in*, but rather *as*, a 'space of appearance'. In other words, it is the contingent actuality of the disclosure and assembly of bodies that brings the *polis* into being: '[The *polis*] is the organization of the people as it arises out of acting and speaking together, and its true space lies between people living together for this purpose, no matter where they happen to be' (1998: 198). In other words, although the spatial component is crucial to the coexistence that brings the *polis* into being, the *polis* is not to be reduced to the physical space of disclosure and appearance: it can be always and continually recreated anew through the actuality of people gathering 'no matter where they happen to be':

> 'Wherever you go, you will be a *polis*': these famous words became not merely the watchword of Greek colonization, they expressed the conviction that action and speech create a space between the participants which can find its proper location almost anytime and anywhere. (1998: 198)

In other words, the *polis* is a '*potential* space of appearance' (1998: 200, emphasis added): 'Wherever people gather together, it is potentially there, but only potentially, not necessarily and not forever' (1998: 199). Hence, the *polis* is an indeterminate and continually recreated potentiality arising from plural bodies getting together and 'acting in concert' (1972: 143). And yet, if the *polis* requires people being in some sense and in particular ways present in a public space, itself constituted by particular kinds of ontological claims and power relations, I suggest that we further complicate this disclosive account of political action and its conditions of 'being there' and 'belonging together', through a critical hauntology of (dis)appearing and (dis)assembling.[2] 'To understand history, that is the eventness of the event', asks Derrida, 'must one not reckon with this virtualization?' (1993: 117). By invoking Derrida's reference to virtualisation, and from the perspective of the political subjects with whom I worked, I would like to register and acknowledge the horizon of emergent potentialities that upset the anchoring of the possible in the polarity of concealment/unconcealment.

In these pages, I focus on the agonistic eventness of appearing as reclaiming a public space for remembering others and otherwise in the face – and in the aftermath – of militaristic state violence and war. 'Appearing', in this context, evokes haunting the space of the *polis* and being haunted by it; it also indicates persistent lingering in spaces rendered uninhabitable. In thinking with and alongside my *ŽuC* collaborators, I wish to engage the spectralised plurality of appearing and acting bodies and ask what kinds of political temporalities and spatialities arise from these subjects' embodied practices of unbelonging, or opting out of certain schemes of appearance. More to the point, I ask how those losses, absences, and disappearances that have been brought about by abusive power form all that remains from the space of appearance. To this end, of particular concern to me is how this reclaiming of public space involves bodies appearing out of place and yet reappearing, bodies meant to be eclipsed, bodies whose presence appears not to be present, disconcerted bodies, and, to be sure, bodies to which 'appearance' is always at stake. So, the register of the emergent that I pursue here is indelibly marked by the performative operations of spectral iteration: it does not simply offer material to be added to a supposedly shared, all-inclusive memory but rather contests the conditions of emergence that turn public space into a fixed and immutable landscape of hegemonic memorability. By articulating and transmitting differently positioned memory claims and struggles, the political actors with whom I worked reclaim a public space for making themselves and others vulnerable and accountable to displaced memories, and, ultimately, to the emergence of the other in the *polis*'s 'organised remembrance'. In this regard, they join the Mothers of Plaza de Mayo, the group of Argentine women who since 1977 have been claiming the 'alive appearance' (*aparición con vida*) of their children (Sosa 2014).

In reading Arendt's conception of the *polis*, Judith Butler has importantly asked:

> On this account of the body in political space, how do we make sense of those who can never be part of that concerted action, who remain outside the plurality that acts? How do we describe their action and their status as beings disaggregated from the plural; what political language do we have in reserve for describing that exclusion? (2011)

I would like to attend to this question of how we reckon politically with the enforced effacements that render the political a space for appearing and visible bodies, which is, for me, also a question of how to politically reckon with visibility tropes and their relevance to power and control. And so I ask what kind of *polis* would emerge from performing the spectral potentiality of displaced and disconcerted memory: an occurrence of memory that, contrary to appearances, incalculably complicates – albeit not incapacitates – the way in which people 'come together'.

I thus engage with the events, practices, and experiences that Diana Taylor has called 'disappearing acts' (1997), ambiguously akin to Peggy Phelan's definition of performance as that which 'becomes itself through disappearance' (1993: 146). What happens then when such 'disappearing acts' come-to-presence not to present themselves in a fixed spatiality and a stable self-same subjectivity but to enact the performativity of becoming-ghostly: that is, the performativity of re-appearing to become responsive to the eventness of (non-present, non-representable) others, in their plural singularity. This agonistic practice of re-appearance is not reducible to metaphysics of presence. Rather, it re-members what remains of presence, by performatively registering that:

> part of the population did not appear, did not emerge into the space of appearance. And here we can see that the space of appearance was already divided, already apportioned, if the space of appearance was precisely that which was defined, in part, by their. (Butler 2011)

What interests me here, in effect, is how the nation comes to command the space of appearance, and yet, perhaps more significantly, how this drive is resisted by embodied practices of critical agency that evoke the 'law of the other, who appears without appearing and watches or concerns me as a specter' (Derrida and Stiegler 2002: 124). Although the nation holds onto the sovereignty of presence, it is also subject to 'the whirlwind of history where all presences are overdetermined and thus negotiable: the contamination with otherness that makes a nation's history contingent' (Gourgouris 1996: 46). Through this perspective of 'contamination with otherness' that makes available the possibility of inhabiting without residing (Derrida 1994: 18), the *polis* is not, ever, one. Rather, it is more than one and other to one: 'plus d' un', to evoke Derrida's formulation (2000b: 301). It is, in other words, multiple and non-identical to itself. It relies on the agonism that establishes ongoing and always contingent spaces of appearance (understood as, at once, reappearance and disappearance). These are cartographies and possibilities for political subjectivation beyond the mastery of self-presence and its concomitant abstract universals, but also beyond 'appearance' and its epistemological premises – that is, visibility, transparency – that have abundantly been used to reify national subjectivities. As we try to make sense of the bodies that assemble in public space and are interpellated to fulfil the conditions of possibility for their appearance through norms of gender, sexuality, nationality, raciality, able-bodiedness, as well as land and capital ownership, we might find ourselves shifting from an analytics of *spaces of appearance* to one of *spacing appearance* (Butler and Athanasiou 2013: 194). In Butler's words, in her thinking about moving from the space of appearance to the contemporary politics of the street, 'the collective actions collect the space itself, gather the pavement, and animate and organize the architecture' (2011). Indeed, collective action *animates* the spaces and the folds it yields. In our context, it is re-collecting the wounds that do not heal as well as the living death of others that animates the space of the *polis* and its embodied apparitions. These acts of collecting and re-collecting space are inextricably bound up with the gestural dimension of taking space, also conceived as taking position, beyond the dichotomy between presence and absence. Furthermore, they are akin to bodies together, bodies apart, and bodies on the line: bodies that (re)appear and (re)assemble for remembering otherwise. It is to these absent presences and emerging spaces that I now turn.

In the Square and Beyond

Mourning is typically either prescribed to the bounds of home and blood relations, or is allowed to enter the public realm as an expression of honour in accordance with the codes of martial masculinity. What has mourning been doing, however, out at the Republic Square of Belgrade since the early 1990s and how is it linked with the question of who gets to inhabit public space? How is the collective, political memory of the 'others' of the national ideal exposed and witnessed in this public space of the Serbian (once Yugoslav) capital? How do assembled female bodies come to enact such an impropriety and how does this public impropriety transform mourning and its gender and national conditions? Finally, how does it inhabit and how does it modify the *polis*?

One afternoon in July 2005, an unexpected delay had made me miss my appointment with my friends, ŽuC activists, at the office of the group. Rushing out to the city to meet them, I easily assumed their site of action and headed to Belgrade's bustling space of urban life, Republic Square. Their action had just started. Eight women dressed in black, silent, lying down on the ground and holding hands, had formed a circle. The bodies of the women, placed like the radii of a cycle, were overlapping the diameter of a feminist symbol that they had previously drawn with salt on the pavement. Outside the circle, by the pillar of the square's imposing statue, nearly forty women were standing still, carrying rainbow flags and posters with feminist, anti-war, and antinationalist slogans: '*Always disobedient to patriarchy and militarism*', '*We remain disloyal to the fathers of the nation*', '*We remember*', '*Not in our name*'. Other placards and flags were placed at the pedestal of the statue. The ephemeral formations of black-clad women – some laying on the ground while others standing still – contrasted sharply with the monumental emblem of the square, the statue of the national hero of Serbia on horseback. And yet, as witnessed by the bodies and the activists' paraphernalia dispersed over the monumental square, the action had reoccupied and provisionally reconfigured the public space defined by this historic site of formal commemoration.

At the same time, outside the circle of the action, a range of varied modes of attentiveness and detachment were at play. The gathered police were on guard, regulating with their bodily posture and spatial placement the proximity between the action and the onlookers. It was decidedly unclear, however, whether they were there to 'protect' the activists from possible attacks or to safeguard the public from the activists. In their narratives, activists have consistently deplored the stance of the police, which, according to my interlocutors, has oscillated between tacit complicity with attackers and hypocritical 'protection' of the activists. Addressing the ironies inherent in police tactics of dividing and disciplining the political stage of appearance, one activist rebuked particularly the practice of creating a 'cordon sanitaire' to separate and isolate the activists from the public:

> They used to harass us in the 1990s, and now they want to protect us! Every time we hold a protest, we find ourselves surrounded by a whole army of riot police, supposedly to be safe from attacks. In effect, however, they don't allow our contact with the public, they make us look like pariahs or monsters.

That 2005 summer afternoon, there was no eruption of violence, in contrast to other *ŽuC* public actions – earlier and later. Some onlookers watched the event, either in silence or making acrimonious comments, while others milled around and eventually walked away indifferently. To some it gave an opportunity, it would appear, for spatial awareness or diversion; to others, a chance for dawdling. In all likelihood, for most of the onlookers that was not the first time they had run into a public action of *ŽuC* in Belgrade. Some of the responses to the group's actions had become overtly violent in the past, as was frequently the case in the 1990s, but also more recently. On 18 July 2004, for instance, the movement organised an action-performance entitled 'Maps of forbidden memory' to mark the ninth anniversary of the Srebrenica massacre. The performance was produced in cooperation with the well-known director and actress Maja Mitić of Belgrade's Dah Theatre, which had been established in 1991, at the outset of the war in Yugoslavia. That action triggered a cascade of reactions on the part of extreme nationalists, who, even before the beginning of the performance, gathered at the square, chanting nationalist songs and verbally assaulting the nearly seventy gathered activists: 'Traitors', 'Whores', 'You are the disgrace of Serbia!', 'Whom do you mourn for?', 'Why are you dressed in black?' Some of them physically attacked the activists, who responded by forming a circle within which the performance finally took place. On another occasion, in July 2005, the activists who were holding an event commemorating the tenth anniversary of the Srebrenica massacre were brutally assailed by neo-Nazi groups in Belgrade's Republic Square. *ŽuC* activist Jasmina Tešanović wrote: '"Srebrenica" is a bad word for contemporary Serbia, even worse than "feminism", and Women in Black place these words side by side' (2005: 35).[3] Indeed, the annihilation of more than 8,000 people on the basis of their ethnic identity by military and paramilitary forces in the predominantly Muslim town in the area of Eastern Bosnia in July 1995 has a special place in *ŽuC* politics.[4] In memory of the Srebrenica massacre and in protest of the crimes committed in the former Yugoslavia, *ŽuC* activists have been standing every year since 1995 on 18 July in Republic Square at the centre of Belgrade.

For many of the onlookers of the 'uneventful' 2005 ŽuC
action, that was a rather unwelcome public enactment and they
therefore turned away, dismissing, in more or less manifest ways,
the 'hysterical women' who, for some, were traitors and, for
others, pathologically attached to their refusal to close an old
wound. The activists insisted on touching a raw nerve all those
years and had attracted bitter accusations regarding their untimely
persistence. Indeed, they have been widely seen as the uncanny
afterlife, some kind of haunting effect, of a disturbing recent past
and its ghostly aspects. The activists, in turn, through their staged
encounters in the contested spaces following war, have been
seeking to make their enactment transmittable: to render the
attending public susceptible to confronting a troubled past and
its lingering traumas. Through their public appearances, which
intimate that the 1990s are still here through their multiple conflicted after-effects and despite the reconciliatory prescriptions of
post-national realpolitik, they pose, again and again, questions of
how to remember (with) the other. It is for this reason that they
inhabit the familiar space of the square as a site of memory. In
appearing in the public space, they haunt it and become haunted
by it. 'Haunting' a space (because haunting is intimately related
with space), as we know from Freud's essay on *The Uncanny*
(2003), signifies both inhabiting a homely scene and disturbing
its homeliness: the familiar (*heimlich*) shifts into the uncanny
(*unheimlich*). By conjuring ghosts in a society that tries to get rid
of them, the activists turn the city's central square into an uneasy
space of appearance: common and uncommon all at once.

The choreography, or haunto-graphy, of the ŽuC action
that summer afternoon conveyed a particular sense of publicness in an urban space pulsating with movement. It produced its
own space, and yet not as a space of self-presence, but rather as
one disowned in order to become hospitable to its absent and
non-appropriable others. Turning the square into a stage, the

action generated a provisional break in the quotidian stream of crossings that usually animate this ample square; a break from which new passages, encounters, and bodily intensities might emerge, one would hope. Each place, Doreen Massey claims, can be seen as a meeting place (2005: 68). Indeed, the meeting place enabled by these actions constitutes both an invitation and a provocation. Aligned in a way with the pedestrian flow, as they placed themselves inside its space, but, at the same time, interrupting and rerouting its routinised tempos, the activists' assembled bodies enacted a discrete yet decisive unsettling of the square's monumental time and space. The exposed vulnerability of those bodies transformed the most familiar urban arena of 'power geometries' (Massey 1993) into an event of counter-memory. Rather than a mere surface or container, then, public space emerged as a taking place (Casey 1997; Massey 2005). The bodies of the assembled activists interfere with normalised rhythms and spatial structures in a way that resonates with José Muñoz's queer utopian engagement with performatives that interrupt 'the coercive choreography of a here and now that is scored to naturalize and validate dominant cultural logics such as capitalism and heterosexuality' (2009: 162).

In their citational reciprocity with layered choreographies and cartographies of memory, those bodies intervene into, and wrestle with, the founding assumptions and exclusivities of the bounded locatedness that is incorporated in national imaginaries. They do so not only in the city's central square and other significant public landmarks, but they also engage with translocal and multilateral commemorative solidarities in different post-Yugoslav regions: for instance, by cutting across the siege of Sarajevo, by actively participating in the Srebrenica commemorative events, or by doing solidarity work at refugee camps. Saša Kovačević has spoken with me about the years of the war and her devotion to refugee support work:

People would see only our street actions, every Wednesday. That was the most relaxed part of our political work. In reality, we were operating on various fronts. We were working with the refugees at the camps around Belgrade, with those expelled from Croatia and later from Bosnia. But contrary to NGOs and international peace organisations, we were interested in the political work of building relations of solidarity and mutual support.

In our many encounters, Saša often emphasised the ways in which their political work of solidarity involved intervening in the matrices that regulated the possibility for affirming relationality with others:

The refugees were like family to me. Some of them wanted to talk, others did not. We would sit with them for hours, drinking coffee, talking. They saw that we were different from organisations like UNHCR [United Nations High Commissioner for Refugees], just administering numbers. I remember an old couple from Croatia, who had lost their daughter. I was trying to comfort their pain. They didn't care that I looked different, wild, with my hair cropped. They accepted me as I was. And I would talk to them about my own injuries. I remember a funny story, within that dreadful situation: the old lady hadn't realised that my father had died before the war, in 1979. She had the impression that he had died of heart problems on the road, on a tractor, during the war. And so, as I was in tears once, affected by her pain of dispossession, she tried to comfort me: 'Don't cry, my girl, it was for the best that he died, better than being tortured.' 'What are you talking about, grandmother', I say to her. 'My father died many years ago.' And she turns to me: 'Even better, then, my girl, even better.'

Therein lies the political relevance of a poetics of vulnerability to reclaiming histories of loss and grief: far from being obstacles to solidarity, previously unrelated lineages of loss and affective anachronisms lend their insubordinate energies to a shared, renewed commitment to responsiveness. For those political actors, in effect, the political affectivity of solidarity was performed at the refugee camps as an alternative, relational mode of inhabiting and modifying the *polis* from its fringes and routes of displacement.

So, the work at the square was combined with the work at the refugee camps, as the activists turned the camps at the outskirts of the city into public spaces of solidarity and co-presence. Moreover, *ŽuC* dis-placed public space by displacing the properness of mourning itself, as the political affect of grief was not the only figurative mode these activists deployed in their public performances in order to intervene in the norms that, in Arendt's terms, organise the remembrance of the *polis*. It was also the joys of camaraderie, and a critical sense of belonging beyond and despite its normative conditions that the war state had prescribed. Marija, an artist from Belgrade who had to dis-continue her postgraduate studies because of the war and because of the extreme conservatism that she encountered among the university faculty, recounted, in an emotionally charged tone, an international gathering of *ŽuC* during the war, which took place in Ribarsko Ostrvo (Fisherman's Island), an island on the Danube River, near Novi Sad:

> It was 1993, in the middle of the war, and it was the first time that women from Croatia had joined the meeting. There were no women from Bosnia, however; the meeting took place during the siege of Sarajevo. At the end of the meeting, I had a feeling that I would never get to see these women again. I was completely ruined. You cannot imagine how happy I was, however, when I met them in the following year. It was after that meeting that I recognised that there would be no place in this world where I could not connect with women.

And this is how Senka Knežević, an activist and schoolteacher in her late sixties, recalled that meeting:

> The first major event I remember with *ŽuC* was the international meeting at Ribarsko Ostrvo. I had prepared sandwiches for all women, I thought that we would get hungry and in 1993 there was nothing to be found in the shops. The meeting was a revelation. I realised that I was not alone in those difficult years.

In a context of numbing and normalised political violence, the actual labour of political activism involved not only the articulation of trauma but also forging critical affective networks of endurance, commitment, and hope. It also involved exposing the ethnocentric but also the heteronormative conditions of what lives and deaths become memorable in the time and space of national belonging. Amidst escalating militarisation, the international annual Women in Black gathering took place in 1996 on Fishermen's Island: a gathering remembered by activists as the one attended for the first time by women from Bosnia and Herzegovina – Selma and Belma from Sarajevo had crossed the border on foot (Urošević and Mlađenović 2013: 302). But that meeting was also remembered for a public lesbian union between an Albanian woman and an English woman which was celebrated: 'On an open-air stage, amid the Danube landscape, and the ceremony that we devised, which was conducted in three languages: every sentence was translated into Albanian, English and Serbo-Croatian-Bosnian' (Urošević and Mlađenović 2013: 302). If queer unions were reduced to the realm of unliveability by the war state, refashioning such 'improper' relations into public rituals of merriment in times of war altered the established propriety of public space. A *ŽuC* activist described her experience from one of the international annual meetings that were held in Vojvodina in the 1990s: 'These three days

167

were actually a rapture of joy and tears that through little sleep, much talk, music and wine brought to a catharsis' (Women in Black 2001a: 17). As in Carrie Hamilton's study of activism of mourning (2010), politics of trauma is transfigured into a politics of pleasure and a pleasure for politics. Ernesto Laclau has provided an analysis of the interconnections between hope, passion, and politics in the social imaginary fostered by the Left: 'at any moment in time we have to construct partial social imaginaries of transformation' (2002: 124).

Mourning and merriment have been attuned by these activists as critical affects addressed beyond the dualisms between positivity and negativity. In other words, their desire for change, at once aberrantly mournful and passionately hopeful and joyous, has remained 'faithful to the positive/negative dialectics' (Stavrakakis 2007: 282). Indeed, either in the city's central spot or in the folds and fringes of the public space, either through mourning lost relationality or through celebrating new actualities of togetherness, it is their performative action that creates the space of the *polis* as a flow of affective intensity and 'partial social imaginaries of transformation' (Laclau 2002: 124). To paraphrase Arendt's citational formulation: Wherever they go, they are a *polis* (1998: 198).

Every Wednesday, at Half Past Three in the Afternoon

During the 2006 anniversary event entitled 'Always disobedient', which celebrated the fifteen years since the founding of Belgrade's *ŽuC*, Ljuba Minić recalled the first weekly actions at the square during the war:

I needed to declare that I was opposed to what was going on. I was no public figure; nobody asked me what I believed, but as a citizen I felt the need to express my opposition. Standing on the street with anti-war messages – that was an obligation and a responsibility towards myself, my children, all of us who live here, who were born here. Every Wednesday, at half past three in the afternoon, we met and stood at the Square. Those moments in which we stood and whispered to our friends, exchanging information about what was going on, and having the opportunity to do so, to struggle together, made us able to endure anything, the disapproving look of onlookers and their distressing words.[5]

Standing in the street or the square every Wednesday at half past three in the afternoon was a ritual not only of collective protest but also of political dignity and survival for many activists. It was not easy, but there was nothing else they could do. Standing together, as Ljuba put it, made them able to endure onlookers' disapproving words and acts. Many of my collaborators talked to me about that secret ritual of endurance that they used to perform every time their public assemblies turned tense: amidst the silence of the action, they would beckon one another, occasionally whispering not only political news outside the war state's propaganda mechanisms, but also words of courage and sustenance.

Another *ŽuC* activist and member of the Belgrade Circle, Jasna Bogojević, referred to her own experience of participating in the all-night actions at the Republic Square:

I came on the first day and since then I missed none. They lasted six months. The first poster read 'For all the dead.' They called us traitors and sell-outs. The main placard read: 'Solidarity with all those who rise up against the war.' Once, Bokan, the leader of the paramilitary group White Eagles, approached us and tore up the placard with a knife. The police intervened. However, 72,000 candles were lit. We continued doing the same throughout the winter, against the strong wind.[6]

The activist referred to a time when the *ŽuC* public actions often ignited raged attacks, such as that launched by the militarist extreme right-wing group Beli Orlovi ('White Eagles') in 1993.

But even among the activists themselves the idea and the physical gesture of standing silently in the street entailed some sense of discomfort. And that was so not only and always because of the hostile responses of the public. Lepa Mladjenović, activist and counsellor for victims of violence, recalls her participation in the very first public vigil thus:

> I was very embarrassed at that time to stand in the street. I felt strange. I felt that something was missing . . . After weeks and weeks of standing, this missing element was found or created by our own standing: we created our own tradition, sense, and language.[7]

Coming out as an anti-war feminist in times of war normalisation was often a source of embarrassment, even shame. It involved bodies appearing out of place and yet being exposed. As a public statement put it, in a pronouncedly self-reflective tone: 'It is not easy to find new ways and codes to express women's resistance to war.' As Lepa noted, however, that new way was 'found or created by our own standing' in the face of the feeling that 'something was missing'; and in response to the necessity to devise another possibility for public language. This political language of responsiveness was ultimately created through the critical imagination and disposition of the activists' bodies, which transfigured the discomfort of public exposure into a collective affect of political activism. In the movement's political work, such contingent possibilities and impossibilities of transforming the traumas of war into a collective agonism required the invention of an alternative poetics that would performatively put into play – rather than pretend to fix – the political aporias inherent in the acknowledgement of memorable lives and deaths. Lepa's self-reflection suggests that the political genre and ephemeral gesture of public standing in mournful protest is by no means without its hazards, as it runs the risk of reinstating gendered clichés of voiceless suffering, empathy, political quietism, or romantic pacifism. Something is always missing (Bloch and Adorno 1996; Muñoz 2009). 'After weeks and weeks of standing', as she put it, the activists created an inchoate and expansive space where mourning would turn into a disruptive performative event haunting and transfiguring the biopolitical fractures that sustain the conventional imaginaries of the nation at war.

As a performative field of emergence in the face of 'something-is-missing', the collective agonistic appearance of *ŽuC*, every Wednesday at half past three in the afternoon, is akin to what Michel Foucault has called 'event', referring to the unpredictable and transformative singularity that does not give in to the regulatory power of the already existing (Foucault 1972). In the context of *ŽuC* activism, the event is enacted through assembled bodies that alter space by appearing out of place and yet reappearing and being exposed in solidarity to those who cannot appear. In this sense, a potentiality of disappearing is at play in the matrix of exposure that enacts 'the eventness of the event' (Derrida 1993: 117). As Staša Zajović commented, referring to the regular weekly public vigils of *ŽuC*, 'we expose our bodies in Belgrade's central square dressed in black, transmuting the familial and national convention of mourning into a subversive act of public critique of nationalism and an act of solidarity with our unmourned enemies'. Through the affective-performative actions of public mourning for the nation's dehumanised others, *ŽuC* political actors evince a non-prescriptive accountable ethics: an ethical and political responsiveness to the memory of those whose loss has been expropriated.[8] They do so by interrogating, time and again, the conditions of possibility of their own becoming other. Indeed, the performative event of public bodily exposure created topographies of empowering interconnection among the participants, especially at a time when they had to cope with various instances of political isolation and alienation amidst a pro-war public sentiment. Saša suggestively addressed this overwhelming sense of 'standing in public, exposing your body, your face with your comrades, and in the same afternoon, attending a class at the university, where fascism was the dominant discourse'.

In their street actions of counter-memory, whenever the *ŽuC* activists appear publicly in concert, they not only expose their bodies to established regimes of intelligible appearance. They also expose these regimes as incomplete and layered. In other words, through their embodied engagement with the spectrality of appearing and disappearing, they come to critically lay bare the matrices of power that uphold the public space's 'make-believe-ness' (Navaro-Yashin 2012: 11). In performatively inhabiting the scripted public setting, they induce an affective touch that echoes what Yael Navaro-Yashin, in her own evocative study of a violently partitioned spectral space, has called 'make-believe space': a concept that indicates incompleteness, fabrication, and fragility, all of which are suggestive for the post-war political-national space she describes, a landscape imbued with ghostly traces of loss and misrecognition. By amplifying the absences they infinitely and imperfectly invoke through their performances of political grieving, the *ŽuC* political actors spectralise the artifice of the nation: they put its present — but also its order of presence — out of joint. Thus, those women, who, like Slavica, had 'turned off the television to take to the streets' during the years of nationalism and war, inhabit the site of the possibility — precarious though it may be — for affecting the 'power geometries' that produce and sustain (albeit not in a finished and definitive manner) the 'throwntogetherness' of space (Massey 2005).

This 'throwntogetherness' of space, created by different routes and unpredictable encounters, invokes the ways in which *ŽuC* activists enact a strange proximity in the square of Belgrade, in contrast to the fantasies of exclusive commonality. They hold public demonstrations as an injurious yet enabling mode of 'concerted action' in conditions of multilayered demarcation of public space and belonging. As my friends led me to understand, their collective project of critical be-longing refers to a longing for a different way to inhabit and cohabit the *polis*, alternative to the normative definitions of homogeneous and exclusive community, with all its fundamental implications of masculinism and heteronormativity. Through their spatial poetics of self-estrangement, not only do they make strange the existing space, but they also actualise another space for a politics of throwntogetherness. They bring to the fore what is at risk of being lost in the ethos of nationalism: the possibility of cohabitation; moreover, a mode of cohabitation which would not be based on, but rather actively opposed to, entrenched inequality (Butler 2012).

In meditating on the figure of the female mourner outside the boundary wall of the *polis*, Gillian Rose writes: 'In these delegitimate acts of tending the dead, these acts of justice, against the current will of the city, women reinvent the political life of the community' (1996: 35). The dissident memory of *ŽuC* takes place at the centre of the city rather than 'outside the boundary wall of *polis*'. The boundary is a phantasmatic topology, however; a technology of demarcating the proper place of non-sanctioned and abjected identities. No other place in Belgrade is perhaps more 'proper' for a political action of unsettling such boundaries in the politics of memory than the Republic Square.

'Serbian Bastille' between National Imaginary and Performative Displacements

Trg Republike (Republic Square), the hallmark of Belgrade's urban vivacity and the emblematic site of the *ŽuC* public actions, has played a key role in the contentious negotiation of national memory in critical moments, but also in the everyday ordinariness, of Yugoslav, post-Yugoslav, and Serbian history. Since the first demonstrations against Milošević's regime in March 1991, the square has been a nodal point of protest events. Nearly 100,000 protestors took part everyday in the many gatherings of the opposition movements over several months in 1996 and 1997 (Jansen 2001). In 1997, dissident protestors suggested that the square be renamed Freedom Square (*Trg Slobode*) (Jansen 2000). When, the same year, in Terazije Square, Belgrade's designated administrative centre, the regime staged a pro-government gathering of citizens from several places in Serbia, a parallel counter-demonstration of citizens opposing the regime took place in Republic Square (Lavrence 2005: 41). During the three-month NATO air raids in 1999, the Square was the hub of massive anti-NATO events (described as *pesma nas je odrzala*, 'the songs that helped us endure'). Some of the large anti-regime demonstrations of 1999 also took place there.[9] When Milošević was impeached in The Hague in 2001, his supporters organised a demonstration in the square. In July 2008, Republic Square became the theatre of violent clashes that were instigated by the extreme nationalist Radical Party of Serbia when the former Bosnian Serb leader Radovan Karadžić was arrested in Belgrade and brought before the International Court in The Hague to face charges of war crimes, particularly for the Srebrenica massacre. What had also fuelled the ire of nationalist crowds was the conviction of seven Bosnian Serbs for the ethnic cleansing in Srebrenica, a decision reached by Sarajevo's Special

Court after a two-year trial for the war crimes committed in Bosnia.[10]

A few days after the Milošević extradition in June 2001, several LGBTQ groups attempted to hold the country's first gay and lesbian pride march at the square. The event was violently attacked by a huge crowd of opponents. Subsequent attempts to organise pride marches have failed due to either official banning or violent attacks by anti-gay protesters. The second Belgrade Pride was cancelled amid fears of violence in September 2009, after the fatal attack against a French football fan in Belgrade, before a Europa League match. Police told organisers they could not guarantee the safety of the participants. The city centre was already full of far-right organisation *Obraz*'s graffiti and posters warning those planning to participate in the march: 'We are waiting for you' (*Čekamo vas!*).[11] The ultra-nationalist Serb Popular Movement 1389 hailed the cancellation of the march as 'a great victory for normal Serbia'.[12] *ŽuC* has worked very closely with queer groups, such as Labris, Gayten LGBT, and Queeria Center. In the early morning hours of 10 October 2010, the morning before the Pride Parade, two men broke into the *ŽuC* premises 'looking for queers' and attacked activists with a bat (Urošević and Mlađenović 2013: 299–300). The Pride Parade of that year was attacked by members of *Obraz*. Members of the same organisation had dispersed the Pride Parade in 2001, had shouted 'Kill, kill, stamp out the fags' in 2009, 'Belgrade will shed blood but there will be no Pride Parade' in 2010, and 'We are waiting for you' in 2011 (Urošević and Mlađenović 2013). On 27 June 2012, however, Gay Pride took place and activists of *ŽuC*, Belgrade Pride and Queeria Center held banners at the Republic Square: 'I have the right to love', 'My parents kicked me out of the house', 'I was beaten up at this square'. One of the banners was dedicated to LGBTQ people who were expelled from the public space – those who had to leave the country and those who had committed suicide amidst life conditions of unliveability: 'I am no longer here'.

In effect, *Trg Republike* is for Belgrade what Navaro-Yashin has written about Taksim Square in Istanbul: an 'emblematic site in urban public consciousness for the enactment, production, and regeneration of the political' (2002: 1). Some of the most prominent public buildings and national monuments of Belgrade are located at the square: the National Museum, the National Theatre, and the statue of Prince Mikhail. The square took its present form after the construction (1869) and the official inauguration (1873) of the National Theatre (*Narodno Pozoriste*): the sole monumental building that had existed in the square for over thirty years, hence the square was called Theatre Square (*Pozorišni Trg*). In 1944, the square became the site of the public burial of the 976 Red Army soldiers who fell in that year's battle against the German occupation, while in 1951 the relics were exhumed and reburied in another place in the city. In 1945, during his ceremonial address to the new Yugoslav socialist confederation from the balcony of the National Theatre, Tito officially renamed the square Republic Square, in a gesture meant to signal the Yugoslav unity that was forged under conditions of resistance in World War II (Lavrence 2005: 38).

In the area where the square presently lies, the Stambol Gate (*Stambol Kapija*) had been erected by the Ottoman Empire in 1723, marking the spot where disobedient Serbs were publicly executed by the Ottoman administration, but also Serbian national insurrections were initiated against the Ottoman rule. The designation of the square as the 'Bastille of Serbia' originates in these echoes of rule and revolt that have made the square thick with competing narratives of memory (Lavrence 2005). The demolition of Stambol Gate in 1867, amidst the tumult of the last Serbian insurrection, marked the liberation of the nation after 500 years of Ottoman rule, as well as the national will to eliminate Ottoman architectural residues in an attempt to 'Europeanise' the city. Since the national insurrection brought about not only the liberation from the Ottoman Empire but also the restoration of the Serbian monarchy, the place of Stambol Gate, that memorial trace of colonial subjection, was replaced by the statue of the liberator prince: the first official monument built in the city of Belgrade under the aegis of the Serbian state. Hence, the statue of Prince Mikhail conferred on Republic Square the epic character of the national state's birthplace.

Dedicated to exalting the birth of the Serbian nation, the vertical bronze statue of *Knez Mihailo* at Belgrade's Republic Square is a primary marker for directing public attentiveness through a declarative monumental architecture that symbolises military honour and power (Sturken 1997: 53). It was erected in 1882 in honour of the Serbian hero who had liberated the remaining seven Serbian towns that were still under Ottoman rule. It depicts the prince on horseback and with his hand allegedly pointing to Istanbul, indicating to the Ottomans the direction to leave the city, in a defiant gesture that echoes the liberatory national ideologies of the nineteenth century. In an ironic twist enabled by the polysemic appropriations of the monument in different historical contexts and by different actors, today's passers-by do not seem to notice the panoptical monument that looms over them. The statue itself seems to have lost not only much of its declarative force but also even its 'proper name', as in recent years it has become known simply as *kod konja* (by the horse). Thus, monumentality is ambiguously rescripted through the ambivalent intimacy that marks the masculinity of the Serbian hero. In this sense, through its unpredictable appropriations and misappropriations, *Knez Mihailo* monument produces, and at the same time, distracts cultural memory.

The hero's statue consolidates – albeit with a demystifying twist – a historical 'awareness of belonging' (Simmel 1976: 41).

Therein lies the performative force of national memorials erected at the squares of national modernity: they spectacularise the way in which blood and soil become inextricably intertwined components of the national sense of belonging (Boym 2001; Huyssen 2003; Ignatieff 1993; Nora 1996–8). They 'produce space' (Lefebvre 1992) by means of constituting public signposts of national memory, nostalgia, and compulsory exaltation. War memorials are imagined projections of the nation, according to Benedict Anderson's account of how the memorials of the Unknown Soldier constitute paradigmatic cultural construc-tions of modern nationalism.[13] Like military cemeteries, war memorials are markers of the historical nationalisation of massive death through the immortalisation of the dead warrior (Anderson 1991). The planning of military cemeteries and war memorials from the nineteenth century onwards, but especially after World War I with the massification of death in the battlefield, works to sacralise war covering over its horror and sanctifying the memory of its losses (Mosse 1990; Winter 1998). The European national capitals of the late nineteenth century, in whose squares the modern drama of the nation-state was staged, are the epitome of what Christine Boyer has called 'ritual cities' (1994: 7). At the squares that are decorated with national and war memorials, various memory techniques of national founding myths are put on stage. Military parades and other phantasmagorical public spectacles, like the ones described in the previous chapter, become condensed moments of national commemoration at work. In the topography of the modern square, the collective imaginary of national identity is grounded and affectively transmitted through rituals of collective memory and oblivion.

Nevertheless, although the national monuments and memorials that most often decorate modern squares are destined to last, they become inevitable markers of the 'ongoing possibility of a different inhabitation' (Grosz 2001: 9). In other words, they become – even despite themselves – the performative displacements, distractions, and reconfigurations to which they resist. It is in one such embattled arena where the *ŽuC* activists assemble and perform their dissident memory, turning the *monument*, typically built to commemorate and glorify national victory, into a *memorial*, usually signalling defeats and signifying grief (Sturken 1997). The public appearance of the black-clad political actors re-memorialise the monumental public space, 'break[ing] the continuity of glory' (Foucault 2003a: 70) that is immortalised in its architecture and ambient qualities. As the *ŽuC* actions in Belgrade's Republic Square suggest, the heterodox uses of the square demonstrate that public space is neither an inert substratum nor an instrument of social control and subjectivation, but *becomes* an agent of agonistic social relationality (Kohn 2003).

Agonism 'at a Standstill'

The *ŽuC* activists dress in black and stand still and silently, usually at rush hour, at central spots of the city and noisy crossroads, or in front of iconic national landmarks: squares, historic monuments, and dividing lines. Their ephemerally 'monumental' standing-in-silence, as a bodily mode of perseverance and protest, reoccupies and perturbs the monumental topography of memory and turns it into a performative field of contention and dissent. Since the years of the war, standing in silent actions for an hour, early in the afternoon every Wednesday at the Republic Square, had become the trademark of *ŽuC* political activism.[14] *ŽuC* actions of *stajanje* (standing still) resignify the territory of the memorable, despite and against the normative premises of blood affiliation, fatherland, and gender and kinship codes that found and sustain it. They transcribe a typical national monument into a landmark of anti-war activism. Indeed, a public space charged with contentious narratives of national history and politics, in all their idealised property and propriety of the 'common place' (as a suitable and familiar space, national fatherland and home), is *spaced* by these activists' bodies and their 'art of associating together' (Arendt 1972: 97). Public space does not come to be presumed as an empty and unmarked container waiting to be filled with things, processes, and embodied encounters. Rather, it is re-appropriated through a process of becoming, as Derrida has shown through his concept of spacing (*espacement*): '*Spacing* designates nothing, nothing that is, no presence at a distance; it is the index of an irreducible exterior, and at the same time of a *movement*, a displacement that indicates an irreducible alterity' (1981: 81).

Events of *stajanje* – or, standing as spacing – at the Republic Square take place in suggestive juxtaposition to the pre-eminent *Knez Mihailo* spatial marker, which underscores the constitutive role of militarised masculinity in the production of 'National Symbolic' (Berlant 1991). The activists' bodily posturing, steadfastly but also fleetingly counterposed to the monumental architecture, textures and complicates the imperative to remember by opening it onto the disconcerting question of whom the remembrance of war requires effacing. In effect, the activists re-mark what has been established as remarkable about the monumental landmark. Their agonistic performance in public are akin to what Cecilia Sosa, in her work on the Mothers of Plaza de Mayo in Argentina, so aptly describes as an experience of 'live architecture' (2011: 63). Over the last thirty years, Sosa argues, this group of women has become a live installation of an endless trauma: a monument 'that has colonized the landscape of the central square of Buenos Aires in the name of the 30,000 missing' (ibid.). Similarly, *ŽuC* activists occupy Belgrade's central square, performing a spectralised plurality of bodies, present and absent, living and non-living. Their silent 'stubborn choreography' (Sosa 2011: 70) embodies an acting monument, or a monument of collective acting: a monument that defies monumentalisation.

Instead of acquiescing to public forgetting of an unwanted past in the name of national reconciliation, and instead of repairing the wounds inflicted on the nation's body and psyche by war as their gender position would prescribe, these political actors seek to politically mobilise the haunting affect of the injuries and injustices of the past in the present. The temporality of their activism does not refer to a linear and progressive passage of time, but rather to the historicality that arises at the articulation of what Walter Benjamin has called, throughout his unfinished *Arcades Project*, 'the now of recognizability' (*Jetzt der Erkennbarkeit*) (1999: 473, N9,7): an incalculable moment, or a 'flash', of new and intensified awareness, which might take the form of a crack, even a revolutionary occasion, into the order of homogeneous, chronological time. The event of the political emerging from this formulation of history as interruption involves a 'now', a present moment and a momentary present, which is not reducible to the continuous and ordinary flow from the past to the present.[15] Rather this 'now', an instantaneity that might occur only in the context of a particular recognisability, indicates what Benjamin referred to as a state of 'dialectics at a standstill' (1999: 463, N3, 1). For Benjamin, this standstill marks the moment for acting.

In this spatial poetics of 'standstill' as a moment for acting, activist subjects stand in principle outside themselves: affected, estranged, non-presupposed, and constantly-being-made outside in the *polis*. Their collective bodily presence evinces an agonistic way for performing the political as a space for appearing bodies. 'We are still in the streets', as one of the key *ŽuC* mottos has it.[16] Marija had taken part in the anti-Milošević demonstrations in 1991 and later in the student demonstrations, before joining *ŽuC*: 'I cannot even remember in how many demonstrations I have participated with *ŽuC*. We were in the streets all the time.' The enduring becoming-plural of the activists signals how 'we' (with all the trepidations and uncertainties that mark this pronoun) can prompt an agonistic way of living with one another not without but rather through attending to the injustices of former violence. Because 'we' are in the street while others cannot, as they have been reduced to the haunting absence that has come to form 'our' space of appearance. Hence, this 'we' – a 'we' at a standstill – also mourns, through a spectral logic, the lost or delimited possibility of getting together and living with one another.

Therefore, *stajanje*, as standing and stasis, at once produces and complicates a spectralised plurality of appearing and acting bodies. Hence, this standing still of time and space emerges as a precarious but defining moment of suspension that yields a new actuality of embodied loss and remembrance: one that derails, if only partially and temporarily (like a 'flash of lightning', to invoke Benjamin's phrase), the normative presuppositions of what and who can 'appear' in public in times of war exigencies and post–war normalisation.

Stasis as Dissensus

Activist Miloš Urošević, in a conversation with me, addressed the exposure of activists' bodies in public as a performativity of constituting a bodily space for combating collective cultures of political amnesia:

> In the most official place, in the centre of Belgrade, we bring the citizens of this country face to face with what they want to forget. . . . Our politics is simultaneously and non-hierarchically

antinationalist, anti-sexist and anti-homophobic. . . . In our vigils, we are in the place of those who have no way to speak and, at the same time, in the place of those who are alive but commonly viewed as lives not to be lived.

In Miloš's words, *ŽuC* breaks with the monological discourse of mourning and loss. The bodies of the activists are exposed to others and to norms that administer the distribution of relationality in the realm of grief. Having routinely confronted state violence, public attacks and misrepresentations, and having become strangers and castaways, they continue to this day to declare their political demand for acknowledgment, accountability, and justice, mobilising the power of injury against its interpellating impulses.

By re-positioning their political bodies at the centre of the *polis* as a means of embodying their own and others' ambivalent and precarious (un-)belonging vis-à-vis its demarcation lines, *ŽuC* activists actualise the multilayered modalities of stasis as standing still but also taking a stance and taking the stand: at once motionlessness and insurrection (Douzinas 2013; Loraux 2002a; Panourgiá 2009; Stavrakakis 2007; Vardoulakis 2009). In Nicole Loraux's theorisation of tragic mourning as central to the ways in which the *polis* imaginatively invents itself, the notion of stasis denotes simultaneously strife and sedition − both an occasion for contemplation and an occasion for revolt (2002a). The double etymology of the word has been obscured through its coming to signify, through reduction, 'civil war'.[17] In Loraux's meditation (2002a), stasis was an ontological condition of the ancient Greek state, connected with the problem of publicly commemorating the dead killed fighting for democracy. She draws on the historical context of 403 BCE, when, after the overthrow of the dictatorship of the Thirty and the victorious return of the democrats to the city, Athenians call for amnesty:

that is, they agreed to forget the unforgettable, namely the civil strife. In officially promoting this wilful obliviousness to political divisions that had been revealed in the course of the civil conflict, they also denied the place of internal discord in democratic politics. In other words, the memory of the city was founded on an injunction to forget. Loraux suggestively argues that the self-images of unity that the Greek city promoted in radically regulating memory were modelled upon a priori assumptions of normative, autochthonous kinship (Panourgiá 1995).[18] Drawing on Loraux's account of the polysemy of stasis in *The Divided City*, Dimitris Vardoulakis has probed into the connection between its two contradictory clusters of signification – namely, mobility and immobility – arising from the same root, as a way to think of democracy in agonistic terms, that is, as being involved in a struggle with sovereignty (2009). In critically engaging with the conventional sharp distinction between (the ethics of) assuming lack and (the politics of) assuming to act, Yannis Stavrakakis has also addressed Loraux's invocation of the element of division as a way to elaborate an awareness of contingency and the constitutive impossibility to impose a closure of the political (2007: 270).

The *ŽuC* immobile, contemplative standing ensemble becomes a restless performative occasion of stasis. In standing at and across the border, in its multiple tropes of external and internal frontiers, enclaves, refugee camps, routes of mass expulsion, and states of siege, these political actors embody the *polis* in ways that echo what Loraux has described as 'divided city', constituted on the basis of that which it disavows. As marked subjects of gender, women, Loraux argues, performatively embody the awareness of this internal stasis – as both division and revolt (2002a). These embodied traces of the 'divided city' recurred constantly in my interactions with *ŽuC* activists. One such occasion was my encounter with Senka Knežević, a retired schoolteacher in her late sixties, who lived with her husband at an apartment located in Sremčica, about an hour by bus from Belgrade's centre. She was waiting for me at the bus stop and took me right away to see 'the graffiti', three huge drawings decorating the external walls of buildings in the neighbourhood. One was a larger-than-life painting of Mladić, in military uniform and military salutation, accompanied by the inscription 'Serbia' in Cyrillic script. The other depicted Mladić again, but this time with the inscription *xero beli* (white hero). And the third one was the figure of an unidentified military man, captioned with the phrase *Vrati se Vojvodo* (come back, Vojvodo – a military title for top commanders[19]). As Senka explained to me, she wanted this 'tour' to serve as a prelude to our conversation. We held our conversation inside the living room: 'I have a strong voice', Senka said, 'there is no need for the neighbours to listen to us.' It was only after we were done talking about *ŽuC* histories and her own activist biography that we went out and sat at the balcony, enjoying the nice spring afternoon and the delicious pastries Senka had made. I had spent time with Senka many times in public actions at the city's central square or another public landmark. This time, however, in the hospitable ambiance of her house, my interlocutor's embodied and narrational practices of ambivalent belonging and unbelonging had produced an alternative space within the *polis* – a *polis* that did not have to listen our conversation that afternoon. The graffiti that she wanted to make sure that I would see as an introduction to her life history, the distribution of the inside/outside boundary according to available modes of audibility, and her narrated stories – all indicated various layers of a divided city, but also her own ambivalent, marked positioning.

Division came up in Senka's narrative about the ways in which ethnic dividing lines started permeating and traumatising people's everyday sociality even before the war:

> I was working as a schoolteacher in a small Serbian town with a
> Muslim minority. The division couldn't escape anyone's notice

at some point before the eruption of the war. I was deeply hurt
to see barriers forming between Serbs and Muslims in that little
town. It was as though someone had taken a pair of scissors and
cut the two communities apart. Just like that. After all those
years of coexistence, some power games had managed to pull
us apart. The town where I was teaching was like a miniature
of Yugoslavia. The school was a Milošević bastion. Conflicts
immediately erupted, people changed within a night. Some
Serbs started behaving with an air of superiority. Perhaps the
same thing was going on among the Muslims. I don't know,
I am telling you what I experienced. So, I had to retire earlier
than I was supposed to, because the atmosphere at my work was
unbearable. For six years, from 1993 when I stopped working
until 1999, I couldn't get myself to take care of the paperwork
required for my retirement, because I couldn't face my nationalist colleagues at the school.

Stasis emerged as an embodied practice of inhabiting the *polis*
through discord, in Senka's narratives, especially those of the
train: Senka was living with her family in Belgrade, while the
school where she was teaching was at Sandžak, a region that
stretches from the south-eastern border of Bosnia and Herzegovina to the borders with Kosovo and Albania, so she had to
commute. Those train journeys haunted her experience of the
early 1990s:

> One time, on the train, some people started singing nationalist
> songs, and they were abusing me, insisting that I sing along.
> I said: 'Leave me alone. I am not your sister. I don't want to
> sing.' There was another man from Podgorica sitting nearby. I
> thought he would help me, but he didn't say a word.

As Senka's train stories manifest, the *polis*, in all its dividing
intensities, travelled with her. Riding that train everyday, within
a country in violent conflict, she embodied and reconfigured

what it is that would render the *polis* impossible, and, ultimately, uninhabitable:

> One time, I was travelling on the same train as some members of *Beli Orlovi* [White Eagles], a group of weekend soldiers. They tried to snatch the food I was carrying. I used to bring pre-baked food when I was going to the city, so that I could spare some time to go and work with the women [*ŽuC*]. And it was like that, accidentally, that I heard from their conversations about one of my old pupils. He must have been around twenty at the time. I used to be very fond of him, because he was coming school from a remote village. I would ask him every day how he crossed the road, how his train journey was, I was concerned about him. So, I heard from those paramilitary men on that train that my old student was joining them in the weekends. I asked them to give him a message: that his old teacher is now ashamed of him.

Within a public space traumatised by dividing lines, those who acknowledge and account for a loss not symbolised as a loss are identified as traitors, or as 'dangerous citizens' (Panourgiá 2009). At a moment of fabricated consensus, those who refuse to 'sing along', like Senka, become strangers and enemies. It was in this vein that in the Women in Black International Conference in the summer of 2005 in Jerusalem, Staša Zajović proposed the infringement of 'national consensus' as a crucial political project for feminism (2005). In contexts where politics is transformed into a police order, in Rancière's terms, the critical estrangement from the normativising call of consensus defines the political power of dissensus: the manifestation of a rupture in the existing distribution, or partition (*partage,* as both sharing and dividing), of the sensible (*le partage du sensible*) (Rancière 2004). The inscription of 'a part of those who have no part' (*le compte des incomptés*) (1999: 39) perturbs and redistributes the existing sensual and consensual order of things in the *polis*: 'The distribution of the sensible reveals who can have a share in what is common to the community based on what they do and on the time and space in which this activity is performed' (Rancière 2004: 12).[20] In this vein, *ŽuC* activists, committed to losses unrecognised as such by master narratives, redistribute the space, time, and bodily disposition required by the commonly recognisable affectivity of mourning. In the context of my argument and my interlocutors' thought and praxis, dissensus – as 'part of no part' – does not refer merely to 'rationality of disagreement' (Rancière 1999: xii). Rather, it registers the possibility of disrupting the established order that authenticates certain properties, senses, memories, and languages as 'rational' while rendering others unintelligible. If shared language is conventionally considered a prerequisite for a community to appear, these activists do not consent to the hegemonic conventions of common sense as qualified con-sensus. Theirs is a feminist 'ethics of dissensus', which conveys an agonistic pursuit of justice (Ziarek 2002, 2007). Ewa Ziarek has perspicaciously proposed a radical democratic mode of ethics as a contested terrain whereby sexual and racial differences are mobilised to call into question not only the depoliticisation of ethics but also the disembodiment that marks notions of citizenship, democracy, and political subjectivity. This is about an agonistic ethics of dissensus that rethinks and reformulates responsibility for the other, through feminist undertakings of embodiment, passion, and the implications of *sensus*. Such performativity of dissensus was encapsulated in the emblematic mottos of *ŽuC* – 'Not in our name' (*Ne u naše ime*) and 'We will not be fooled by our own' (*Ne dajmo se prevariti od svojih*) – which denoted opting out of the dominant schemes of consensual belonging.

In foregrounding the concept 'partage de la raison', or 'partitioning/partaking of reason', Rada Iveković (2003, 2013) has explained that the double meaning of 'partage' as dividing and sharing with others impels one to engage with 'the dialectics of their interaction as in-compossibles' (2013: 149). What makes a community compossible is precisely what diverges from, and is rendered incompossible with, the actualised and established order of commonality: as Iveković argued, normative constructions such as (hetero)sexual difference and the nation are indefinitely and infinitely constitutive to the community and its logic/reason (ibid.). What is at stake in the becoming-incompossible of *ŽuC* politics is to address belonging differently, dissidently, in ways that allow it to remain undetermined.[21]

Đorđe Balmazović, known as Zole among his friends, started being engaged with *ŽuC* political activism in 1994, through his partner. When I met Zole, he had recently come back from London, where he had attended a postgraduate programme in graphic design and politics. He talked about how *ŽuC* puts to work a performative language to intervene in the sensible and to politically re-articulate the divisions between what is visible and invisible, sayable and unsayable, audible and inaudible. He narrated to me one such occasion: in December 2007, *ŽuC* invited Zole and his choir, called *Proba* (Rehearsal), to join an antifascist action in Republic Square. 'It was a very tough occasion', he recounted.

> Hundreds of extreme rightists, *Obraz* members and neo-Nazis had gathered at the square. Those guys really wanted to kill us; they were screaming to us all their famous slogans, like 'Knife, barbed wire, Srebrenica' [*Nož, žica, Srebrenica*], 'Death to Muslims', 'We will slash the throats of gays and lesbians'. A huge crowd of them had gathered. The choir and the *ŽuC* activists were standing together by the statue. Police were deployed in-between the two groups. We performed after all, we sung our song 'Reword'. The extreme rightists were screaming their songs, but we had sound equipment, a huge loud speaker and amplifiers, so we could be heard much better than they could.

We repeated our song six times. That was a significant part of the performance: repetition itself. And they went crazy. They left the square under heavy police protection. And then police surrounded us and escorted us up to our office.

In effect, collective action of publicly rehearsing a song suggestively named 'Reword' managed to dismantle, even temporarily, the affective regime of authoritative in-audibility. In fact, activist choirs emerged as a new genre of collective action and public intervention in the 1990s. The use of public space is a crucial aspect of such public performances, which upset conventional formulas of choir singing and enact a plurality of voices to perturb the prescribed monovocality of post-Yugoslavia. As an articulation of counter-nationalist plurality, the collective public singing of the choir *Proba*, in its repetitive intensity, unsettled the conventional links between affect and discourse, Logos and politics (Cavarero 2005). The performative resonances of the singing 'rehearsed' the voices yet to be heard. The dissonance generated by the embodied and passionate implications of their agonistic dissensus worked to reformulate the partition of politics and *sensus* – as configuration of sense and distribution of the sensible.

Performing a dissonant and dissident distribution of bodies, affects, voices, and memories, *ŽuC* activism seeks to recover the political potentiality of *aesthesis* and aisthetics. Activist Goran Lazin is a designer – he was completing his studies at the time of our conversation – who makes the distinct knit patterns on the *ŽuC* placards. He is interested in political art, but he also loves knitting and embroidering, which he learnt from his aunt. Goran was a child in the 1990s, so he only has a meagre memory of the war. As he hastened to add, however, he remembers quite vividly the 'heavy atmosphere' at home and at school. He joined *ŽuC* in 2010, after having seen the group protest in the street. He had been particularly attracted by the way in which the group translated its antifascist and feminist politics into a public aesthetics of standing silent in public and wearing black. As he explained to me, he was wearing black himself even before joining ŽuC, but he now associates this bodily practice with a situated 'political aesthetics' of anti-nationalist political solidarity. Similarly, in developing what she called 'aesthetics of resistance', Staša Zajović referred to the street action named 'A pair of shoes – one life', which took place on 7 July 2010, at Knez Mihajlova Street, and was conceived and realised by ŽuC together with numerous artists and art collectivities – that is, Škart, Dah Theater, Spomenik/Monument, Art Klinika, and Center for Cultural Decontamination. That 'artistic activist' event involved the gesture of citizens' offering shoes in the memory of the victims of the Srebrenica massacre. The action continued until 8,732 pairs of shoes were collected: a number corresponding to the officially reported number of the victims. On Zajović's account, the action was articulated on several levels related simultaneously to 'addressing victims, addressing the citizens of one's country of residence and addressing the state' (2013a: 22). The action was designed as the first phase of the campaign for the construction of a monument dedicated to the memory of Srebrenica, in Belgrade.

Ever since its inception, ŽuC has been working together with politically engaged artists and artists' collectivities to re-configure the ways in which the banality of public memory has been archived and lived in post-Yugoslavia. In previous pages, I have referred to the 2006 street action 'In memory of the deserter', whereby a live monument was performed by ŽuC activists in solidarity with the deserters and conscientious objectors, but also to the 2010 performance 'We are returning your tank: Homage to the rebels against war and violence', in which ŽuC activists worked together with the Novi Sad art group Art Klinika. It was the reclaiming of public space as a scene for performing dissensus that Daša Duhaček addressed in referring to 'the importance and the need for (a public) scene or stage . . . where this revelation before audiences is to take place' (2010: 46). Thus, the 'aesthetics of resistance' invents a public language that performs hitherto inadmissible political sentiments. Such aesthetic intervention as a performative recon-figuration of what counts as memorable was also manifested in an exhibition organised on the occasion of the twentieth an-niversary of *ŽuC* 'Always disobedient – We leave an imprint'. The exhibition addressed the erasure of particular lives, affects, and actions from a homogenised community, but also a story of resistance and dissent that 'has left a deep and permanent imprint in each one of us, in our activist community, and also in our society' (Zajović 2013a: 36). The event was 'an active creation of a different re/presentation of the pluralism of the public in Serbia and beyond' from the perspective and political standpoint of becoming 'outside and above consensus' (ibid.).

ŽuC actions engage with a labour of standing up as dissenting and as enduring; above all, as repartitioning and reconfiguring the political realm of appearance (and audibility). In talking with me, Slavica recalled her experience of standing at the square as an experience of responding to the enforced erasure from the *polis*'s space of appearance:

> I remember the feeling of such isolation, like we didn't exist, we were completely ignored. People passed by and passed by. That was an awful feeling of just being erased. I remember one day, it was a rainy day, some women from Switzerland had come and joined us, and it was a wonderful feeling that someone cares, it was as though we were born again.

She referred to the violence inherent in apathy, as a mode of erasure from the *polis*'s matrix of compassion:

Attacks happened later. At the beginning, people's reaction was apathy. They could not understand what we were doing there, standing still and silent, dressed in black. Nobody would see us. Maybe they looked at us but they did not see us.

For ŽuC activists, erasure from the *polis*'s available space of appearance has been the price for their stasis and dissensus. At the same time, however, Slavica's narrative pointed not only to the traumas but also to the ek-static potential of standing against the will of the *polis*: 'Each standing was like a catharsis for me. I remember very clearly that at the beginning of the vigil I was in a certain state of mind, and after an hour of standing I would find myself somewhere else.' Collective endurance in spite of the ordained matrix of appearing was not only an occasion of affective alienation, but also one of an immanently critical affect of becoming and belonging.

The traumas and the ecstasies implicit in reclaiming a space for admitting the inadmissible denote, in ŽuC activism, the possibility of opening to a new partaking. The question at stake in this performative configuration of the space of the *polis* as an event of being-with is precisely who has 'a share in what is common to the community' (Rancière 2004: 12). In taking up the position of the internal enemy, these political actors depart from where they (un)belong in order to address the departures of others: 'What is thus remarked is its *departure*, that to which it no doubt belongs but from which it departs in order to address itself to the other: a certain (im)parting [*partage*]' (Derrida 2005f: 13). Clearly, departure, partition, partaking, and *partage* as sharing of belonging, in all their multilayered and incalculable intensities, are at stake in the appearance of the liminal figures that haunt and threaten the nation's indivisible sovereignty from within and from without.

Since October 1991, when the weekly actions started in Republic Square, the silence of the standing women was accentuated by written slogans – simple and affirmative: 'Women, traitors of war, protest for peace', or 'We are disloyal'. Through such self-identifications of dissensus, the activists' non-belonging would become not a deplorable state of alienation but rather an act of collective agonistic forbearance for them. In Saša's words:

> One time, during the war, it was just three of us at the square. Because of the heavy cold? Because of the war? In any case, only the three of us appeared. It was in 1993 or 1994. You cannot imagine the prevailing atmosphere and the reactions. Three women standing at the centre of the city, protesting against the war. Unthinkable. Passers-by were cursing us, spitting on us. But I was feeling proud, not scared at all. I was so devastated that I did not care. Our gatherings every Wednesday were like a breeze saving my life, again and again. It was a way for me to assert my difference; a way to say that I, Saša, have nothing to do with them.

ŽuC remained committed to the political performativity of dissent in times when the latter was condemned and foreclosed as incompatible with shared sentiments of patriotic loyalty. It continued to organise vigils until October 1998, 'at the verge of civil war, and renewed threats of NATO bombs. We went to the vigil carrying our documents and small refugee bags; we weren't sure what awaited us'.[22] They opposed the NATO bombing of Serbia but without subscribing to the logic that seemed to reduce anti-imperialist resistance to a nationalist recuperation. They raised, once again, the difficult questions: 'I wonder what a Women in Black vigil would look like today' if the NATO bombs hadn't united the majority of civilians on one side whilst silencing the other, reducing it to invisible, useless dust . . .'[23] Adriana Zaharijević joined ŽuC in 2004 and she was very young at the time of the NATO military operation against the Federal Republic of Yugoslavia during the Kosovo War.[24] In a conversation with me, she addressed the tormenting ambivalence that the NATO imperialist intervention provoked among those activists who were vehemently opposed to the Milošević regime but did not endorse the NATO military intervention:

> During the bombings, I was a philosophy student reading Plato and Aristotle, and in my punk phase. Those were times of devastating ambivalence, but not of apathy. You could not say who the good guy and who the bad guy was, it was not an either-or situation. I was extremely angry with the Serbian government but that didn't mean I was supporting the bombings.

And she added: 'I did not wear the target sign, but my best friend, who later joined *ŽuC*, did.' Adriana referred to what became a symbol of Serbian reaction to the NATO bombing campaign: a black bull's-eye surrounded by two concentric circles that was ubiquitous – adorning billboards, bridges, newspapers, people's clothes and lapels – and designed to convey defiance but also to mock official NATO claims that the aim of the aggression was not the Serbian people, only their leaders. Indeed, despite claims that the target sign campaign was organised by Milošević's government, not only people who supported the regime but also people who were critical of it and actively involved in the resistance movement used the target sign to turn themselves into human shields against NATO aggression.

My interlocutors described this precarious stance as a painfully impossible one. Clearly, in the context of a reinvigorated national sentiment triggered by the NATO air strikes, the accusations of treason and disloyalty, to which *ŽuC* activists were summoned, would be considered more than ever a justified ground for abuse. At the time when NATO was threatening to bomb Serbia (which eventually began in March 1999), Vojislav Šešelj, head of the hard line nationalist and anti-communist Serbian Radical Party (appointed deputy president of the Serbian government

in 1998), issued a statement targeting 'Serbia's inner enemies':
'Maybe we cannot reach every [NATO] airplane, but we will
grab those who are close to us. . . . If we find them in the
moment of aggression, they shouldn't expect anything good.'[25]

That was a period when the portrayal of *ŽuC* as an internal
enemy was drastically invigorated. When Belgraders held
anti-NATO protests defiantly wearing the target symbol that
indicated the resistance of a small nation to an imperialistic
superpower, *ŽuC* activists, even those who vehemently opposed
the air strikes, had to keep a low profile or even go underground along with numerous other dissident citizens and groups
who opposed the bombing but could not relate to the way in
which nationalist discourses found legitimacy in anti-NATO
gatherings. As feminism and antinationalism were demonised
and discursively conflated with NATO and other international
forces lurking to harm the Serbian nation, *ŽuC* activists had to
'disappear' from the public scene. In Saša's words:

> We were under persecution. We were just a few and tired. We
> found ourselves in an impossible situation. They had smashed
> us. They had broken into our office. We were considered worse
> than the bombs. It was at that time that we became the worst
> enemy.

Some of the activists went underground, others to self-exile in
an attempt to avoid arrest. Others stayed in Belgrade, however.
Ljiljana Radovanović described the everyday anxieties that
permeated the social space of the city:

> In 1999, during the NATO bombing, several of my daughter's
> friends were trying to avoid being drafted. They were all
> gathering in our house, even sleeping there. They would come
> over with their bicycles so that they did not have to use the
> public transportation. That would be extremely dangerous,

since the whole city was under police and military occupation. I was feeding them, I was hiding them, and I was bringing them cigarettes. I was going to Hungary to bring them food. On my way back from Hungary at night, I used to take the Pancevo Bridge, the one that, as they were saying, was going to be bombed. I remember that sometimes I had to take tranquillisers in order to handle my fear and manage to pass that bridge. I was afraid because the kids were waiting for me.

Slavica, who also was in Belgrade at the time, talked about the political atmosphere of that period, when appearing in public was not really an option for ŽuC:

In 1999, we could not go public. I felt the danger immediately, especially in the first days and especially at street corners, where secondary school boys were gathering and secret policemen were drinking beer. It was an atmosphere of hatred. I knew I was different and I was prepared for street lynching.

Pro or against the bombing was, for Slavica, 'an impossible choice'. She did not share, however, the consensus of national unity that the NATO attack cultivated, with disastrous effects for dissident groups. Opting out of idealised anti-Americanism was a way in which she performed her difference from that newly formed national consensus:

I didn't want my son to be misled politically by the prevailing anti-American mood. At that time, American rock 'n' roll was banished. So, I went and bought him stereophonic equipment and CDs of American rock music. It was the first time I was so generous to him. I even took him to the shop during the curfew.

That was when, in response to threats, ŽuC publicised a statement and held a performance in Republic Square in Belgrade, called

'I Confess', which was structured as a public confession for their anti-war activism:

> 'I confess that I did not agree with the beating of people of other ethnicities and nationalities, faith, race, and sexual orientation.
> . . . that I was not present at the ceremonial act of throwing flowers on the tanks headed for Vukovar in 1991 and Prishtina in 1998.
> I confess that I am opposed to political repression, apartheid, and war.

More than 100 members of the group wrote statements, which were then compiled by Jasmina Tesanovic into a collective narrative on the occasion of the seventh year of *ŽuC* anti-war activity:

> I confess that I am disloyal to all forms of authoritative power . . .
> . . . that I have lived two lives, one in Sarajevo and one in Belgrade.
> . . . that I love Sabahet and Mira and Vjosa and Ana.
> To all the charges, I confess that I am a traitor in every sense.[26]

In all, through the *ŽuC* performance of stasis as standing and dissensus, the *polis* emerges as not-one: more than one and other to one (Derrida 2000b: 301). Ultimately, what is at stake in the performative configuration of the *polis* as not-one through *stajanje* is the aporia between stasis and ek-stasis.

Public Mourning and Its (Gendered) Discontents

As their public statements and appearances manifest, *ŽuC* political actors 'take black out to the square as a political colour'. During the time of my research, I witnessed material traces of

this embodied theatricality not only in the staging of demonstrations, but also at the 'backstage' of public events: before and after
them, black clothes would occasionally circulate among activists,
along with other props such as rainbow flags and placards. Some
activists, like Ivana, a young activist whom I only fleetingly met
once, who went to the bathroom to change clothes when we
sat for a coffee after a street action, preferred to relinquish their
black outfit after a street action. Some of my interlocutors stated
that they like to wear black in their non-activist life, while others
wear black as a kind of political 'uniform' of public protest.
Either way, the political temper of black colour as an activist sign
of mournful protest came up many times in my encounters with
ŽuC members, who described its performative use as signalling:
'mourning and struggle', 'war testimony', 'cruel mourning',
'opposition to militarist violence', 'mourning for those not
allowed to be mourned', 'resistance to national amnesia', and
'solidarity with the victims of nationalism and racism'.

In the political life of ŽuC, black clothing creates a visible
critical space of public protest but also constitutes one of the
embodied idioms that make up the palpable everydayness of the
activists, their 'scene of the ordinary' (Das 2007: 218). Through
the affective nuance of black clothing, the movement brings
forth a mimetic excess that replays and simultaneously refracts
the proper formulas of mourning. The activists I engaged do
so, to unpredictable effect, by enacting a poetics of gendered
embodiment, which draws on the female body's awkward
position in nationalist imaginary between procreative fetish and
object of abjection, between mothers of the nation and internal
enemies. Hence the disquiet that the activist black clothing has
occasionally generated among foes but also intimates. An activist
recalls an uncanny encounter of another activist with her family
in Montenegro: the daughter, dressed in an urban black outfit,
visits her mother, an old peasant woman dressed in black: 'You

are no good', says the mother ... 'you haven't married, you have no children, you don't have a flat . . . the things you are doing . . .'[27] Apparently, the daughter's black clothing was not recognised by her mother as a familiar women's outfit, but rather as a disturbing marker of unruliness: an aberration from the customary propriety of both mourning and femininity. In this specific context of her ambivalently familiar native home, the activist's black clothing seems to have entered a homely scene in a way that disturbed its homeliness and produced an uneasy, barely recognisable, space of appearance.

In a similar vein, Ljiljana Radovanović conveyed the uncanny public effects produced by the performative expropriation of black colour's un/homeliness:

> I personally like black clothing. Politically speaking, however, I believe that the black colour expresses at once mourning and protest. It is irritating to some people, because they think that we bring bad news. In older times, when people saw me wearing black, they were concerned that someone had died in my family, but nowadays my black clothes signal for them that I am a *ŽuC*.

Indeed, this theme of 'bringing bad news' and also 'looking like ghosts' was recurring in my interlocutors' narratives when they talked about the ways in which they think they are perceived by others. Ljiljana described the uneasiness her black clothing generates in her neighbourhood 'which is like a small village', when a familiar outfit for expressing grief for 'one's own' turns into an upsetting sign of estrangement and even treason:

> Every time I come back home dressed in black, on the 11th of July [*ŽuC* commemoration for the Srebrenica massacre], they ask me if I am going to go to Bratunac tomorrow. [Bratunac: a town located in eastern Bosnia and Herzegovina, in Bosnia's

Serb entity, the Republika Srpska, where Serb civilians and soldiers were killed by Bosnian forces in July 1992.] In contrast, my friend Zinaida does not face provocations like that, because it seems normal to most people that a Bosnian does not participate in commemoration ceremonies of the Serbian nation. They see me as a traitor, however, as someone who does not take part in the memory of her own nation.

It is precisely the established intimacy of public recognisability that the activists' black-coloured appearance defamiliarises. An impossible contemporaneity emerged in my interlocutors' narratives and practices: in making themselves appear to others through their characteristic black clothing and silent standing, they take on the quality of a spectre in order to perform an unauthorised relationality with those who can no longer appear. As a *ŽuC* public statement puts it: 'Women wear black in our countries to show grief for the death of the loved ones. We wear black for the death of all the war victims.'[28] The syntax of the statement – *women* do this, while *we* do something different – is suggestive of the differential impulse it introduces into the established realm of feminised and nationalised mourning. The statement introduces a differentiation that illustrates dissonant modalities of mourning vis-à-vis its role in en-gendering the nation. In embodying a state of 'not being at home', the poetics of black clothing is mobilised in ways uncanny and troubling to the available 'distribution of the sensible' (Rancière 2004).

As we were walking in the city once, after a demonstration, with Miloš and Saša, we were talking about the lived experience of black clothing, gendered perceptions of black clothing, and perceptions of oneself in activist black clothing. In responding to my enquiry, Miloš explained that for him black colour signals mourning 'as women's exemplary position in, and instrumentalisation by, the nation'. Saša interjected: 'In Yugoslavia there is a strong cultural tradition of ritualistic female lamenting. A quite heavy tradition, like the one bore by lamenters in Montenegro. You cannot imagine the black things going out of their mouth.' Saša was referring to *narikače*, the lamenters who perform death rites and mourn dead heroes in the Yugoslav tradition but also in various other Balkan contexts. To be sure, the protest of *ŽuC* has been associated by some commentators with the particular role assigned to women in the Balkan 'death cult' (Devic 2000; Slapšak 2002). As Svetlana Slapšak argues, *ŽuC* replots the powerful cultural sign of mourning as miasma. Being polluted by nature, women are culturally constructed as being closer to the contaminated dead bodies, and thereby qualified, by virtue of the rules of social defilement, to tend dead bodies – and, in national narratives, the dead bodies of male heroes. Slavica, however, shed light on another aspect of this genealogy and explained that the tradition of the Balkan weeping woman is a retrospective invention of nationalism, in outright juxtaposition to the Yugoslav value-system:

> Women's restriction to the home is not a Serbian tradition. *Narikače* can be found perhaps in some remote villages in Serbia. But the Yugoslav tradition was women's participation in the workforce. Our mothers used to work. This image of 'traditional women' is a retrospectively produced tradition, a part of nationalist iconography.

In Slavica's narrative, mourning is no longer presented as timeless. It rather reveals its own genealogy of citationality. Subversive recitation of mourning in activism expropriates the domestic economy of mourning, thereby revealing the contingent and ambivalent potential of all mourning.

As Saša was talking about the critical ways in which *ŽuC* engages and re-articulates the nationalist definition of women as attendants of death, Miloš insisted on the ways the material apparatus of activist black clothing opens up the possibility for the emergence of other sites of cultural inscription: 'Through or positionings, we play with this tradition. At the same time, we break with it.' Indeed, the *ŽuC* activists 'play' with the (nationalised and feminised) matrix of grief while giving a radically political dimension to this social prescription. Staša Zajović mentioned in another instance that the black colour of *ŽuC* is a 'public, political colour for revolution'. As she further explained, it is a sign for the revolutionary dislocation of the dominant presuppositions – be they gendered, national, or sexual – of memory and mourning. In its political life as a performative colour of feminist anti-war activism, it entails a break with the memorial ideology of the dead warrior's worship.

As I observed in my interactions with members of the movement, the use of the black colour in their public actions illustrates how a conventional inscriptional surface of patriarchal and national femininity might be transformed into a bodily disposition of public protest. In the performative politics of this movement, mourning becomes a critical language of and about the repressed mourning of the other, officially coined as 'enemy'. The black–clad bodies in the public space of the square re-occupy and displace the binding norms that regulate the performative modalities, the time and the position of mourning and memory. In this sense, performing public mourning for the ungrieved enemies of the nation, and doing so from a gendered internal enemy perspective, represents a treasonous deviation from, and a bodily refashioning of, the established national and gendered propriety of mourning and memory.

However, subversive expropriation of a sedimented norm always involves uncertainty and risk, which are related to the involuntary nature of performativity. 'How will we know the difference between the power we promote and the power we oppose?', Butler asks (1993: 241). And yet, the effects of performatives are incalculable and cannot be reduced to a matter of 'knowing'. Some activists conveyed a sense of creative ambivalence about the visual effects of *ŽuC* public performativity. Nađia Duhaček, a young anthropologist in her late twenties at the time of our conversation, was no longer involved with *ŽuC* but continued to be in solidarity with the group's political commitments. She described her involvement with *ŽuC* as 'a coming-of-age experience', which enabled her to negotiate her own positionality – national, gendered and otherwise – within the complicated, multinational space of Yugoslavia after the collapse of communism. Nađa spoke passionately about the *ŽuC* embodied performativity as an intensifying experience that involved visual signs, tactile bodies, spaces, movements and practices. 'Bodies taking over public spaces – it feels wonderful and liberating to participate in such public performances', she commented. In her activist days, Nađa had tried, successfully, to bring an air of creative innovation to the street practices of the movement. I remember her participating in a springtime street performance, where some women were laying down while others were drawing the feminist symbol with salt around the circle of the women's bodies lying on the pavement. As she explained to me, she was also the one who initiated ideas of holding visually different demonstrations, like the one that she helped to organise in 2006 which involved activists changing colourful costumes, thus creating a lively performance in front of the parliament. 'For me, that performance was interesting because it was powerful', she recounted.

> I understand the idea of wearing black, especially for the days of remembrance, like the 11th of July. I think it was important and creative that the symbol of mourning was taken over and reclaimed into something completely different during the war. But time has passed since then and we need to explore different ways of communicating with the public. The idea of that performance in front of the parliament was that we all had to wear

and change costumes. Finally, we all ended up wearing rainbow colours and hanging up flyers. I don't think that black is doing it. Not because it is threatening, actually that part I like. But it doesn't relate anymore. People just pass by us.

Nađa maintained that *ŽuC* needed not only to add colour, but also to keep pushing the boundaries of available codes of public appearance and recognisability in order to invent new and unforeseeable performative ways of action without compromising the tenacity of its message.

The *ŽuC* activists with whom I interacted do not simply identify with the visual terms of their public appearance, such as the black colour. In fact, their performative appearance in the public space is beyond affirmative identification. It is, rather, about dislocating and departing from these terms. Slavica shared with me her differentiation from the dominant meaning of black clothing as a feminine language of mourning:

> The black colour is not close to me. The culture of mourning women's black attire is alien to me. I always have to borrow clothes to go to our vigils. But I understand that for us this is about deconstructing the tradition of mourning. In a way, it is some kind of a uniform; we have to have a uniform, because we want to create one body out of many bodies. It is a uniform which is not a uniform. It is something which actually belongs in some way to women's culture. Black is indeed serious and sad, but we cannot deny that war is sad. Black is also a minimalistic colour, a way to remove all sentimentality, including the sentimentality of mourning. We take the opposite direction from women who mourn. Ours is a cruel mourning. It is a mourning without sentimentality.

The black colour of agonistic mourning opens up to multiple antinomies, even regardless of its agents' intentions. Agency is 'not the same as voluntarism' (Butler 1993: 241). As Slavica put it, the colour of mourning is itself partially and ambivalently inscribed in a realm of gendered belonging: it 'belongs *in some way* to women's culture'. It cannot be fully owned and controlled by either the power that binds it or the intentions of its agents. It embodies a binding potential that remains self-critical and non-homogenising. It also embodies the potential, and the pleasure, of bodily self-fashioning: a costume, or 'a uniform which is not a uniform'. And so the alternative space that the activists struggle so poignantly to claim produces a plural performativity of appearing bodies. The expropriated black colour marks the workings of an agonistic mourning that 'creates one body out of many bodies'.

(Not) Taking Space as 'Woman'

Through the performative introduction of the non-sanctioned mourning into the square, the epitome of the open and the outside, unstable re-articulations of the categorical association of space and the feminine are occasioned. The sign of mourning is expanded to unsettle the national and gender propriety of the memorable, as it is grounded in the normalising division between public and private. These contentious practices of embodied appearance destabilise the regulatory regime of en-gendering space through qualities that are typically attributed to the feminine: a passive, inert, amorphous, material receptacle that awaits, and is susceptible to, formative fulfilment. In Western metaphysics, space is en-gendered through the feminine-as-maternal. The category of the feminine is defined as the constitutive other and, at the same time, as the necessary material, reproductive condition (the 'matrix') of the phallogocentric topographical distinction matter/form (Butler 1993; Grosz 2001). By virtue of this constitutive displacement, 'woman' has no space of her own but she provides the mute substratum for imaginary communities and their reliance on sovereign and possessive masculinity (Irigaray 1993).

Bringing catachrestic mourning to public space, a space associated with reason and passions that are authorised by established memorability, is an abuse of the prescribed spatial coordinates of mourning since 'public space is regulated by keeping it free of passion' (Duncan 1996: 140). As Elena Pulcini and Luisa Passerini have argued, in the name of her historic identification with sentiment, the female subject undergoes two fundamental dispossessions, namely the exclusion from both the right of citizenship and the right of passion. On the one side, she is excluded from a public sphere defined as the cornerstone of the liberal conceit of the rational (qua male) individual, and, on the other, she is excluded from the excesses of passion, as her realm of intimacy is demarcated by the norms of heterosexual and reproductive love (2002: 101). If, however, mourning is associated with either the invisibility of home or the phantasmagoria of authoritarian public spectacles, then the *ŽuC* catachrestic mourning, against the authorised boundaries between the public and the private, as well as between the affective and the political, constitutes a public impropriety. The embodied performative politics of improper mourning introduces social passion into the public space of the city and, by the same token, it politicises affectivity.

As the cultural idiom of mourning is historically imbued with the nationalist fiction of the 'mother of the nation' who has sacrificed her sons to the nation's military glory, *ŽuC* activists show their solidarity with mourning women, undermining, however, the normative role stereotypically assigned to women by nationalism and patriarchy. As Ljiljana put it: 'I am a mother but I am not in *ŽuC as* a mother. I am proud of my two children and of the fact that we share some political principles, although

I have never exercised any pressure on them.' These activists perform disobedience to the gendered and nationally marked idiom of mourning by re-appropriating its ambivalences and by pushing them beyond the established boundaries of *home/ oikos*, which denotes the everlasting, familiar, and memorable community of life and death, in its multiple forms: national fatherland, patriarchal heteronormative blood kinship, and family tomb (Panourgiá 1995).

Hence, even the way in which activists administer the 'home' of *ŽuC*, the space 'of their own', is dissident. Occasionally, it entails strategically occupying the position of the feminine as the 'home manager'. Senka used to go to her sister Staša's apartment, in order to take her laundry and that of their refugee friends from Sarajevo, as there was no washing machine at Staša's place. She would take the laundry back to her home to wash and then return it clean. One time, due to an unexpected and rather hostile visit, Senka had to conceal her identity as Staša's sister:

> Staša was renting a tiny place, sixteen square meters. I used to wash her clothes and also the clothes of Jadranka, as there was no washing machine in the apartment. So, one time, Staša was not in, I had gone to the flat to bring clean clothes and to tide up a little. Three policemen knocked on the door, looking for Staša. 'Are you the lady of the house?', one of them asked. 'No', I answered, 'I am just the cleaning woman.' He insisted: 'What is it here to clean, in such a tiny space?' And I say to them: 'You must know that a woman always finds something to clean.' He persisted to ask for my ID, though. And then I take this fragile, feminine tone and say: 'I will give you my ID, but what are you going to do to me?' They never realised I was Staša's sister.

When Staša was not at home, her sister 'cleaned' for her. From different standpoints, they both occupied restless spaces of 'not being at home'.

It is precisely the embodied *oiko-nomy* of home as an allegedly common and familiar place but also as subject to the operations of distribution that is displaced by the *ŽuC* border-crossings. This performative estrangement of the biopolitics of 'home' releases the latter from its phallologocentric connotations of administered peace, stability, and familiarity. Such stereotypical representations notwithstanding, home implies anything but a well-ordered, coherent, and integral place. Being at home already contains the possibility of homelessness, the possibility of displacement from it and within it, as well as the possibility of 'strange encounters' that this displacement may entail (Ahmed 2000).[29] *ŽuC* returns to traverse and estrange the place of home by recalling the gender-marked historical foreignness and homelessness, and by forging improper relations with those situated out of home and out of place. Rather than essentialising otherness and placing it thereby 'in its place', the situated epistemology of *ŽuC* makes room for the ghosts that demand regard: those remaining other to the ordained preconditions of appearing and belonging.

In engaging with the spectralised plurality of the (dis-)appearing and alienated elements of the national order, the *ŽuC* performative enactment of public appearing involves standing at and across the border of the *polis*. It involves an itinerant politics of ongoing passages. Rosi Braidotti has aptly addressed the nomadic, post-nationalist idiom of feminist cross-border activism in the former Yugoslavia as part of a critical cartography that bears on 'the 'becoming-minor' of Europe' (2005: 175). As she explains, this cartography of feminist struggle embodies a nomadic subjectivity that seeks to account for, and make a difference in, a Europe marked by the proliferation of internal territorial borders and internally displaced people. Similarly, *ŽuC* cross-border activism draws political cartographies of an alternative and differential mode of becoming – that is, embodied and embedded (Braidotti 2002).

In fact, the embodied and embedded critical cartography of passing was crucial to *ŽuC* during the siege of Sarajevo. Zinaida recounted the ways in which she and her friends participated in initiatives of collecting and sending packages by cutting across the siege of Sarajevo:

> We had to arrange things to fit and be sent in the maximum allowed number of parcels. And then we had to help loading the trucks. My husband's salary was in foreign currency and so I was not in a very difficult financial situation. But there was a huge inflation and no merchandise in the shops. One had to buy immediately some food or else change the money. So, I would buy cans and instant soups and store them under a couch. People organised themselves and gathered everything they could. Every once in a while, my neighbours would hand me a can to put in the parcels. But the problem was how the parcels would reach their recipients in Sarajevo. They would be informed through street posters but sometimes they had to go far away from their homes, under the sniper fire, to get them.

Zinaida's words capture the materially grounded, embodied, and affective intensity of border crossing. The latter emerges as an alternative economy of bodily immersion in infrastructures and flows of endurance and relationality.

Either in cutting across the siege of Sarajevo, or doing solidarity work across ethno-national lines, a guiding principle of the movement is, as Staša Zajović has put it, the body politics of crossing national boundaries and walls, even embracing the accusation of treason (2002). Cynthia Cockburn – a member of the Women in Black network, whose research has focused on areas of conflict and division, such as Bosnia, Cyprus, and Israel and Palestine – has called this politics 'transversal politics' (Cockburn 2004; Yuval-Davis 2006). Through their political performativity of stasis within and across the gendered *polis*, these political actors become themselves 'other' and turn the *polis* into a scene of dissensus. Acting within, across, despite, and against the spatial differentials of power, they embody the question of what happens when the one who does not belong returns and reappears to reclaim a space of appearance. 'Without a fixed place, without a determinable *topos*, mourning is not allowed', writes Derrida (2000b: 111). Yet, these activists draw a horizon from which to redefine the topos of mourning as a register of the emergent. By re-appropriating an ambivalently 'feminine' position within the fixed places of proper mourning, they perform response-ability with regard to the memory of lost others whose very loss is eliminated in the *polis*'s space of appearance and remembrance. In Olga Taxidou's words:

> mourning comprises a discursive *topos* that examines the function of the law, the citizen, gender, and the power over the dead and the past in the new democratic *polis*. It becomes the site where the subject-in-the-making is confronted with the *polis*-in-the-making. (2004: 187)

Thus understood, subject-in-the-making but also *polis*-in-the-making give rise to a new possibility of political subjectivity: one that is marked not by self-identity but rather by the undecidability of subjection and relationality. This is about the political subject – no less than a politics of the subject – that persists not as mere presence (although there is nothing *mere* about presence), nor as mere absence, but as doppelgänger (Vardoulakis 2010). The 'effective presence' of the doppelgänger is relational, differential, and transformative, as Dimitris Vardoulakis has indicated. It figures the political in the sense that it enacts the conditions of the possibility of action. Although the motif of the doppelgänger cannot be reduced to any canonical example or pragmatic occasion, it does allow us to reconfigure or disfigure political subjects as liminal and spectral 'double-walkers' who persist and mark the ongoing present of the space of appearance with their appearing and disappearing acts.

It is the spectrality at work in the space of appearance that concerns me here. It must be noted that Arendt's account of the public space of apparitions and the 'who' of appearance-as-action allows for spectral transfiguration of the sovereign subject, when she refers to the *daimon* figure:

> [I]t is more than likely that the 'who', which appears so clearly and unmistakably to others, remains hidden from the person himself, like the *daimon* in Greek religion which accompanies each man throughout his life, always looking over his shoulder from behind and thus visible only to those he encounters. (1998: 179–80)[30]

The 'whos' of the space of appearance/apparitions cannot be reified as essential and self-transparent subjects. Rather, they denote non-sovereign performative conduits for public emergence: a public emergence that takes place largely behind the actor's back and in ways hidden from oneself and witnessed only by others. Actors are acted upon in a process of non-sovereign subjectivation, whereby acting over and being acted upon are not external to each other.

Veena Das has made us acutely aware of this when she addresses non-heroic ways and everyday efforts to make the world inhabitable (2014). Drawing on the work she has done among the urban poor in Delhi, she has raised important questions regarding the relation between action and subjectivation, as it might be investigated on the terrain of the everyday and through the figure of the spectral, 'when it (the subject) becomes a shadow of the real or ghost-like' ('On singularity', n.d.). In this context, she asks how one might 'think of subjects as singular but not sovereign' (ibid.). In other words, singularity cannot be reduced to a 'who'. It divides itself in response to another. Elsewhere, Das has discussed Derrida's critique of presence, examining not only the critical possibilities it offers but also its perils, when the state deploys the critique of presence and intentionality as a tactic of self-exoneration and negation of the authenticity of testimonies. She describes how the words of women and men with whom she spoke were often imbued with a spectral quality, as they had been uttered by the person with whom the anthropologist was having a face-to-face encounter but had been animated by another voice (2007: 8). In the context of her enquiry, related to failures of grammar in moments of world-annihilating violence, spectrality occupies an ambivalent position with regards to event and actuality, thus giving rise to frayed and fragile temporalities of potentiality: 'Potentiality here does not have the sense of something that is waiting at the door of reality to make an appearance as it were, but rather as that which is already present' (2007: 9). Indeed, the spectral is grounded and embodied in the power routines that institute and distribute the possibility of acquiring a presence according to the conventions of property and the proper.[31]

Clearly, the element of uncanny encounters is a key dimension of Arendt's own account of non-sovereign freedom. The 'who' of the political subjective space is more than one and other to one. It is haunted by the 'demon' of otherness. It is always other and in excess to itself, exposed and exposable, formed in and through the presence of others (see also Cavarero 2000; Honig 1995). However, if appearingness is the condition of being recognised as member of a community, ecstatic and expositive relationality that marks the space of appearances/ apparitions requires the operation of power that governs the matrices of recognisability (Butler 2005, 2011). Performative exposure comes to involve again and again, today and tomorrow, the violation and agonism of bodies appearing *and* disappearing despite and against established regimes of recognisability. This intensified performative dialectics of affirmation and disappropriation involves struggles over what is public, who is to appear in it and according to which visual and spatial norms. The space of appearance is riven and haunted, but also spaced-out and refashioned, by such partitions and departures, violations and losses, including the loss of oneself in another that has disappeared. Appearing is a scene always haunted by the phantom traces of another. 'There is no *Dasein* of the specter, but there is no *Dasein* without the uncanniness, without the strange familiarity (*Unheimlichkeit*) of some specter', writes Derrida (1994: 100). Spectrality, in Derrida, refers to ethical obligation to the past and the future. It is through impossible mourning, but also through mourning impossibly, that these activists enact a sense of spectral acknowledgement and responsibility to the other, thus reminding us of Derrida's point that *spectre* is an anagram of *respect* (2005c: 288). Responsibility towards the other here involves respecting the other's resistance to the technologies of mourning (Derrida 1989). It is through this perspective that I considered in this chapter the aporias within the space of appearance as the 'very place of spectrality' (Derrida 1994: 65). I tried to account for these other 'demons' that haunt the political: the uncanny emergences that exceed the authorised conditions of presence and visibility, as they come to perform all that remains from a unevenly framed and allotted space of appearance.

This peculiar appearance, in Nancy's words, 'consists in the appearance of the between as such' (*Elle consiste dans la parution de l'*entre *comme tel*). Nancy calls this appearing-together, which takes place as *partage* (in the sense of simultaneous sharing and dividing) and being singular plural, a 'compearance' (*comparaître*) (1992). In this chapter, I have considered how the losses, absences, compearances, and differential reappearances that have been brought about by abusive power haunt the *polis*'s space of appearance, traversing and transfiguring its temporalities of presence. I focused on the agonistic eventness of appearing (out of place) as producing spectrality and reclaiming a public space for remembering others and otherwise in the face – but also in the aftermath – of conflict and war. This response-able memory is enacted by the *ŽuC* deheroicised and antiheroic standing as stasis at Belgrade's Republic Square, under the national hero's sleepless gaze and imposing posture. In becoming ghostly, the activists' bodies are embroiled in the *polis*'s politics of appearance and yet are propelled beyond themselves and exposed in solidarity to the plurality of those who are not part of the established order of *polis*. Thus, becoming ghostly emerges as an interstitial trope not only of struggle for appearance, but also of struggle for different cartographies of appearance.

Consider the banner at the Republic Square, in the 2012 Gay Pride, 'I am no longer here', registering the sociality of the uncounted, the ones who opted out from one's uninhabitable world, gave up their place, or were banished from the *polis*. Indeed, heterotopias erupt from such collective iterative inscriptions, or traces, on the body of the *polis*: the spectral present absence of those who have no part. My respondents' appearances in public evoke what it takes to make *these* present absences count. Such instances of counter-memory evoked the spectral presence of minor events and bodies that seemingly had not left any impressions on the normalised and normalising site of archived history and, nevertheless, returned to trouble the ordered regularity of this history. Judith Butler has importantly alerted us against accounts of disaggregation or effacement from the plural that take the excluded and the destitute to be 'simply unreal, or [to] have no being at all' (2011). I would like to make clear that spectrality, as I use it here, does not denote by any means a status of being unreal/unrealised or being outside the political realm itself. Rather, it seeks to signal an emerging and enduring state of appearance within, despite and against existing political arrangements that make certain appearances of bodies in political space impossible. Spectres, as we know, recur to haunt edifices, upsetting ontologically their terms of possession and making them passible, that is, susceptible to other inhabitations. In a different context, but in ways consistent with our purposes here, Achille Mbembe has addressed the structural positionality of the black subject as subjection in terms of ambiguous spectrality, whereby the subject is dead while being alive:

> How is it possible to live while going to death, while being somehow already dead? And how can one live in death, be already dead, while being-there – while having not necessarily left the world or being part of the spectre – and when the shadow that overhangs existence has not disappeared, but on the contrary weighs ever more heavily? (Mbembe 2001: 201)

Becoming ghostly as a performative modality of reckoning with ghostly matters looms large in my interlocutors' political desire to wield public space as a register of the emergent: as a state of what is yet to come and present itself. During a spring afternoon in 2010, at the *ŽuC* office, Marija and Saša were showing me photographs from the movement's actions in the 1990s. Our attention was captivated by one particular photo from the protest against the siege of Sarajevo, organised by *ŽuC* and the Belgrade Circle. Standing with others at the central square of Belgrade, Saša was holding a banner: 'Sarajevo is a grave for living people'. Through the activists' embodied emergence, the living dead of Sarajevo haunted the public space of Belgrade. At the same time, the photograph itself becomes what Ariella Azoulay calls a 'locus of appearance' (2012: 54): it is indeed a political image 'to the extent that people make it exist among themselves, in plurality, in public' (ibid.). The action captured in the visual document registered what it takes politically to affirm relationality with others – especially those present in their absence – by intervening in the matrices that regulate the possibility for conditions of living and re-presenting together in public. It is through such performative idioms of body-archive that *ŽuC* decentres the space of national memory as a haunted space of political death. Thus, the square of national memorialisation becomes a re-public square (rather than a square of *the* Republic). It is through political subjects' corporeal and affective practices of opting out of normative schemes of appearance that public space becomes, even if only temporarily, a plural one, open to the contingencies of finitude and social contention.

Notes

1 Statement of Women in Black of Belgrade, available at <http://zeneucrnom.org/index.php?option=com_content&task=view&id=22&Itemid=15&lang=en> (last accessed 19 July 2014).

2 The concept hauntology was first introduced by Jacques Derrida, in *Specters of Marx* (1994), where he argued that Marxism, but also the utopian notion of revolution, would haunt Western society even after its apparent 'end'. Hauntology becomes a heuristic methodological conduit that allows Derrida's reading of Marx's onto-eschatological conception of history (i.e. 'A spectre is haunting Europe – the spectre of communism', *Communist Manifesto*). The word 'hauntology' is almost a homophone to 'ontology' (in French), which it alters by introducing 'haunt' to signal the paradoxical state of the spectre – neither present nor absent, neither dead nor alive, neither being nor non-being. Writes Derrida: 'We will take this category to be irreducible, and first of all to everything it makes possible: ontology, theology, positive or negative onto-theology' (1994: 51).

3 Enacting solidarity to Srebrenica was not only considered a despicable act by Serb nationalists, but it was also a delicate matter among activists of the 'opposing sides' of the Yugoslav war – Serbian and Bosnian. In 2002, women's groups from Serbia (including *ŽuC*) were invited to the commemoration ceremony that was held in Srebrenica, after the hard work

of preparation and communication between the 'two sides', and after the organisation Women of Srebrenica had visited Belgrade in order to work together with Serbian women's collectivities with this end in view.

4 In July 1995, Serbian military and paramilitary forces, under the command of General Ratko Mladić, chief of staff of the Bosnian Serb Army (1992–5), had expelled 40,000 people from Srebrenica, and, after gathering the inhabitants of the small town in football fields, schools and factories, annihilated more than 8,000 on the basis of their ethnic identity. Mladić's aim was the extermination of that predominantly Muslim town in the area of Eastern Bosnia, in an attempt to establish the territorial integrity of the new political entity of Republika Srpska (the Serb-dominated entity of Bosnia and Herzegovina). The UN had declared Srebrenica and six other besieged towns UN-protected zones, which, however, did not prevent the massacre, even though 400 armed Dutch peacekeepers were present at the time. The government-commissioned report of the Dutch Institute for War Documentation concluded that the mission was not well conceived; as a result, the Dutch government accepted partial responsibility and the second cabinet of Wim Kok resigned in 2002. In 2004, the International Criminal Tribunal for the former Yugoslavia (ICTY) located in The Hague, the Netherlands, ruled that the atrocities committed at Srebrenica constituted an act of genocide. In 2007, the International Court of Justice concurred with the ICTY judgement, but determined that Serbia itself was not guilty of the crime. President Boris Tadić of Serbia welcomed the ruling and urged the Parliament to condemn the Srebrenica massacre. Nevertheless, committee findings and court jurisprudence remain generally disputed by Serb nationalist groups who still subscribe to the Milošević-era propaganda that the massacre never happened. On 10 November 2004, the government of Republika Srpska issued an official apology. On 10 April 2007, a Serbian war crimes court sentenced four members of a paramilitary group known as 'Scorpions' to a total of fifty-eight years in prison for the execution of six Bosniaks (Bosnian Muslims) during the Srebrenica massacre. In his article 'Srebrenica: Between denial and recognition', Obrad Savić, the Acting President of the Belgrade Circle (one of the NGOs involved in the drafting of the 'Declaration of the Obligations of the State of Serbia'), examines the question of the public recognition of Serbian war crimes committed in the 1990s, and speaks of a 'national policy of denying a criminal past' (2005).

5 Minić, from the meeting 'Always disobedient', ibid.

6 Bogojević, from the meeting 'Always obedient', ibid.

7 Women in Black 2001a: 12.

8 The demand to assume responsibility for the commitment of nationalist atrocities by Serbia in the Bosnian war now pervades the official discourse of Serbian politicians. Boris Tadić, in his first public address after his inauguration as President of Serbia – in July 2004, on the anniversary day of the Srebrenica massacre – spoke of a 'confrontation with the crimes committed by our nation', avoiding, however, any direct reference to the ethnic cleansing in Srebrenica. Tadić's social-democratic party ('Democratic Party') had participated in the broad coalition of political forces against the Milošević regime. He was elected leader of the party in 2004 (after the assassination of Zoran Djindjić), and then was elected President of Serbia in 2004, prevailing over his political opponent, the candidate of the nationalist Radical party. In 2007, Tadić made a public apology for the crimes committed against Croatia in the name of Serbia during the war in Croatia. In May 2008, Tadić's coalition 'For a European Serbia' won the parliamentary elections.

9 Zoran Djindjić, who in 2001 was elected Serbia's prime minister and was assassinated in 2003, played a principal role in those anti-regime public gatherings, as the leader then of the opposition parties. Djindjić was the head of the opposition when NATO's assault on Yugoslavia started. A photo showing him shaking hands with US President Bill Clinton during the bombing of Serbia was used by his political opponents who accused him of treason. Djindjić played an important role in the September 2000 presidential elections and the October uprising, which brought about the collapse of Milošević's regime. He led a grand coalition ('Democratic Opposition of Serbia'), which won the December elections, leading to his appointment as prime minister in 2001.

10 The arrest and extradition of suspects for war crimes has been a condition for Serbia's accession to the European Union and, according to the post-Yugoslav national narrative, for the country's definite 'deliverance' from the burdens of Balkan legacy. In 2007, Serbia initialled a Stabilisation and Association Agreement (SAA) with the European Union. Mladić was arrested on 26 May 2011, and in December 2013 the Council of the European Union approved opening negotiations on Serbia's accession in January 2014.

11 Serbian far right and racist organisation *Obraz* (honour) was founded in 1993. It praises war criminal indictees Ratko Mladić and Radovan Karadžić, and calls for eradication of 'enemies of the Serbian people': ethnic minorities, democrats, and LGBTQ people. In 2012, *Obraz* was

officially banned by the Constitutional Court of Serbia. On the web site of *Obraz*, queer people are described as 'sexual perverts' and 'enemies of Serbia'.

12 BBC News, <http://news.bbc.co.uk/2/hi/europe/82 4514.stm> (last accessed 4 September 2014).

13 The memorials of the Unknown Soldier denote a displacement from the exclusively memorial exaltation of army generals and kings towards a 'democratisation' of the national memorial, during the nineteenth century (see Anderson 1991).

14 These actions were organised from October 1991 to October 1995. After that, they continued on a monthly basis or on specific scheduled dates.

15 For the event in history in Benjamin's philosophy of history, see Cadava 1997; Ferris 1998; Löwy 2006.

16 'We are still disobedient and we are still in the streets': title of a *ŽuC* performance held in Belgrade, in 2002, 2003, and 2004.

17 In her study on Greek civil war and its production of 'dangerous citizens', Neni Panourgiá (2009) significantly extends Nicole Loraux's gesture of distinguishing between *stasis emphyl(i)os* and *oikeios pólemos*, in their different ways of summoning the political significance of gender, race, kinship, and the city. Loraux makes a distinction between *stasis emphyl(i)os* and *oikeios pólemos*, whereby the former denoted a war that happened within the *polis* understood as belonging to the same *phýlon*, while the latter means a civil war happening in the *polis* taken as part of an *oikos*.

18 In juxtaposition to the decree of amnesty in late fifth-century Athens one would perhaps consider another public treatment of memory, posited centuries after the Athenian amnesty: namely, the Truth and Reconciliation Commission, in South Africa, especially with reference to the injunction to recount and narrate, to tell the story, to speak the truth (see Feldman 2004). The *ŽuC* poetics and politics of counter-memory would not be comfortably positioned in either of these.

19 'Vojvoda' is a Slavic military title, denoting the principal commander of a military force. In the Balkan Wars and World War I, this title designated the highest military rank in Serbian Army. In the same period, the Chetniks used the title to designate their top commanders. It was used again by the Chetniks in World War II. Most importantly, the word has been used to refer to the leader or 'duke' of the Serbian Chetnik Movement Vojislav Šešelj. Because of its name, this party was denied registration, but was merged in 1991 with the National Radical Party to create the ultraright Serbian Radical Party under Šešelj's leadership.

20 In *Dis-agreement*, Rancière draws a distinction between two heterogeneous orders of political rationality: politics as counterpolitical 'police', that is, ordered demarcation of the sensible, and politics as dissensus, that is, disagreement and disruption of the dominant order of the sensible. Politics is an event that happens when the 'part of no part' appears and speaks (as if it has the right to do so), thus dismantling the existing 'distribution of the sensible', that is, the force of the police order to keep the sensible in order. A word of caution is in order lest we posit the two logics in terms of rigid opposition and pure exteriority.

21 It is through this perspective that Iveković addresses the present-day constellation of global capitalism, whereby sovereignty is transferred from the state to the market: she is critical of the re-emerging communalisms and nationalisms that are mobilised as responses to the 'desovereignization of the state' (2013: 160).

22 Women in Black 2001b: 19.

23 Ibid.

24 The NATO operation supposedly sought to terminate violence used by the Milošević regime and stop human rights abuses in Kosovo. It was the first time that NATO used military force without the approval of the UN Security Council. The bombing killed around 500 Yugoslav civilians and caused extensive infrastructure damages, including destruction of public and civilian buildings, industrial plants, bridges, historic sites, cultural monuments, hospitals, and military establishments.

25 'Serbian Deputy Prime Minister Šešelj threatens journalists and human rights organizations', *Human Rights Watch*, 2 October 1998. Others have reported Šešelj's statement as: *Jedan NATO avion ubiti jednu ženu u crnom* (one NATO plane for one Woman in Black).

26 *ŽuC* annual statement: 'Seven years of Women in Black against War: 9 October 1991 to 9 October 1998'.

27 Women in Black 2001b: 11.

28 Women in Black statement, 10 June 1992, cited in Mladjenović and Hughes 2001.

29 See also Fortier 2000.

30 Elsewhere Arendt refers to the 'shadowy interior of the household' (which consists of women, children, and slaves) to indicate a (problematic) distinction between the public and the private. However, as I argue here, the 'public' itself is circumscribed and yet crossed and haunted by such 'shadowy' present absences of the excluded. This is about what Butler calls 'melancholy of the public sphere' (2000: 81).

31 The etymology of the word 'daimon' is suggestive in this respect, as it implies the 'divider', or 'distributor'.

4

Political Languages of Responsiveness and the Disquiet of Silence

When the body 'speaks' politically, it is not only in vocal or written language. (Judith Butler 2011)

[T]hose historically excluded from liberal personhood have proceeded against the spectrum of silences limning the universal claims of humanist discourse for the past several centuries. Jews, immigrants, women, people of color, homosexuals, the unpropertied: all have pressed themselves into civic belonging not simply through asserting their personhood but through politicizing – articulating – the silent workings of their internally excluded presence within prevailing notions of personhood. (Wendy Brown 2005)

Silence itself – the things one declines to say, or is forbidden to name, the discretion that is required between different speakers – is less the absolute limit of discourse, the other side from which it is separated by a strict boundary, than an element that functions alongside the things said, with them and in relation to them within over-all strategies. There is no binary division to be made between what one says and what one does not say; we must try to determine the different ways of not saying such things, how those who can and those who cannot speak of them are distributed, which type of discourse is authorized,

223

Vesna Pavlović, *Saša, Staša and Violeta, Republic Square, Belgrade, 1994*. Gelatin silver print.

or which form of discretion is required in either case. There
is not one but many silences, and they are an integral part of
the strategies that underlie and permeate discourses. (Michel
Foucault 1981)

Inaudible Voices, Disqualified Discourses

How might reflective responsiveness unsettle the regimes of
audibility and speakability associated with the political discourses
of dealing with the enduring aftermath of war atrocities? How
does gendered silence speak the languages of the political? How
might it trouble the acoustic and linguistic matrices that make
the political possible and sensible? And, finally, how is activist
bearing-witness constituted as counter-tale or dissonant voice
in post-conflict Serbian society? Over the course of this chapter,
I elaborate on the political performativity of responsiveness
that is articulated or withheld in the context of antinationalist modes of being haunted by, and accounting for, the past.
In acknowledging the dead of the rival side, who have been
treated as dispensable during the wars of Yugoslav succession,
ŽuC public assemblies intervene in the ways in which violences
of dispossession committed in the name of national interests
came to be perceived, heard, embodied, and remembered in
Serbia, but also in other former republics of Yugoslavia. Both
during and after the violence, these political subjects have been
seeking to counter the attempts of various agents – that is,
official authorities, media, and public intellectuals – to trivialise
or deny the violence that 'their own' national intimates inflicted
upon others. Through a performative enactment of silence in
their public vigils, but also through their bodily appearances
and utterances, they reshape the vocal registers that implicitly
condition the configurations of the political.

I would like to suggest that in engaging in bodily acts of witnessing, in which the body is not a 'mute facticity' (Butler 1990: 129), *ŽuC* activism yields an account of the political subject's social becoming and unbecoming as a performative event of responsiveness to others within specific constellations of power. Such an account of responsive political subjectivity involves a critique of representing the other through discursive devices of sovereign authenticity, as mourning is an occasion in which the other resists its own horizon of language: 'Speaking is impossible', Derrida writes, 'but so too would be silence' (1989: xvi). Indeed, the politics of mourning raises questions concerning the 'appropriation of the other and resistance of the other to that appropriation' (Deutscher 1998: 176). The question for these activists is how to respond when speaking is impossible, but silence is as well. The incalculable contingency of engaged and responsive silence vis-à-vis regulatory grids of audibility and speakability in light of the 'incalculability' of loss is the central concern of this chapter.

The *ŽuC* collective ethics and praxis of responsiveness carries the obligation to rethink the possibility of justice as disengaged from vengeance, retribution, and resentment. This is about a demand for justice as an ongoing process, not simply reduced to jurisprudence that takes place within institutionalised settings. In this regard, it echoes Derrida's distinction between justice and formal regimes of law (i.e. bureaucratic, administrative institutions of law-making and legislation) (1992a). Arguably, domestic and international official discourses and institutions have generated a public record – no matter how diverse, layered, and controversial – of the events of the 1990s. The indictments issued in 2005 by the International Criminal Tribunal for the former Yugoslavia (ICTY), founded in 1993, have played a crucial role in the process of determining responsibility at an official, legal level. This process has not brought forth a definite 'closure', however, not even at the institutional level. More recently, there have been major reversals of earlier assessments by the Tribunal. In May 2013, for instance, the ICTY decided to acquit state security officials who had been held responsible for creating, arming, and directing paramilitary groups that had committed a large number of crimes in Croatia and Bosnia–Herzegovina. In another case, a former general convicted of aiding and abetting crimes against humanity in Sarajevo and Srebrenica was acquitted on all charges and released (Gordy 2013b).

These acquittals, which rejected the basis of responsibility for officials accused of facilitating crimes committed by the Bosnian Serb army, worked to mitigate the feeling among many ethnic Serbs that the tribunal was biased against them, but at the same time generated distrust among various activist organisations regarding the commitment of tribunal jurisprudence to secure justice for the victims. According to these activist groups, the 2013 dramatic exoneration of paramilitary officials by The Hague Tribunal left little or no feeling of justice for the victims. *ŽuC* and seven other organisations from Serbia, Bosnia and Herzegovina, Croatia, Montenegro, Kosovo, Macedonia and Slovenia, which have taken the initiative to organise the Women's Court in Former Yugoslavia (*Ženski Sud za bivšu Jugoslaviju*), maintain that the work done by ICTY has been important, but not sufficient in itself. These collectivities that emerged from that post-Cold War historical moment aim at enacting alternative modes of justice, legal subjectivity, and testimonial process, whereby the affective and the political intertwine to make stories of violence, survival, and resistance audible and transmissible. These critical political subjectivities are led to grapple with various quandaries regarding the internal limitations of transitional justice, the freighted politics of memory and oblivion, the possibilities and impossibilities of witnessing, and the ambivalent event of testimony.

Explicitly inscribing itself within the legacy of the Women's Court Movement, *ŽuC* is a core participant and coordinating agency of the project 'Women's Court – A feminist approach to justice', which started in 2010 (Zaharijević 2012). Under the rubric 'women's court is a space where women's voices can be heard', the Women's Court in Former Yugoslavia initiative was started in 2010 to provide space for testimonies about the daily injustices suffered during the war and in peace, and about resistance to this violence of injustice. A fundamental aim of the women's court is to foster a feminist concept of responsibility directed at building a just peace through transnational alliances. In the context of this court, women, but also all those who experience unequal distribution of resources and public voice, are encouraged to testify about various forms of structural violence, including poverty, work exploitation, and racism. As political scientist and *ŽuC* activist Adriana Zaharijević put it:

> If one begins with an assumption that formal legal systems do not side with victims and that, even if the trials prove to be fair, they do not necessarily bring justice to the victims, then one is bound to seek alternative justice. Alternative justice is needed for those who are deprived of power in political, civic and social terms. (2012: n.p.)

And in the words of the women's court initiators: 'we write alternative history'.[1] By creating 'alternative' paradigms of reflective justice, this endeavour seeks to intervene in the narratives and silences that make up the public memory of the 1990s, especially at the level of the banal ways in which people remember, forget, embody, narrate, and keep secrets about the 1991–9 conflicts in the former Yugoslavia in the course of everyday life.

Nevertheless, *ŽuC* is also concerned with an agonistic politics of responsibility beyond and beside official jurisprudence, be it incriminating or exculpatory. For *ŽuC*, the question of justice cannot be put to rest through juridical frameworks, including those of formal recognition or misrecognition. As Staša Zajović mentioned in one of our conversations:

> It is disheartening that the European Union asks from the Serbian government to close the case. They are asking from us [*ŽuC*] to become the laundries for the bloody clothes. It is as though they say: let's move on, without assuming responsibility. No one, not even the European Union, posits that Milošević's party should be denounced as a prerequisite for Serbia's accession to the EU. It's only us who do this, but our persistence puts us in a vulnerable position.

Therefore, rather than promoting logics of closure, these activists' emphasis is on responding to the futurity of justice, that is, on the opening of a horizon for justice. This is about an ongoing and indeterminate interrogation of established recognisability with regard to justice, which cannot be subsumed under fixed juridical accounts of culpability or moralist accounts of self-rebuke and guilt. For these activists, the legacy of the war remains animated – if in ingrained economies of normalisation and disavowal – through various instantiations of contemporary sociality, including silences and presumptions that are thoroughly infused into the everyday. For them, present and future possibilities of responsibility are shaped through, and against, wider assemblages of power – certainly wider than juridical configurations.

It is this contentious legacy that has constituted over time the condition of possibility for these activists' and their fellow citizens' subjectivation as heirs of the memory of Yugoslavia's breakup in the 1990s. It has formed what they have become and how they have become undone in the face of this violence; it has also shaped their demand for justice as an indefinite demand and as a site of continual contestation. And so they ask: What is it that still remains to be accounted for in the public memory of the wars that followed the disintegration of Yugoslavia? What kind of political and affective language would such response to past injurious injustice and its trivialisation require? *ŽuC* bears the political burden of taking up, again and again, these questions, in all their openness and indeterminacy. It does so by politically mobilising the sign of responsiveness to reconfigure power differentials that condition univocal speakability. This necessitates, according to *ŽuC*, a reformulation of responsibility as responsiveness and response-ability, which, in turn, requires forming new possibilities for relationality, that is, for living together in the aftermath of loss and violent disposability. Judith Butler has cogently addressed response-ability as the ability to formulate affective responses to war within frames that, in being infused by right-wing, neoliberal, sexist, homophobic, and racist norms, establish particular sensate ways of regarding loss (2010).

In order to pursue the critical task of response-ability, then, *ŽuC* claims for itself a collective voice to deal with the disputable limits of language, as a crucial component of the group's commitment to making room for a critical and just relation to the past. The genre of holding silent public vigils is meant to attend to the silenced memory of the nation's histories of injustice that demand witness when nothing is left to be said and when the pains of injustice cannot be fully reducible to the available idioms of language and representation. At the same time, it is meant to echo what has gone unsaid and what remains to be said in light of the historic voicelessness of the gendered and racialised others of discursivity. In their struggle for recovery of a certain possibility for language despite conditions of irrecoverable silencing and speechlessness, these political subjects register their political distrust of what Wendy Brown has called 'compulsory discursivity' (2005: 85). Thus, they put their silenced gendered agency to use. One of the written declarations that the movement issued during the years of the war conveyed its emblematic practice of using silence to defamiliarise and destabilise the fixed configurations of identification and belonging that sustained the war. That declaration called attention to the ways in which women's victimisation becomes the ground upon which the national body politic takes place in war:

> We refuse to add to the cacophony of empty statements that are spoken with the best intentions yet may be erased or go unheard under the sound of a passing ambulance or a bomb exploding nearby . . . Our silence is visible. We invite women to stand with us, reflect about themselves and women who have been raped, tortured or killed in concentration camps, women who have disappeared, whose loved ones have disappeared or have been killed, whose homes have been demolished.[2]

By ambiguously incorporating the bewildered muteness of the witness as a means to politically mobilise the historicity of silenced gendered agency, performative silence takes the form of refusing complicity in the injurious discourses of subordination and trivialisation, but also in the depoliticised routine of post-conflict, post-Yugoslav NGO-isation (Helms 2003; Malkki 1996). It echoes, at the same time as it means to dissipate, the sound-surplus of war: the 'passing ambulances', the 'exploding bombs', but also the post-war rhetoric of 'good intentions' that works to silence those abjected by prevailing regimes of enmity and disposability. The statement 'our silence is visible' disrupts the equation of visibility with the presence of a voice; an equation so operative in the ways in which political action is perceived in the discursive order of liberal representation and recognition. This is a politically situated silence through which *ŽuC* political subjects reckon with the experience of being excluded from the domain of speakable and audible national narratives.

The agonistic silence of the activists' vigils lays claim to the political imagination by attending to narratives yet-to-be-heard. It is a way to reclaim the testimonial performative power of inaudible and disqualified voices beyond the authoritative premises of speech, or, at least, beside them.[3] The wager of these activists is to mobilise politically the aporias at the heart of languages of responsiveness and not to do away with work of language. One cannot evade the necessary structure of language and the violence engendered by it, of course, not even by resorting to silence. Either by engaging speech or by remaining silent, one is susceptible to what Butler calls 'linguistic vulnerability' (1997b), that is, one's becoming a subject and surviving subjection depends on the structure, or infrastructure, of language. And so there is surely nothing unmediated and uncontaminated about silence, as it necessarily draws on existing and largely unmasterable discursive conditions and conventions. As Foucault has demonstrated, silence is, after all, an integral part of discourse (1981). In the hands of *ŽuC* activists, silence becomes a self-reflective position, which pushes the limits of performativity beyond the referential formulas of the speech act. For them, the question becomes: how might silence work to make susceptibility toward silenced memory politically enabling?

Aporias of (Un)Speakability

The *ŽuC* way of laying claim to the public through performative silence is meant to reconfigure the conditions that make speech 'the paradigmatic form of action' (Butler 2011: n.p.). As Butler has put it, in her reflection on the shift from the space of appearance to the contemporary politics of the street: 'when the body "speaks" politically, it is not only in vocal or written language' (ibid.). And so we ought to rethink the register of appearing bodies and the linguistic register in their intimate connections, 'through a performativity of the body that crosses language without ever quite reducing to language' (ibid.). It is precisely this modality of performativity, neither merely linguistic nor merely theatrical, that the *ŽuC* activists come to articulate, as they reinvent silence as an affective political lexicon through which to acknowledge the injustices at the heart of unnameable and ungrieavable losses.

Lepa Mladjenović, member of *ŽuC* and a counsellor for female victims of male violence, explains the 'infuriating silent technique' of the *ŽuC* vigils: 'It is a very loud silence ... It mocks the silence that is imposed on women . . . [I]t is a rebellion against the way that women are politically and socially silenced' (in Prince-Gibson 2005: 16). In Lepa's words, silence is not an absence of voice, as is often assumed. It is a resounding medium of political engagement, which retains revolutionary potential as a public expression of deep discontent with authoritative grids of intelligibility, including gendered domination. In taking up the silences shrouding injurious national and gendered histories, these activists reconfigure the discursive associations of mourning with the feminine, the familial, and the patriotic. In 'mocking' the gendered imperatives of silencing, as Lepa put it, this activist silence reveals the factitiousness and radical contingency of discursive truth-effects and, furthermore, works to unfix the norms that have historically enabled the production of such regulatory inscriptions. Indeed, the evocative way in which Lepa and her comrades spoke about the crucial significance of silent standing in public for the *ŽuC* agonistic politics implicitly recalled a complex historicity of feminist silent protesting. The Silent Sentinels, for instance, were a group of women who protested quietly in front of the White House during Woodrow Wilson's presidency in the USA, in support of women's suffrage. At a time when women's speaking in public was thought to violate gender norms, the suffragists held banners that contained messages such as 'how long must women wait for liberty?' and 'democracy should begin at home'. Throughout the vigil, many of the Silent Sentinels were harassed, arrested for 'obstructing sidewalk traffic', charged with treason, imprisoned, tortured, placed in solitary confinement, and force-fed when they held a hunger strike (Southard 2007).[4]

Mourning as an appropriate feminine language, oscillating between resounding silence and incomprehensible bodily enactment, also has been radically appropriated in contemporary instances of political activism. In her ethnography of the political subjectivity of women participating in Catholic resistance to British rule in Northern Ireland, Begoña Aretxaga has shown how the theme of the sorrowful Mother Ireland was both deployed and challenged in the context of women's political activism in the 1980s. Through various non-verbal signifying practices of resistance – either as relatives cladding themselves in blankets to bring the prisoners' reality to the streets, or as prisoners defying the penal system by smearing their prison cells with faeces and menstrual blood – these activists sought to break the silence on state violence. In so doing they articulated the experience of being excluded from dominant – speakable, audible – political narratives and unsettled the connotations of asserting a distinctively 'feminine voice' (Artxaga 1997). The mothers of Relatives Action Committees in Northern Ireland, much like the Argentinean Mothers of the Plaza de Mayo who demand the return and the remembrance of the thousands of 'disappeared persons' in their two-decade long silent vigil in Buenos Aires (Sosa 2014; Taylor 1997), depart from the stereotypical trope of nationalist motherhood and turn their grief into a motivating force of political radicalisation. *Women in Black* in Israel/Palestine and *ŽuC* in the former Yugoslavia emerge from this tradition, which they resignify, by further expropriating the kinship prerequisite of grief. *ŽuC* in the former Yugoslavia draws on and further radicalises the Argentinean Mothers' motto 'None of the mothers is looking only for her child', by seeking to dismantle the discursive normativity that makes women-as-mothers stand for the idealised suffering of the nation.

The signifying practice of agonistic silence is taken up and restaged by *ŽuC* activists in ways that mobilise a whole inherited figuration of performative citationality – both as a forcible process of normative repetition and as an enduring possibility for repeating differently and subversively, whereby these two practices are inevitably implicated in one another (Butler 1990, 1993). Indeed, becoming silent has been historically reduced to incapacity to speak or act. It also stereotypically signifies the gendered language of the 'hapless victim', or the language of the unspeakable – of harms and losses that cannot be spoken in conventional idioms of language (see also Husanović 2009). The performative quietness of *ŽuC*, however, opens up spaces for muddling conventional divisions between the affective and the political, between word and silence, as well as between body and language. Lying beyond the metaphysical dichotomy between the phonic and the semantic, the political work of *ŽuC* brings forth the ambivalent implications of silence as unforeseeably and incalculably open to the forces of the performative: discursively constituted and yet potentially disruptive.[5]

Social anthropology has historically retained a constitutive connection to the work of recuperating and documenting gender – and sexually specific silent voices (e.g. Messick 1987).[6] More significantly for the purposes of this enquiry, silence has been a productive site where the naïve realist and monovocal conventions of ethnographic writing have been contested (Clifford and Marcus 1986). A crucial aporia of ethnographic writing lies in that it not only documents but also produces silence, as it necessarily evokes partial discursive and affective encounters. Tracing the possibilities of this impossibility, anthropological writing seeks to unravel who can and who cannot speak, who speaks for whom, whose speech or silence is expropriated, and who does not speak in authorised ways. But anthropological accounts that remain critical to normalising discourses of official archival imagination engage with the discursive, affective, political and ethical forces played out in the aporetic production of silences and minor voices without succumbing to the positivist epistemologies of collecting and recuperating the presumed authenticity of suppressed voices (Papailias 2005). Other anthropological work also has identified the verbalisation of the 'silent' and the 'unutterable' dimension of the social as one of the most vexing problems of ethnographic work (Hirschauer 2006; Pereira 2008). Especially in research contexts of testimony, witnessing, and memory as they connect to past violence, the anthropological recuperation of survivors' voices has been complicated in ways that have made us alert not only to the precarious linguistic limits of testimonial narrativity in all its gender-specific connotations (Das 1997), but also to the bureaucratisation and commodification of the 'voicelessness' of trauma by new transnational regimes of humanitarian power and expertise (Cuéllar 2005; Fassin and Rechtman 2009; Pandolfi 2003). Valentine Daniel (1996) has grappled with questions of violence and testimony in his riveting account of wounded testimony emerging from the collective violence that occurred in Sri Lanka in 1983: the wager of his 'anthropography' was to get around the question of what it means to give an account of the pain and passion of violence, in its complex interrelations with demands for justice and claims of forgiveness, without submitting to the prurience of violence, but also without betraying the victims of violence. In sum, as in João Biehl's pursuit to unravel the cryptic words of Catarina, a presumably mad young woman living in a zone of social abandonment in Porto Alegre, anthropologists and their interlocutors are 'both up against the wall of language' (2005: 11): most notably so in contexts of intensified precarity, injurability, and social death.

Feminist scholarship has importantly contributed to the exploration of the links between gender, sexuality, silence, and power by engaging not only with struggles about 'gaining a voice', but also with the paradoxical power of women's silence as both reflection and deflection of assigned or purported powerlessness.[7] Contemporary social theory has provided ample evidence that silence is not necessarily a sign of powerlessness, but rather a socially and culturally devalued genre through which 'subjugated knowledges' (Foucault 1980) are performed and hegemonic discourses potentially contested. In Michel Foucault's writings, silence is intimately connected to apparatuses of power, in a multiplicity of different contexts: the silences at the fringes of normalising epistemes, the institutional power and the discursive operations behind silence, the performance of silence in the contexts of religious truth-bearing confession, the potential of heterotopias to 'undermine language' and 'desiccate speech' (1994: xviii), and, finally, the tacit workings of power, but also the subversive potential of silenced and subjugated discourses.

Not only is silence positioned in a non-oppositional relation with speech and Logos, but it also constitutes part of the social effects of discourse. In the famous Foucault–Derrida debate on the nature of silence, Foucault argues for the necessity of an 'archaeology of silence' in the context of writing a discursive history of madness (1961), while Derrida questions whether a history of silence can be ever possible, claiming that this would ultimately involve a (phonocentric) metaphysics of presence and thus would inevitably restore the order of Western reason (1978: 35). The question emerging from this debate might be formulated thus: can silence contest the assumptions of logocentrism and enact an unquiet, deconstructive rupture in the metaphysical enclosure of Logos, or is it bound to embody the positivist impulse of authorial and authorised verbalisation? Or, to put it slightly differently: is it possible to write a history of silence or would this amount to a silent history? And what would be the political consequences of such dilemmas given the hegemony of the logocentric tradition whereby politics is irrevocably tied to the emergence of the human in language?

In criticising Foucault, Deleuze, and Guattari for their un-reflexive and irresponsive politics of representing the 'masses', Gayatri Chakravorty Spivak (1988) has powerfully addressed the epistemic violence that allows Western Logos to speak for 'others'. Western intellectuals, including essentialist bourgeois feminists, remain complicit in the modes of Western/colonialist/ postcolonial representations of the 'other' that silence the subaltern by means of speaking of/for a self-speaking subaltern subject constituted as an 'authentic voice' of irreducible alterity. Spivak sides with Derrida in acknowledging the discursive and linguistic matrices, with all their privileges and exclusions, in which forms of representation are always already embedded. Through the prism of a deconstuctive and antipositivist ethics and politics of representation, Spivak poses a radical challenge to the question of representation as 'speaking for' and as 're-presentation', thus theorising the im/possibility of subalternity as either representable or non-representable. She has importantly shown that it is through acknowledging and responding to such im/possibilities of representation that the echoes of the silenced can be listened to.

Taking such conundrums forward, Wendy Brown has proffered a perceptive analysis of the relationship between silence, speech, and political act. In theorising silence as a force normatively produced and yet potentially subversive, she reposi-tions the powers of silence beyond the 'norm-making process in traditions of "breaking silence"' (2005: 92). Brown importantly reflects on the political potentials of silence as a mode of resistance to power, in opposition to both passive aggression and historical habituation to being silenced. Addressing the embattled ambiguity of silence in relationship to normative discourses, I explore here, along with my interlocutors, the performative operations through which disquieting silence can derail, if only temporarily and incalculably, the truth claims of what qualifies as audible and intelligible discursivity in the master narratives of nationalism and phallogocentrism.[8]

Any critical account of mourning cannot do away with a critique of claims to master the past by appropriating, representing, or assimilating difference. This is something that Derrida addressed, apropos of his mourning of Paul de Man, in critically engaging the historicist pursuit to recover the past and translate it into recognisable discursive forms (1989). Attentive to the im/possibilities that haunt available linguistic and representational devices through which Yugoslav and post-Yugoslav memory has come to make sense, *ŽuC* activists situate themselves where fractured memorability is archived, while remaining unarchivable, in the body of the public space. Through practices of 'live' embodied performances but also by means of collecting testimonies and using the spoken word and various other media, their critical accounts of re-membering are alternatively documented and transmitted over time beyond silence/speech dichotomy, beyond the reductive relation between the recorded and the embodied, and without claims of full recovery. As I argue throughout this chapter, their performative medium of engaged silence enacts – rather than claims to retrieve – what was hitherto unheard of, that is, what was eclipsed by the common languages of political or judicial speech. It seeks, in other words, to do justice to unspeakability; as if this were possible.

Speaking For Others? Relational Structures of Address

Hélène Cixous has written that 'no political reflection can dispense with . . . work on language' (1981: 45). The *ŽuC* political work on language lays bare the limits of authorised enunciability and explores a new relational sense of address. Since the movement's inception, its silent standing in public, in commemoration of those excluded from the domain of memorability, has rendered it one of the most contentious 'alternative voices in public space' (Fridman 2006). Throughout the years, as several of my interlocutors have explained to me, the movement has been the target of attacks from far right-wing and fascist organisations, it has been prohibited from conducting solidarity work in refugee camps, materials have been confiscated from its office by state security forces, and its rallies and street actions have been banned or accompanied by heavy police presence. The emblematic silence of *ŽuC* public assemblies has not stopped them from being stigmatised and treated like an 'inner enemy' who purportedly engages in disruptive political mobilisation. It is precisely because of the persistent disquiet the group brings to the public space of presence and presentability that, rather paradoxically for an anti-war movement, it has been accused of derailing the process of restoring peace and normalcy (Fridman 2006).

The performative public stance of *ŽuC*, however, does not intend to establish silence as the only way of speaking back to existing discursive premises. In a conversation with me, Staša Zajović narrated her experience of 'talking' (back) to power in public as a way to bring forth possibilities for performing critical agency in contexts that incite silence:

> It has been important to me, since the time of old Yugoslavia,
> to address police officers in public. I do so in order both to

stand up for my friends and to stand for freedom: to relay the
message that we are free before the law. Also, this is a way to
alter the public perception of us: a way to show that we are not
what they think we are. We don't yell, we don't swear at them,
we just speak openly in public. In my experience, this attitude
leaves them in a state of bewilderment. This doesn't mean that
I am not aware of the police's malicious role, but I contend
that this stance towards the police is my way to act against the
violence and the hatred that have been accumulated since the
time of the war.

Staša 'submits' to an available modality of interpellation in order
to re-frame it. For her, addressing the police in public is a way
of countering the conditions that have demonised her and her
comrades, and practicing courage with others. It is, therefore, a
way of articulating dissent.

The disquiet these activists insert into the public domain of
speakability manifests courage – a notion that Foucault associates
with critical work (1977) – as not restricted to verbal acts of
truth-speaking, but rather performed through a multiplicity of
embodied acts, gestures, and aesthetics that enable the elaboration of critical matrices of de-subjugation and relationality.
In his investigation of relations between the speaking subject,
the courage of *parrhesia* and the agonistic virtue of critique,
Foucault has unravelled the activity of dangerous truth-telling
as 'speaking truth to power' (2001).[9] His question about critical
work is intimately connected with the question 'who is able
to tell the truth, about what, with what consequences, and
with what relations to power' (2001: 7). Drawing on Foucault's
insights on critique as located within the field of self-formation
and de-subjugation (*désassujettissement*) (1997: 47), Butler has
defined 'virtue' as the practice by which subjects form themselves in de-subjugation, which is to say, by risking their own
deformation as subjects, thus posing the question: who will be

a subject here (2001). Indeed, resisting one's own subjectivity is a crucial part of this embodied practice of critique as courage with others. As Costas Douzinas puts it, in theorising dissident subjectivity: 'Resisting subjectivity emerges when this initial call of refusal perseveres in the care of self with others' (2014: 93). For our purposes here, then, we might ask: what kinds of relations between truth and power determine whose *parrhesia* is authorised and whose undermined? How are we constituted and deconstituted as speaking subjects with others within and despite specific contexts of speakability? And how do realms of speakability work to determine 'who will be a subject here'?

Critically drawing on Foucault's notion of 'fearless speech', but also taking into consideration the Foucauldian conception of the impossibility of disengaging truth from power, one might further complicate the ethics and politics of truth-telling through positing the performative act of silence as bodily exposure and resistance by which the truth-effects of discourse are contested. It is through this perspective that the political performativity of *parrhesia*, conceived here neither as merely verbal nor as necessarily 'fearless' activity, is related to concerted forms of courage in the face of impossibility and at the cost of danger. In the words of Holloway Sparks: 'Courage, we might say, is a commitment to persistence and resolution in the face of risk, uncertainty, or fear' (1997: 92). In the context of our enquiry, then, rather than a state of individual honourable self-mastery and heroic, manly, moral transcendence through verbal acts of truth-speaking, courage emerges as a historically situated performative ethos of collective endurance, resistance, and political engagement. At times, it does in the presence of fear. In criticising 'the historical symbiosis of courage and manliness', Wendy Brown has insightfully suggested that: 'we need courage to *sustain* life . . . A courageous deed is one which sets identity and security at risk in order to bring forth new possibility' (1988: 206).

If, on the one hand, the *ŽuC* performative enactment of silence signifies the risks and iniquities that are inherent in the normative reduction of the wounded other to the silenced status of abjection and victimhood, on the other hand, it implies the unanticipated potential for a rupture in the established matrix of speakability and the gendered, racialised, and class-related violence it carries with it. This is a performative occasion inextricably tied to the question of how to critically wield the normative violence of rendering unspeakable, without repeating the mystification of unsayability and without reinstalling an exclusionary domain of singular speakability in the forms of authoritative naming. The agonistic silence of *ŽuC* is calibrated to counter the 'epistemic violence' that subjugates or eliminates the space from which 'the subaltern can speak' (Spivak 1988). The question of whether and how the subaltern speaks, a question inevitably invoking the very genealogy of feminine suppression in language, resonates in an article published by the head of the Belgrade Circle,[10] Obrad Savić, which discussed the memory of war crimes in the former Yugoslavia through the questions: 'Can victims speak?' and 'How can we testify in their name?' (2005).

In ways not always relying on actual words, *ŽuC* brings forth the forced silence of improper victims, and, along with it, the vexed question of whether and how one can possibly testify in their name. The *ŽuC* performative silence, construed as a sign of the unspoken and unspeakable aspects of discursivity but also as a sign of the impossibility of voice in the face of exposure to sovereign violence, is entangled in the question of 'who speaks': a question which, in exposing the traumas through which the speaking subject is constituted as sovereign and memorable, can be a rallying point countering the processes of subjection that are always already inherent in the production of the narrative itself. As Butler puts it: 'Who speaks when convention speaks? In what time does convention speak? In some sense, it is an inherited set of voices, an echo of others who speak as the "I'" (1997b). Indeed, the 'I' of speaking and testifying cannot be fully appropriated as one's own. Rather, echoes of 'others' (other subjects, times, voices, conventions, and voices of conventions) constantly subtend the scene of speaking, which is inextricably bound up with a modality of speaking *to*, as exposure and response to others, within grids of sociality (see also Papailias 2005). And so all language is necessarily implicated in a relational structure of address (Butler 2005). How does speaking one's 'own' memory, then, involve or interrupt the stories, memories, psychic investments, and lives of others? And, even more crucially, how might speaking one's 'own' memory constitute the condition of the emergence of an 'I' who 'speaks' her memory only in relation to others? So, response, as openness to being interpellated by another's address, is always already embedded in the very scene of subject formation and its required resources – linguistic, mnemonic, corporeal, or otherwise.

Through bearing witness to what remains unsaid or inaudible and to what lies always already outside oneself, the relational affectivity of *ŽuC* involves a performative reclaiming of the agency of language as it takes place in both registers of the compound formulation 'who speaks' – 'who' *and* 'speaking' – with their manifold forms of opacity, undecidability, and unforeseeability. What is more, this relational affectivity critically acknowledges the exclusions, complicities, and narrative conventions that condition the constitution of 'who', as a speaking subject echoing 'an inherited set of voices', in Butler's terms, and called into linguistic being by the interpellation of another. In the context of this affective structure of encounter, subjects do not pre-exist as moral selves but rather come to be *with* others, and also *as* others, in reclaiming a critical space of being-with-others.[11] Such an ek-static and reflexive conception of agency as address poses a critical challenge to moral agency, in its conventional reliance on insular, individualistic self-identity and representational transparency. As Butler states: 'Agency begins where sovereignty wanes. The one who acts . . . acts precisely to the extent that he or she is constituted as an actor and, hence, operating within a linguistic field of enabling constraints from the outset' (1997b: 16). The question to be addressed, then, is what kind of non-sovereign agency is implied in the relational formation of the speaking subject, when the field of relationality is troubled by fractured experiences of unspeakable political destitution that exceeds documentation and representation.

Standing within and across such impossibilities and impermissibilities, the *ŽuC* performative silence is the event of an agonistic exposure of the possibility of being undone in language, undone by language. A relational structure of address is at work as these activists act politically in performing a mode of non-sovereign subjectivity, whereby not owning one's words (and silences) has critical political consequences,

> since speaking is always in some ways the speaking of a stranger through and as oneself, the melancholic reiteration of a language that one never chose, that one does not find as an instrument to be used, but that one is, as it were, used by, expropriated in, as the unstable and continuing condition of the 'one' and the 'we', the ambivalent condition of the power that binds. (Butler 1993: 241–2)

Activism as Responsiveness

As I elaborated in the previous sections, the *ŽuC* agonistic silence is about breaking the linguistic and representational structure open as a means of becoming disposed to be undone in relation to others and others' losses. This social passion of activism – or, social passion as activism – is emblematically manifested in the public assemblies of non-nationalistic memory, which offers space for reconsidering the disembodied and affectively purified subject of political action in conventional liberal constructions of politics. These activists put into play the ek-static character of political subjectivity as constituted through the address of the other (denoting both being addressed by and addressing others). As they become 'moved' by, through and toward, the disavowed losses that haunt injurious memoro-politics, they deal with the question of how responsiveness might appear in the languages of activism. In other words: how might we think activism in terms of responsiveness, rather than in terms of achieving sovereign autonomy through transcending structures of subjugation? How might we think activism as one's being collectively moved and moving despite and against the powers by which one is subjectified?

As Veena Das reminds us, reflecting on how women's bodies were made the passive witnesses of violence during the Partition of the British Indian Empire, the language of passion and pain can only be heard as an incoherent bodily language of hysteria: a 'language having all the phonetic excess of hysteria that destroys apparent meanings' (1997: 86). In this perspective, passion as activism, in its assigned connotations of sentimental femininity and uncivilised primitiveness, inserts an element of disagreement and disquietude into the 'intimate public' (Berlant 1997, 2008) of Yugoslav and post-Yugoslav memory, a public affect that has been formed by contexts of uneven intimacy and disposability. Thus conceived, the public affectivity of activism does not rely on a divide between public and private, but rather carries with it the performative possibility for a disruptive sense of belonging, homeliness, and publicness. Against sentimental political fantasies of generalisable immediacy and homogeneity, the intimate public fostered by *ŽuC* activism denotes the social passions of relationality and dissent, or relationality *as* dissent, that stem from shared histories of injury, abjection, and courage with others, in times when dissent is delegitimised as uncongenial to the patriotic urgency of public ordinariness.

Ildiko Erdei, a social anthropologist at the University of Belgrade, who used to be active with *ŽuC* and has organised vigils at Pancevo (a city located in the southern part of Vojvodina, in Republic of Serbia), which was heavily bombed by NATO forces in 1999, talked to me about her experience in the movement by intertwining an ethic of courage and the concerted action of dissident politics in the face of unliveable political conditions: '*ŽuC* saved my life in the 1990s', she said. As Ildiko put it, what puts our bodies on the line is often precisely what can save our life. 'Saving one's own life' is not a private matter here (if it ever is), distinct from the public realm of assigned, or destructed, conditions of liveability. Quite the contrary, bodies on the line and in alliance, in all their exposure and persistence, come together to perform dissenting practices in order to sustain one another's life, thus crossing the conventional line of what counts as 'private' and 'public'.[12] After recounting the multiple ways in which her participation in the movement's dissenting practices 'saved her life', Ildiko referred to the present situation of the movement: '*ŽuC* is the last remaining group that resists the incitation to mainstreaming and insists on holding on to the element of dissent. This comes with a price, however: it is marginalised and demonised.'

In this regard, *ŽuC* dissident performative action resonates with what Ewa Ziarek calls an 'ethics of dissensus', whereby at stake is a reformulation of the agonistic politics that conveys an infinite pursuit of justice. Opposing depoliticised, disembodied, and privatised moral discourse and self-present subjectivity, a feminist ethics of dissensus, in Ziarek, involves the political potential to contest the mutually constitutive forms of racist,

sexist, and class domination, and, at the same time, an ethical obligation to those who cannot voice their damages (2002, 2007).
In this respect, the force of 'dissensus', based on an agonistic
notion of relationality, is fundamental to how the political and
its subjects come to 'make sense' in the context at hand. Adriana
Cavarero's ethics of relationality might offer us insightful means
to grapple with the texture of public affect as it pertains to the
formation of a collective political subjectivity alternative to
the conceits of the self-possessive and self-constituting subject
(2000). In a similar vein, Butler's ethical account amounts to re-
imagining of subjectivity in terms of the dependency of subjects
on others and on norms, and hence relies upon the idea of a
subject excessive of oneself. The practice of giving an account of
oneself, understood as an always partial and incalculable response
to an address posed by another, is made possible and necessary
despite the opacity at the heart of the speaking subject – opacity
to itself and to others (Butler 2005). In the ethics and politics
of responsibility, not everything gets across (Spivak 1995), and
this is not only a delimiting but also a formative condition.
The question is how activism as responsiveness engages and
mobilises politically what Gayatri Spivak, drawing on Levinas
and Derrida, calls 'the impossible intimacy of the ethical' (1993:
171). As Spivak suggests, it is only by learning the hard lesson
of 'the impossible intimacy of the ethical' that an ethical engagement can ever take place, albeit with no guarantees. This
is the political burden and potential that undergirds the *ŽuC*
gendered ethical account of responsiveness as the experience of
the impossible (Spivak 1995), which entails conflictual articulations of, and ongoing painstaking negotiations with, established
configurations of intimacy, body, and language.

In conversing with Shoshana Felman (1983), Butler com-
prehends speech acts not as occasions for pre-existing speaking
subjects to exercise sovereignty through language (as in 'doing

things with words', according to Austin's (1975) famous phrase), but as bodily acts, whereby the interrelation of speech and the body is by no means causal or deterministic: '[T]he body is the blindspot of speech, that which acts in excess of what is said, but which also acts in and through what is said' (1997b: 11). It is from this vantage point of body–speech interrelation, which refuses the reduction of one to the other, that we might view the ŽuC activism of performative mourning as a responsive, bodily 'speech act', which works 'in excess of what is said' but also in and through what has remained unsaid or inaudible. The body, in this context, is not presupposed as a hypostatised foundation of agency or merely an inert surface of inscription, but rather becomes a performative occasion for the citational eventness of social agonism through relating with others. 'Indeed, the body can appear and signify in ways that contest the way it speaks', writes Butler, 'or even contest speaking as its paradigmatic instance' (2011: n.p.). ŽuC activism brings forth a politics of address that recalls and re-enacts the ways in which the terms of recognisability are bound up with vulnerability to language. As words fail it, the body of this activism contests speaking as the paradigmatic modality of political agonism.

It is this possibility for contestation that Veena Das engages by means of reflecting on the 'transactions of language and body' directed at transforming an uninhabitable public space by means not reducible to the language of recognition: 'In the register of the imaginary, the pain of the other not only asks for a home in language but also seeks a home in the body' (1997: 88). In a context of violent appropriation of women's bodies as cultural media by the project of nationalism, Das addresses women's gesture of mourning as a gesture of presenting their bodies in public rather than making their bodies speak through traditional laments or standardised narratives of suffering. As she writes: 'it was the ability to recraft the symbols and genres of mourning

that made them active in the highly contested domain of politics'
(2007: 217).

In this scene of activist relationality, engaging with the other's
singularity in her political vulnerability is not to be taken as
predicated on an affirmation of the other according to the model
of self-present and self-sufficient subjectivity. Nevertheless, it
does not amount to a conceptualisation of the alterity of the
other as an invariably negative thing either, that is, as radically
and ineluctably elusive. Rather, it is the impossible relation to
alterity that compels to bearing responsibility to others. This
act of engagement gives an account of the other neither as a
sacrosanct alien nor as an object of rehabilitation, as both such
accounts of the other would presuppose the restoration of a self-
sovereign 'I'. In other words, this is not about shifting from the
self-sovereign subject to a subject beset by, or given over to, the
other. With regard to the *ŽuC* act of relating to vulnerability as
a 'painful availability' (Barthes 2012: 80) (rather than a disembodied observer's will to document the pain of 'the other'), the
lives and deaths of those violated or annihilated are addressed
not so much in terms of restoring the presumed authenticity and
representational transparency of subjugated voices, but rather in
terms of simultaneously exposing the shifting and precarious
limits of what partakes of common memorability and reckoning
the impossibility, and impertinence, of taking the other within
oneself. In this context, then, activism emerges as shared persistence, resistance, and vulnerability, including vulnerability to
power.

The Labour of Witnessing

I became a witness of the war. I was influenced by the women
of my family who took the arms themselves but were fond of

those men who had abandoned the arms and the war. When the war broke out, I took it to the street in order to say this story in public.

This is how Staša narrated to me the story of her becoming a 'war witness' as a story of not only enacting her own anti-war commitment, but also of being interpellated by the call and memory of others: namely, the women partisan fighters of her family, who had fought with the anti-Nazi resistance movement. In claiming a sense of agency, Staša bears witness to her contemporary injustices of war and nationalism and, at the same time, to the historical violence of gender oppression: her point of reference is women partisan fighters who took the arms against Nazism but resisted men with arms. She actually becomes a subject of her enunciation through witnessing the history of anti-Nazi resistance women fighters. In my friend's words, witnessing, as bearing witness and giving testimony, is politically mobilised with others, and as a response to – and address of – others. It entails relationality but also critique. It opens onto the possibility of address-ability and response-ability (Oliver 2001) beyond the descriptive, the juridical, and the representational: does witnessing always necessitate the apparatuses of self-present observation and observable self-presence? What kind of subject position is the one occupied, performed, and reconstructed by the witness? Is it a subject position that counters or repeats the violence? Is it a position fundamentally determined and destroyed by violence?

Giorgio Agamben opens his famous essay aptly titled 'On potentiality' (1999b: 177) by citing an excerpt from Anna Akhmatova's tremendous poem cycle of agony and witnessing 'Requiem', where she narrates an incident that took place in the years of the Stalinist terror. In a context of physical exhaustion and political destitution, another woman in the prison queue waiting to hand in parcels to beloved ones 'jolted out of the torpor characteristic of all of us, she said into my ear (everyone whispered there) "Could one ever describe this?" And I answered, "I can.'" It was out of that encounter, or interpellation, that grew her 'Requiem'. As Agamben develops, the potentiality of witnessing lies precisely in this aporia, whereby the speechless subject speaks while bearing the impossibility of speaking – her own and the other's. Indeed, it is through this aporia that witnessing can be politically mobilised as a mode of persistent, relational potentiality. Agamben offers an account of a potentiality that persists in the actual world, remains irreducible to determinate actualisations, and lies beyond the binary of potential/actual.

In her compelling reading of Agamben's essay, Ziarek (2010) puts forth the ways in which Akhmatova's poetic testimony bears witness to the systematic destruction of the potential of subjugated people and, at the same time, reclaims powerlessness as a resource for infinite possibility – possibility of speaking, of writing, of endurance, of relationality, and of action. This is, for Ziarek, a recovery of feminine possibility from powerlessness. And it is, crucially, a recovery enabled in response to another woman's despair. The arising possibility entails being-with others. Unravelling the unheard-of, gendered possibility of this intersubjectivity, Ziarek asks: 'How can transformative capacity and potentiality survive their destruction by political terror? How can its victims and survivors be "jolted out of their torpor"?' (2010).[13]

In expropriating feminised silence as address-ability and response-ability, *ŽuC* deals with the 'lacuna' of language that prevents the survivors from testifying.[14] The silent mourning that it performs in public places of official commemoration inhabits language in its most intense unpronounceable losses. It puts into action the naked experience of language – language being at a loss; drawing on the very recesses of speech, it enacts a language that might yield new avenues of witnessing. In this context, then, the labour of witnessing in the transnational 'age of testimony' (Felman and Laub 1992: 206) emerges not as a moral imperative, but rather as mnemonic and testimonial sensibility aware of its own limits, aware of the precarious status of the witness as biopolitical remnant: as that which, having undergone and endured the inhuman, remains human and remains between the perished and the survivors (Agamben 1999a).[15]

As Derrida suggests, in his essay 'Poetics and politics of witnessing', witnessing can never be transparent and re-presentational. It necessarily involves the poetic. As such, 'all responsible witnessing involves a poetic experience of language' (2005b: 66). Testimony cannot be reduced to the constative language of documentation and confirmation or to a representational model of language, then. It cannot be reduced to the representational devices of activism either. But also, put the other way around, activism cannot be reduced merely to the constative language of documentation. So we might ask for our purposes here, what kind of intersubjective event in language might be activism of/ for those forced outside language? What kinds of performative contradiction would it mobilise but also what modes of complicity with the violences of belonging would it risk? By bearing witness to unwitnessable lives and by mourning unmournable deaths, the silent language of *ŽuC* does not give itself over to a semantic destination, to a proper place either in gender normativity or in the nation-state; it always slips away, into unexpected routes of address-ability. At the same time, it does not revert to pursuing 'pure' models of language and representation or a self-exonerating moralism of non-representation. In effect, it is an unending agonistic 'event of language' (Agamben 1999a: 142) that contests the violences that the mother tongue carries in itself. In this respect, the *ŽuC* catachresis of mourning is to be read as testimony, that is, as an event of language faced with the impossibility of witnessing, and, thus, brought up against the limits of speakability:

> Testimony takes place where the speechless one makes the speaking one speak and where the one who speaks bears the impossibility of speaking in his own speech, such that the silent and the speaking, the human and the inhuman enter into a zone of indistinction in which it is impossible to establish . . . the true witness. (Agamben 1999a: 120)

In Agamben's elaboration of an account of ethical response to biopolitical subjection, testimony emerges from the indistinction between the silent and the speaking, the human and the inhuman, the subject and non-subject. In other words, testimony occurs when 'the "I" stands suspended in this disjunction' (Agamben 1999a: 130). It is through the intertwined processes of subjectivation and de-subjectivation that testimony can arise as bearing witness to the impossibility of witnessing. Testimony, as bearing witness to something that cannot be borne witness to, requires the subject's risking of her own de-subjectivation in language. In providing the witness with the means of responding to another's de-subjectivation, testimony also bears witness to her own expropriation in/by language. The decentred and non-sovereign sense − but also scene − of political subjectivity performed by *ŽuC* is indebted to and enabled by not so much the question of the 'true witness' but rather the aporias of testimony. Ultimately, testimony takes place where the impossibility of speaking becomes a resource for the enabling possibility of address-ability and response-ability, albeit one not easily reducible to the figure of the speaking subject as a paradigmatic figure of sovereign will. What does the *ŽuC* performative silence call for, then? How does its call for response entail the troubled register of the vocal?

Vocal Registers of the Political

The genre of women's public mourning works through the connections among political violence, gender, language, and the body, by exposing the political possibilities in the resignification of memory and mourning. It thus resonates with what Veena Das, drawing on Nadia Seremetakis, calls 'the antiphony of language and silence' (Das 1997; Seremetakis 1991; see also Butalia 2000).[16] The event of 'antiphony', in its suggestive etymological implications of *both* alternate or responsive singing as different soloists and the chorus 'take' the lament from each other (i.e. *instead of*, or *in place of* each other's voice) *and* the counter-vocal (i.e. *against* voice), opens new performative routes of audibility and acoustics through which injustice might be recognised in the collective language of political mourning. It is through thrusting the limits of representation and referentiality that the silence of the *ŽuC* vigils enacts the silent death, that is, the unlamented death, to which are subjected those outside the national or familial demarcations of affective recognition.

For the activists I worked with, in other words, antiphony as a means of call-and-response cannot be dislodged from questions of power. In a context of unevenly distributed figures of strangeness and estrangement, like the one of hierarchical loss precipitated by the breakup of Yugoslavia, the most embattled force of antiphony arises. Here antiphonic response is not premised upon the banality of kinship filiation; its forces of collective authentication and authorisation are short-circuited by fractured communal ties. Antiphony emerges thus as a dissonant performative conduit that contravenes established protocols of reciprocity and referentiality, and is beset with an agonistic politics of difference. Address, transmission, recognition, and responsiveness are rendered contentious, as they are troubled by all those voices left unaddressed and unacknowledged. And so all 'voice' (including, significantly, the voice (*phonê*) of *anti-phoné*, anti-phony) is the provisional, spectral embodiment of a certain order of enunciability and audibility, but is also always already imbued with the multifarious powers of difference and dissonance. In the context we are concerned with here, sonority is a site of simultaneous producing contestation and forming a possibility for responsiveness. This subversive mourning for the unmournable other is a performative occasion that introduces ambivalence, nuance and dissonance to the formulations of 'speaking in one's own voice' that rest on the conventional lexicon of post-war trauma objectification and management. While appropriating the 'voices' and 'silencings' of the others of Serbian nationalism as the site of its solidarity, the activism studied here also mobilises this incommensurable ethico-political complexity and complicity to resist dominant structures of address-ability. In attending to the voice of the other, *ŽuC* enacts the etymology of the Latin *vox*, whereby the voice implies a call, an invocation addressed to the other (Cavarero 2005: 169). The engagement with this troubling but also troubled modality of address-ability is what makes the realm of the vocal, including its silences, political. And this politicised vocal realm is what *ŽuC* activists probe in order to reclaim the *polis* and its affective and political lexicon.

As I have laid out above, silence has been abundantly perceived in Western thought as the passive other of speech and the negative of a voice. And thus, in revisiting silence as the 'other side' of the speaking subject's phallic and colonial constitution, feminist and postcolonial critics have engaged with the suppression of Echo's narrative in appropriations of Ovid's myth. By a divine punishment, Echo is deprived of the ability to articulate a speech of her own, to speak for herself and in an inaugural fashion, but is bound to speak after others repeating their words in an incomprehensible way, as she only reverberates

with the last sounds of utterances. As the sonorous performance of muteness that verbalises the other side of language
by repeating, sending back and also deforming and interrupting the voice of Narcissus as the discourse of the same, Echo
instantiates the designation of the feminine to the realm of the
passive, derivative, and imitative; the realm of the feminised and
colonised, or, in other words, the *in-fans* (speechless) realm of
the gendered subaltern (Spivak 1995: 188). In Spivak's rendition
of the scene between Narcissus and Echo, voiceless Echo figures
the potential undoing of Narcissus's self-absorbedness, the
potential disfiguring of his ego that resounds with the effacement of the other. She is a catachrestic figure as such, one that
has no language proper to itself – deludingly and deridingly
oscillating between silence and voice, while embodying the
disruptive potential of iterability. Echo also becomes the voice
of death and memory, as she bears witness to the vanishing
trace of the speaking subject: 'Echo comes to echo farewell, to
echo the rites of mourning' (Spivak 1995: 184).[17] While clearly
conversing with Levinas, Spivak departs from his account of the
ethical engagement with alterity in criticising his devising of
sexual difference in pre-ontological and pre-discursive terms,
and in illustrating the ways in which dominant ideologies of sex
and gender come to form ethics of difference.

Being inscribed in the economy of patriarchal symbolic order,
as Cavarero also elucidates, the myth of Echo as mere resonance of
man's voice rehearses the feminine predicament vis-à-vis the disembodied rationality of Logos as the Aristotelian *phone semantike*
(signifying/significant utterance) that, in turn, defines human as
zoon logon echon (speaking animal).[18] In Cavarero's account, by
evading the semantic through the vocalic aspect of repetition,
Echo invokes and, at the same time, disrupts the devocalisation
of Logos that accompanies the history of metaphysics. Echo
disorganises the narcissistic circuit of the 'I' by bringing forth the

corporeal reverberation of the other (Cavarero 2005). What is particularly relevant to the enquiry at hand is that Cavarero calls into question the binary of *phonê/Logos* in developing an account of voice's corporeality. In reading Cavarero's *For more than one voice* (2005) in relation and juxtaposition with Loraux's *Mourning Voice* (2002b), Honig probingly puts forth the consequences of such a deconstructive gesture: 'analytically distinguishing *phonê* and *logos*, though useful, misleads us into thinking of *phonê* and *logos* as parallel and distinct logics. What if instead they inspirit and interrupt each other?' (2013: 142).

Like Derrida, Cavarero seeks to overturn the hierarchical oppositions between speech and writing, or the vocal and the semantic. In seeking to redeem the voice, however, Cavarero problematises Derrida's account of the voice as the privileged medium of meaning and his affirmation that metaphysical logocentrism is a phonocentrism. In the framework of his thesis on phonocentrism, Derrida has identified the voice with meta-physics of presence in Western philosophy and culture, while reserving for writing the possibility of destabilising the phono-centric order of metaphysics through the forces of *différance* (1973).[19] Cavarero, however, perceives *phonê*, in its implications for a politics of sexual difference, as the undecidable supplement, or *différance*, of Logos.

Let us recall at this juncture that in Derrida's allegory of the experience of iterative voice in the figure of Echo, Echo does not merely repeat the sovereign voice in any complete and predictable way. She feigns to cite Narcissus, as Derrida puts it; that is, she fabricates and deceives authorship and its rever-berations (DeArmitt 2009). Rather than a mere duplication of the same, then, Echo figures the idiom of the other who, in effect, returns the call and re-appropriates her silenced position of subjugation to evade and trouble the injunction of the law that has constructed her as other by assigning her to the status

of non-speaking herself. In this way, Echo is mobilised to complicate the fixed demarcations that determine the ownership of
the voice in its relation to Logos but also silence. At the same
time, this figure recalls the meaning of critique as an eventful
practice of reiterating but also reclaiming the object of contestation. But what would be the ethico-political consequences of
recounting and calling upon the resonances of voicelessness?
Rather than political disengagement, silence, in *ŽuC* political
activism, amounts to a responsive way of jamming the machine
of normative repetition that makes the political resound with
sovereign Logos. In the words of Staša Zajović: 'It [silence]
means deconstruction; you remain silent, you do not wish to
repeat what they expect you to say' (2013a: 34).

Drawing on my research engagement, the question for me
became how we might tackle the performativity of political
activism, especially the one engaging the register of silent public
assembly as responsiveness to the suppressed voices of others,
without retreating into metaphysics of presence, which would
either devocalise presence or reduce presence to the phono-
centric order. Following Cavarero's pursuit to redeem the voice
in its mutual and potentially disruptive inhabitation with Logos, I
set myself the additional task of redeeming silence as an agonistic
corporeal presence that troubles and, at the same time, inspirits
the dominant Logos of presentability. In the context of *ŽuC*
political subjectivity, the sovereignty of 'presence' is marked and
displaced by presences that are missing and have been relegated
to the abjected fringes of the presentable. As performed in the
ŽuC public assemblies and vigils, presence also assumes the
modality of *becoming* present to one another, and thus emerges
as an occasion of critical relationality, which already relies on
social norms that produce and regulate ontologies. As much as
'presence' can never quite be disengaged from authorised forms of
self-identity and self-sufficiency, it is not always already absorbed

into these normative conceits upon which conventional, logo-centric conceptualisations of the political are premised. Quite the contrary, becoming present and available to one another comes into play as an uneven and agonistic process, one that fundamentally includes being-with others who no longer are due to prevailing regimes of disposability. The *ŽuC* activists' practices of living-on, performed by affirmative declarations such as 'we are here' and 'we are still in the streets', convey a reliance upon, and responsibility to, others who cannot be here, or whose being-here cannot be acknowledged by existing standards of presentability. And so acts of catachrestic 'making present', as performed by *ŽuC*, work to disconcert the terms by which 'presence' and 'presentability' attain their normative force at the expense of the abject and the dissident. This relation to the other's death is what makes activist presence politically possible as an act of responsiveness to the eventness of (non-present, non-representable) others. This is a presence that displaces one's proper speaking self, and one that cannot be encompassed under the register of the voice construed as immediate self-presence. It is drawing on such performative politics of becoming present, as struggle for emergence, that *ŽuC* activists explore the political potentials of voice through what is other or even refractory to it.

What is of special interest here is the ways in which the rethinking of the exigencies of the voice in the context of acts of living-on and being haunted by the past might illuminate the catalytic role that the feminine plays in resonating the relation between speech and the political. In logocentric discourses of politics, silent or vocal articulations that do not conform to the disciplinary semantics of proper language are to be expunged from the lexicon of *polis*. They are to be relegated to the realm of the pre-political or anti-political: either irrelevant or subversive. In that respect, the feminine is denied access to the abstract, rational, and bodiless universality of meaningful language, as it is 'traditionally represented under the sign of a body that only comes to speech through idle chatter' (Cavarero 2005: 207). 'Idle chatter' – as garrulousness, gossip, babbling or mumbling – designates a voice without speech: a nonsensical sound or noise attached to the body and assigned to 'woman'.

This normative casting of feminine voice as a bodily sound rather than meaningful speech is also critically recalled in Nicole Loraux's account of the vocal register of women's lamentation as fraught with dangers and thus either limited to the stage or set apart inside the boundaries of the home. It is by virtue of its 'antipolitical' implication that women's mourning voice, when public, threatens civic order and its enduring conventions of intelligibility. What Loraux calls 'antipolitical' designates the political act that is actively opposed to the established logic of the political; in her words, 'the other of politics, but also another politics' (2002a: 23). In the activism of *ŽuC*, this 'another politics' would be irrevocably affected by the exigencies of responsiveness, and, as such, it would involve a reclaiming of the *polis*.

Some of the activists with whom I interacted complicated the performative practice of public silence and improvised with alternative usages of sound. Nađia Duhaček for one, who, as I have mentioned before, has been interested in enriching and layering the iterability of the movement's devices of public appearance, has become concerned with the activist performativity of sound:

> One of the things that I like about *ŽuC* activism is that we have been technologically upgraded into using sound and this, in fact, captures public attention. This is a way that marks the space of our demonstrations. When you just stand still and silent in a space, it's easy to get ignored, while sound says 'we are here and if you want to ignore us, you have to make quite an effort, you have to walk on us'. I think it's difficult to impose the silence, because if there happens to be a coffee shop playing music next

to our action, or if there's somebody around promoting the new facelift cream with balloons and loud music, our silence and blackness are being lost.

Sound is performative, Nađa insists, and, rather than distracting or attenuating the silence of the *ŽuC* public assemblies and vigils, aural and sonic experience might work to supplement, echo, or transcribe it. Working as an aural antidote to the unstoppable commercial sounds of the city, the affective soundscape of activism would not let activist silence get lost. Collective listening would redefine the space of protest, as Nađa's critical reflection posed. The *ŽuC* experimentation with sound and choir activism is one such example of how the acoustic materiality of the performance space can open up to alternative vocal registers of the political. As we saw in the previous chapter, when Zole and his choir *Proba* joined a *ŽuC* antifascist action in Republic Square, a possibility emerged for mobilising collaboratively composed performative resonances to enact what activist Staša Zajović calls 'aesthetics of resistance'.

Political Performativity between Subjugation and Insurrection

The political genre of mournful silence is by no means without its performative contradictions and ambivalences, as it runs the risk of reinstating gendered clichés of voiceless suffering, prudence, political quietism, or romantic pacifism.[20] Indeed, it entails not only possibilities for political subversion but also the liabilities of renormalisation: notably, the peril of being drawn into the complicity of the observing bystander who essentialises grief reducing it to liberal–legalistic discourses of humanitarian reason. In the current era of mediatised empathy saturation, appropriating affliction has become the prevalent currency of moral(istic) engagement – all too often reduced to sentimental pathos, and all too easily severed from political responsibility.

Indeed, as my interlocutors have often remarked, one should be wary of either reducing silence to inertia and conformity, or romanticising it as a strategy of dissent available to communities marginalised by virtue of class, gender, race, or sexuality. Wendy Brown has alerted us to the possibility that silence, as ostensibly a tool of insurrection, may converge with techniques of subjugation. Adopting a more vehement critical perspective, Mladen Dolar has posited silence as the ultimate and irresistible weapon of the law.[21] In his account, silence is akin to the way in which the law works by not being enforced, as it is depicted, quite famously, in Kafka's parable 'Before the Law', where the always open gate of the castle has immobilising effects on K., 'the man from the country' who stands in a position of exclusion from the law, but an exclusion that is tantamount to being always inside the law. The land surveyor dies from old age waiting outside the gate, learning that this gate was reserved only for him. The subject's perennial exposure to a 'silent' and inactive figure of the law – accessible and impassable, at the same time – has also been implied in Agamben's description of the relation between sovereignty and the state of exception as exclusive inclusion or inclusive exclusion. The law is voiced through its silence, as it were, and this is another reminder of the paradoxical and elusive political status of silence vis-à-vis the force of the law.

As if tacitly heeding Brown's warning that silence 'may feed the powers it meant to starve' (2005: 84), ŽuC activists arduously wrestle with, rather than claim to transcend or resolve, the perils that their political work of mourning entails: especially, the peril of retreating into self-absorbed modes of moral universalism. Nevertheless, they take the risk of engaging in the ambiguous signs of silence and mourning against their normative implications, while remaining acutely mindful of the vicissitudes involved in such engagement. As is arguably the case with any political project of dissent, *ŽuC* wields the tension between its own constitution by sedimented, formative power structures and the ever-present albeit always deferred possibility of performing freedom with others. Thus, aside from participating in, and reformulating, institutionalised and bureaucratised practices of official or juridical restitution and compensation (i.e. rituals of public remembrance and recognition, apology to the victims, national and international trials), they strive to dismantle the sanctioned norms upon which testimonial and empathetic appeals are typically predicated. In so doing, they remain loyal to the demand of justice as a horizon that exceeds the realms of law and moralism.

As they strive to make the embodied practice of silent public standing a performative venue to new and unpredictable modes of agonistic political life, they assume the responsibility, but also the risk, of naming: naming the victims, naming the perpetrators. Providing a unique perspective on the relation between pain, language, and the body, Veena Das has powerfully shown that the act of naming violence constitutes such a challenging endeavour not merely because of the semantic struggles it involves with respect to the fundamental aporias of language and translation in the wake of devastation, but also because such performative utterances have serious political stakes in the lives of victims (2007: 205). But what I find especially incisive about Das's perspective on an ethic of responding to painful utterances and silences is that while she remains attuned to the criticism that emphasis on the victims' suffering might result in the creation of communities of *ressentiment* and popular cultures of voyeurism, she still addresses the question of 'whether a different picture of victims and survivors is possible in which time is not frozen but is allowed to do its work' (2007: 211).[22] Indeed, the

ŽuC activism is provoked by the dilemmas of how to address victimhood without *ressentiment* (Brown 1995: 68), or how to acknowledge unjust disposability and loss without reducing affected subjects and communities to essentialised objects of representation. Any attempt to respond to such unanswerable questions, however, would have to acknowledge that there is no pure and unmediated position from which to pursue critical agency, and thus would have to begin to critically refashion the presumptions of absolute exteriority and strangeness that often insinuate themselves into constructions of otherness in the context of discourses of victimhood.

The conservative biosociality of compassion, which has become central to the moral economies of post-war crisis management and neoliberal universalism, is rife with clichés of victimhood that produce, while also conveying a certain disdain for, 'victimization' (Cole 2006). In such discourses of 'compassion's compulsion' (Edelman 2004), victimhood is constructed around the figure of the 'victim' as an icon of pitiful vulnerability or public pathology, cultural defectiveness, and individual failure, but also as the ideal recipient of philanthropy and object of international humanitarian governmentality (Fassin 2011). The condition of victimhood delineates disciplinary processes through which an ethics of compassion has come to displace a politics of justice in contexts of contemporary Western moral and political economy (Fassin and Rechtman 2009). As Wendy Brown has thoughtfully shown, 'wounded attachments' is a key route for producing and managing essentialised identities by depoliticising and normalising them within 'the history of liberalism's management of its inherited and constructed others' (1995: 56).

Against the backdrop of an overwhelming hegemony of discourses of suffering and trauma in late modern capitalism, *ŽuC* activism deploys the language of victimhood with attention and in ways that open possibilities for public reflection. While this agonistic politics guards against the moralistic and therapeutic calculus of producing injury-based victim identities inhering in liberal discourses of victimhood, it also disengages emphatically from individuating and stigmatising anti-victimhood discourses so prevalent in right-wing social conservatism (Cole 2006). The challenge, then, for the activists with whom I worked, becomes how to depart from the liberal governmentality of victimhood but also, even more significantly, how to counter 'anti-victimism', to use Alyson Cole's term: that is, the trend of renouncing and vilifying victimhood. The challenge of these activists is how to account for subjugated histories of woundedness away from formulations that close and totalise them into fixed identities premised on naturalised injurability, while, at the same time, opposing anti-victim discourse. In a way, this challenge is about reconfiguring the political affects of agonistic politics as response-ability. In a conversation with me, activist Slavica Stojanović articulated specifically the *ŽuC* demand for justice as one differing radically from an incitation to what she called the 'moralism of guilt'. And for Miloš, one of the *ŽuC* activists who have been monitoring trials on war crimes, keeping track of these juridical procedures is a matter of constituting responsiveness to the silenced voices of conventionally archived memory, through 'establishing a relationship with the victims, and opening an alternative space for them'.

The limits of response-ability are laid bare, however, when victimhood is used as an occasion for reaffirming, instead of disrupting, fixed and reified identities, such as those of 'victims' and 'advocates', in contexts of solidarity coalitions. This predicament emerged when Staša recounted a post-war project of inter-ethnic solidarity that went astray:

We were once involved in a project of solidarity with women from Sarajevo here in Belgrade. But some of them seemed to be thinking that it would be always up to us to bear responsibility and up to them to assume the position of the victim. It was this way that our cooperation ended. There would have been possibilities for us to work together if they were willing to stand critically towards their own community as we do towards ours. But they chose to stress ethnic and religious identity. It was an injurious story. For me, solidarity does not mean to close the eyes.

As Staša sees it, solidarity requires critical engagement with power relations, including those that determine the very terms of building solidarity alliances. This is a process, however, that involves a painstaking, and often painful, 'politics of translation' (Spivak 1993, 1998). Spivak conceives of translation as a crucial strategy in mobilising gendered agency and achieving women's 'solidarity', whereby the task, or the responsibility, of the feminist translator is to learn the language of the other, as an act of intimacy and as 'the most intimate act of reading', rather than imposing a notion of solidarity as an a priori given (1998).

In a relevant conversation with me, Adriana Zaharijević referred to the incommensurable complexities that play out in the *ŽuC* deployment of the discourse of victimhood in terms of 'creating dissonance in the realm of what becoming a victim means'. In the context of this activism, the invocation of victimhood prompts something other, more dissonant, than the moralist attitudes of vengeance and rancour. It puts into play the mark of vulnerability, not as a problem to be resolved but as an aporia that propels an impossible yet necessary possibility of passage, or *poros*. It also involves critical engagement with the uneven power relations entailed in distributing, managing, humanising, and feeling for vulnerability. Ultimately, it acknowledges its unintended complicity with the workings of such power relations.

ŽuC activism engages a form of vulnerability that operates as a performative force that allows the event of solidarity to take place. This force of vulnerability, or vulnerable force, is akin to the Benjaminian idea of a paradoxical force without power, 'on which the past has a claim' (2006: 390). In Benjamin's weak messianic thought, as well as in *ŽuC* activism, 'weakness' does not allude to a quantitative logic of reckoning the effectiveness of the performative in terms of an opposition between force and inertia, or between active and passive. Rather, it breaks with this structure and it instead enacts resistance to history's authoritative closure, as a redemptive gesture towards the unrealised, displaced, or refracted potentialities that haunt the ongoing present. Inspired by Benjamin and citing his 'Theses on the Philosophy of History', Derrida has described the 'weak messianic force' in *Specters of Marx*. In Derrida, this force is related to an alternative form of politics that exists and remains as ambivalent and incalculable potential, one which, as Derrida states in another text, 'requires us to calculate' (1992a: 28). This refashioned form of politics is marked by what Derrida considers in *Rogues* as the possibility of a 'vulnerable non-sovereignty' (2005a: 157).

Rather than a definite and definable category of moral economy, then, vulnerability emerges as a critical force of unsettling prevailing conceptions of politics and unjust distributions of life and death. Thus, in all its tensions and dissonances, it becomes a matter of mobilising in a collective political struggle for bringing justice to victims for losses, injuries, and injustices that have not been accounted for. In other words, it becomes a performative venue through which to articulate the promise of memory and redeem the possibility for justice.

Critical Practices of Political Response-ability

'When you have been present in such events, you do not merely feel empathy, rather you are stunned, you are being affected. It is this being-affected that goes together with responsibility.' This is the way in which Adriana illustrated, in a conversation with me, the workings of affective self-deconstitution and reconstitution as a process of assuming responsibility. It is not about producing fixed objects of empathy and it is not even about feeling empathy, she contended, but rather about opening critical spaces for producing intersubjective relations that mobilise complicity, responsibility, and action. Her self-reflective words also tacitly posed the vexing question of proximity or distance, in all their implications of uneven situatedness, which the language of affect often implies, especially in contexts of humanitarian reason but also solidarity alliances: who is being moved, to whom or to what, and who is assumed to be fixed in the position of the object of one's moving and responding? As Sara Ahmed has argued:

> The impossibility of feeling the pain of others does not mean that the pain is simply theirs, or that the pain has nothing to do with me. I want to suggest here, cautiously, and tentatively, that an ethics of responding to pain involves being open to being affected by what one cannot know or feel. (2004: 30)

This ethics is bound up with a certain sociality of vulnerability and responsiveness, whereby the presumption of intimacy with the other's pain risks confirming narcissistic moral claims to know or feel the other's pain, whereas the invocation of distance and inevitable ungraspability risks dissipating the need, or the obligation, to take responsibility and action for justice. Would this line of questioning imply an ontological distinction between the one who assumes responsibility and the one in whose name this responsibility is assumed? Solidarity implies attempts to build coalitions between asymmetrically and unequally situated subjects. How – if at all – is agonistic relationality and response-ability able to critically engage with such incommensurabilities?

Adriana conveyed an activist mode of responsibility not in terms of 'owning' responsibility and thus reverting to the discourse of a proper meaning and agent or proprietor of responsibility, but rather in terms of being captured, or dispossessed, by the eventfulness of an event, whereby the very self-presence and self-ownership of (ethical) subjectivity is provoked and one becomes undone for the other, with the other, and thus mobilised to act for her, with her. Indeed, the question of responsibility permeates the political, legal, and cultural forces that shape public memory and the workings of international and domestic justice in dealing with the aftermath of the wars of Yugoslav succession. Either in the form of dispute over the character of the violence and the number of victims, or over the issue of what counts as appropriate responses to violence, questions of responsibility continue, persistently and passionately, to engage the ways in which the war crimes that were committed under Milošević came to be perceived by the people of Serbia (Gordy 2013a).

Response-ability, for these activists, is indissolubly wrapped up in a gendered critique of war. Like many of her combatants, Saša often framed her rejection of the idea of female patriotism by invoking Virginia Woolf's declaration, from her 1938 essay *Three Guineas*, as war crept nearer: 'As a woman I have no country. As a woman I want no country' (Woolf 1963). In the spirit of Woolf, Saša and I have talked sometimes about the delicate ambivalence implicit in loathing nationalism and militarism, yet being fond of the language, the literature, and the landscape of one's country. Indeed, Saša's biography was entangled in layered affective loyalties, as her disengagement from patriotic fervour had not compromised her affection for Slavonia and her birthplace, although that was located, as she emphasised to me once in a charged tone, near a 'place of genocide', namely, the town of Jasenovac, which became the largest concentration camp complex in the Independent State of Croatia (Nezavisna Hrvatska Drzava, NDH) during World War II.[23] That fraught legacy, as Saša explained to me, has been one of the key forces leading up to her enduring political commitment to antimilitarism, her love for the texts of Virginia Woolf, and her own sense of perennial displacement and disquiet. For Saša, who was so strenuously critical of Serb nationalism and committed to responsiveness to the 'other side', there is a lot at stake in acknowledging Jasenovac as a place where Serbs had been massively tortured and massacred. For her, that was about articulating a critique of the exclusionary regimes of memorability that enable and legitimise military violence. At the same time, for her, affective attachment to a sense of 'a place in the world' (in an Arendtian vein[24]) is not incompatible with critique and dissent from nation-state policy. A sense of a place in the world cannot be reduced to a desire or nostalgia for 'at-homeness'. Thus, the aspect of Saša's biography that was related to the complicated and distressing geography of her birthplace became the fulcrum for exposing herself – and her activist self – to the ethical and political delimitations implicit in the question of whom to remember in this world. For her, feminist unhomeliness and agonistic response-ability to the others of national memory and affection account for her own reclaimed and transgressive worldliness.

Hana Ćopić, who was twelve when the war started, described herself as 'a second-generation from Belgrade', as the families of her parents were from Bosnia – mostly Serbs from her father's side, although the father of her grandmother was Hungarian. Both families were extensively dispersed at the beginning of World War II and after it. 'Some came to Belgrade, some were killed', she pointed out. 'My parents were not talking about the history of their families, but gradually some narratives started forming as my grandmother and my mother were getting older.'

Hana reported that she learned from *ŽuC* 'a new sense of patriotism': 'In *ŽuC*, you learn to love differently your country. And this is a powerful lesson.' This is for her a matter of taking a position beyond the ethnicised apparatus of belonging. It is a matter of remaking the sense of being in the world by means of 'learning how to take counter-positions'.

In Arendt's spirit, the *ŽuC* political action takes up worldliness and, at the same time, revisits and reactivates the givenness of the world, infusing it with a new, unpredictable, and agonistic sense. This is about a political action that propels the notion of collective responsibility beyond the juridical logic of closure and the post-war bureaucracies of managerial and sentimental consensus, which tend to consolidate injurious allocations of recognisability and responsibility. It engages with the 'here and now' of unjust and repressive conditions, by opening the event of acting responsibly to its own contingencies, unresolved ambivalences, and to ongoing sites of struggle. In *ŽuC* enduring political temporality, responsibility remains to come and it is always in the making. Daša Duhaček, a founding member of *ŽuC*, co-founder of the Belgrade Women's Studies Center and Gender Research Center (1992), and Professor of Political Science at the University of Belgrade, has thoughtfully pursued the question of responsibility as a political category in the process of reformulating political subjectivities in Serbia, in the context of dealing with the legacies of the wars of the 1990s (2002, 2006). Drawing on Arendt's work, against the backdrop of Yugoslavia's breakup, Duhaček offers an account that situates responsibility squarely within the political. In this vein, *ŽuC* performs an idiom of citizenship based on the 'making of political responsibility' (Duhaček 2006: 214).

Embodiment and affective attachments are crucial components of this making of common or shared responsibility (Birmingham 2006). Recounting the outset of the movement,

Staša emphasised the crucial importance of responsibility as an affective incentive for political action:

> We felt responsible to do something against the war, to assume a responsibility that we did not own. We started to think that there were alternative, non-armed, ways to resist the war of one's own country. Neda, who had taken part in the armed resistance during the World War II started thinking, with us, alternative ways of resistance.

Staša offers an account of responsibility as transfiguration of resistance, including resistance to the resisting subject's self-presence. As her words conveyed, for these activists, to ask the vexing question of responsibility is how to assume a responsibility that you do not own and yet you claim in response to another's call that remains unheard in the normative conditions of public discourse. In other words, it is to think through a politics that is responsive to the singularity of the inappropriate other in the face of normative matrices of recognition and misrecognition that work to silence the voices of these others. At stake in this activist idiom of citizenship as political responsibility is the way in which contemporary Serbian society commemorates a 'critical event' (Das 1995) of its recent past, whose narrativisings and silencings have been turned into arenas of fierce contestation:

> We demand . . . that the citizens of Serbia confront the recent past and take their share of responsibility for the dishonour to which we were pushed by criminal leaders and defenders of national interests, but also our lack of strong opposition to the evil around us. (Women in Black 2001b)

Hana, who joined *ŽuC* at twenty-three, after the war, shared with me, in a lively conversation, that she was first attracted to the group by their different kind of energy, the serious political work the group was doing, their way of not solving things but dealing with them: dealing with memory, the past, responsibility, and accountability. And dealing with the question what all these mean not just for us, but for others as well.

In Hana's words, these political subjects are neither capable of nor interested in resolving the inner tensions of 'dealing with' memory and responsibility. Rather, they are enmeshed with others, they get injured by others, and they take courage from others: they are always 'to come' (*à venir*, in Derrida's formulation (2005c)), presenting an infinite transformative potential and urging ongoing engagement in the present. For them, engagement implies constitutive disjointedness and responsive openness to others, even before assuming responsibility. In Jean-Luc Nancy's words:

> To be responsible is not, primarily, being indebted to or accountable before some normative authority. It is to be engaged by its Being to the very end of this Being, in such a way that this engagement or *conatus* is the very essence of Being. (2000: 183)

Responsibility is akin to what Nancy calls a 'law without law' (*loi sans loi*). We are always already before this law without law – one that does not offer guidelines or prescriptions as to how, when, and with whom we should act. We are corporeally enmeshed in, and exposed to, it; and this exposure is what unceasingly constitutes our existence as coexistence (*être en commun*).

Indeed, what emerged from my anthropological engagement with talking, living, standing, and marching on the street with my *ŽuC* friends is that, for them, the 'making of political responsibility' lies primarily in the ongoing question of how to respond to those whose loss has been expropriated in injurious ways. Thus, through their public assemblies, they performatively assume responsibility for the wrongs that were committed in their name in the territory of the former Socialist Federal Republic of Yugoslavia. At the same time, they infinitely complicate and recast what is 'assumable' about responsibility, by performing a dis-identification, or a withdrawing, from the Serbian nation-state and by demanding accountability from it. For them, dissenting from the authority of the Serbian nation-state operates as a necessary and determinate basis for constituting responsiveness to those rendered inappropriate addressees by that very authority. The way in which these dissenters affirm responsibility as response-ability works to complicate the assumptions at the heart of 'assuming responsibility'. They thus struggle with such dilemmas: can one ever assume responsibility for the crimes committed in the name of the Serbian nation? What kind of political responsiveness might become possible in the face of law's insufficiency but also in the face of a certain impossibility of justice?[25] And what kind of engagement – albeit partial and imperfect – would we pursue to open responsibility to a radical democratic future?

Douzinas has importantly complicated the political notion of responsibility as responsiveness by stating that 'when responsibility is defined as consent to the commands of power it is not moral; in such cases, the moral attitude is irresponsibility' (2014: 98). Thus, responsibility is not a universal moral principle but rather an ethical commitment to dissent as 'irresponsibility of struggle' (ibid.). In this regard, it is also worth recalling here that, opposing the concept of responsibility as inevitably contaminated by the juridical domain, Agamben has introduced the idea of non-responsibility, which indicates 'a confrontation with a responsibility that is infinitely greater than any we could ever assume. At the most, we can be faithful to it, that is, assert its unassumability' (1999a: 21).[26] Echoing Derrida's notion of justice as the infinite and incalculable movement that exceeds the calculability and constant 'inadequation' of the law (1992a: 20), Agamben poses a stimulating challenge to moral regimes premised on the calculable determination of responsibility. As Derrida has made clear, however, the 'impossibility of justice' does not preclude the possibility or, in fact, the necessity to pursue struggles to improve the law. Quite to the contrary, justice in its impossibility 'is what gives us the impulse, the drive, or the movement to improve the law, that is, to deconstruct the law' (1997a: 16). Incalculable justice is at the same time impossible and urgently necessary, as 'incalculable justice *requires* us to calculate' (Derrida 1992a: 28, emphasis in the original). Accordingly, unassumability is not a sufficient reason for not assuming responsibility, but rather the very condition of possibility for assuming responsibility. As Derrida writes: 'the condition of possibility of this thing called responsibility is a certain *experience and experiment of the possibility of the impossible: the testing of the aporia* from which one may invent the only *possible invention, the impossible invention* (1992b: 41, emphasis in original). In this sense, ethics and politics can exist only on condition that the experience of aporia, as the only possible experience, is acknowledged. Indeed, how can we assume ethical and political responsibility except by means of persistently recasting, reworking, and testing this aporia?

Taking up the conception of an unassumable or imputable responsibility through this prism of the 'possibility of the impossible', then, I would like to suggest that *ŽuC* activists assume precisely what is unassumable about responsibility. What is at stake here is a certain distribution of assumability and unassumability in responsibility, whereby the latter requires, according to Derrida (with Levinas), the act of responsiveness. These activists assume responsibility, in all its contingency and contestability, not as juridical culpability nor even as a regulatory principle, but as 'the ability to respond', in Gloria Anzaldúa's words (1987:

20–1).[27] And this is an ability that one does not simply own, but invents and assumes as a performative *experience and experiment of the possibility of the impossible* (Derrida 1992b: 41).

Such ethical passion of response based on the 'making of political responsibility', to reiterate Duhaček's phrase, raises urgent questions concerning the implications of responsiveness for agonistic configurations of the political. From the outset, these activists call for response-ability to be mobilised as a relational category and as an incalculable resource for politics. They are called into responsibility while remaining aware that the very possibility of responsiveness, understood as an incalculable disposition toward others and with others, is conditioned by contingent and contestable power configurations through which we come to respond to each other. They are themselves formed and marked by such histories of subjection and agency. Through their own war-scarred biographies that implicate lives and stories of others, and through their activist public appearances with other bodies, these political subjects dissolve categorical distinctions between victim, survivor, witness, and activist, as several of these activists are not situated in either position alone, but inhabit various intersections, interstices, and inextricable relations to one another. They come to be *with* others and *as* others. Here, the encounter with the other exceeds the grammar of the third person. It also requires a change in the status of the first-person speaking subject (Blanchot 1995: 25), as it radically departs from moralistic constructions of self-owning and self-sufficient moral subjects who 'choose' to take responsibility for others. In examining the narrative dimension of nationalist narcissism, Butler has addressed the necessity to find another possibility of language, a possibility for 'a decentering of the narrative "I" within the international political domain' (2004: 6–7). This 'other possibility' would summon up a language performed by the very passage from the proper place – or, the *home* – of the mother tongue to the improper languages of nomadic response-ability. Thus, not letting itself be caught by formal and fixed preconditions of self-grounding representation and third-person othering, the *ŽuC* agonistic performativity opts for the indeterminate and disruptive potentials of responsiveness, whereby speaking is always 'the speaking of a stranger through and as oneself' (Butler 1993: 241–2).

The performativity of provisional belonging and responsive disposition might figure a deconstituting possibility in the apparatus of moral narcissism that occasionally characterises the activist self. These activists' articulation of responsibility lies with the decentring (rather than self-centred presence) of sovereign subjectivity, and thus runs counter to the liberal-legalistic model of liability as based on a contract that reified, individual subjects willingly devise and adopt. The critique to perceptions of political subjectivity as invulnerable and irresponsive self-mastery carries with it enormous political consequences in opening a way to appreciate 'how a theory of subject formation that acknowledges the limits of self-knowledge can serve a conception of ethics and, indeed, responsibility' (Butler 2005: 19). We are thus led to recognise that responsiveness is made possible from the impossibility of a complete, immediate, and transparent 'giving an account of oneself' (Butler 2005). The political work of *ŽuC* sets responsibility to work as responsiveness 'to a call (or something that seems to us to resemble a call) that cannot be grasped as such' (Spivak 1994: 22). Premised upon an awareness of another, who might seem or remain ungraspable, the response to her call does not require and, as a matter of fact, escapes technologies and languages of cognitive mastery. As Butler's and Spivak's important engagements with Levinasian ethical subjectivity have made amply clear, the call of the other precedes, and pre-emptively constitutes, the subject's knowledge and self-knowledge. It arouses one to awareness as it calls one in question. It is this fraying of ego – this undoing of the norms that call subjects into being – that enables engagements with the political in its being affected by the irreducible ambivalences of intimacy and responsiveness.

In accounting for strategies of silencing that are at work in the 'theaters of responsibility' operative in capitalist policies, Gayatri Chakravorty Spivak is concerned with the foreclosure of the ethical singularity of subaltern subjects and voices of the global South by dominant, seemingly self-transparent and benevolent, structures of responsibility and representation (1999: 61). In this context, she maintains that '(the thinking of) responsibility is also a (thinking of) contamination' (ibid., p. 23). She thus valuably draws attention to a certain complicity with the epistemic and political logic that produces and, at the same time, effaces the other. But it is precisely this acknowledgment of fundamental epistemic and ethical complicity with the logic that the labour of critique seeks to contest that becomes, in Spivak's deconstructive ethics of critique, the inevitable and enabling condition for assuming critical practices of ethical responsibility to another as an ethics of the impossible (Spivak 1999: 309; see also Morton 2003: 41). In this realm of deconstructive critique of responsibility, then, complicity and radicality retain a relation of undecidable performative dialectics. It is this undecidable cartography of agonism that the responsive politics of *ŽuC* creates.

Silence as an Event in Language

In the political work of *ŽuC*, contingent possibilities and impossibilities of responding to injustices require the invention of another mode of language, or a mode other than proper language. The agonistic silence that marks the movement's public appearances is to enact such possibility for a political language motivated by responsiveness. This performative silence neither relies on, nor lays claim to, an immediate, not discursively mediated reality. Such a perception would entail a neo-vitalist assumption of affectivity as a sort of immanent somatic force that escapes the order of utterability, discourse, signification, and representation. The agonistic silence of these activists, however, performatively exceeds the sharp split between discourse and affect (Glynos and Stavrakakis 2003; Laclau 2003, 2004). As I suggested earlier in this chapter, there is nothing unmediated and uncontaminated about silence, as it necessarily draws on, and partakes of, existing discursive conditions and signifying conventions. Instead of instantiating an ostensible prevalence of sensation and affect over subjectivity and discourse, the activist silence at hand embodies a postfoundational political articulation that intervenes in, under-mines, disarticulates, and transforms the hegemonic milieu. At the same time, it is not reducible to a mere 'articulation of demands' (Laclau 1990, 2005), although this might be part of its contingent and precarious performative effects.[28] As a demand that can never be fully 'satisfied', Laclau's trope of 'demand' is a powerful device to explain important aspects of radical democratic politics, precisely because such an understanding of articulatory signifiers as 'irrepresentable' in mainstream terms keeps the potential of political articulation and re-articulatory agency open and the processes of social subjectivation always deferred. In this light, it might be worth underscoring that 'demand' is not to be reduced to merely a rhetorical operation or verbal persuasion. Rather, the 'demand', in a generalised form, exceeds the scope of its utterance, and Laclau's overall work has surely enabled such a multilayered and wide-ranging account of radical democratic articulatory practices. Butler makes a similar point when she criticises Althusser's scheme of interpellation: as useful as it is, she argues, it 'restricts the notion of interpellation to the action of a voice'. And she suggests: 'Interpellation must be dissociated from the figure of the voice in order to become the instrument and mechanism of discourses whose efficacy is irreducible to their moment of enunciation' (Butler 1997b: 32).

Accordingly, in accounting for the disruptive configurations that defy capture into, and are expelled by, the totalising calculus of representation, the affectively invested agonistic silence of *ŽuC* – occasionally punctuated by written and uttered slogans, watchwords, and rallying cries – further complicates the horizon of all verbal and non-verbal political articulation and representability. This agonistic silence, avowing and mobilising a co-constitutive entanglement of discourse and affect, responds to that which is as-of-yet unspeakable and unhearable. Such pursuit of instituting alternative idioms that are more hospitable and less harmful than established discursive matrices of articulation, does not pertain only to the activists' public appearances but also to an overall sociality of living otherwise. As such, it was inscribed in the words of Miloš, a queer *ŽuC* activist, during an interview: 'When I say "I love you" to another man, I feel that a prohibited language emerges (*jedan zabranjeni jezik ponovo rađa*): a language that somehow exists but cannot be heard.' Miloš's affectionate address to his lover, made possible against all odds in a context unfavourable and inhospitable to such intimacy, exceeds what can be presently phrased and heard, and thus defends and institutes an idiom that counters the dominant domain of speakability and audibility. This new language of intimacy does not evade the public but rather constitutes one.

In the public politics of *ŽuC*, silence, as a performative language of response-ability, can never be one with itself. It is akin neither to a pre-discursive, ahistorical speechlessness, nor to a sublime metalanguage lying beyond speech and above history. It does not exist outside language and it is not a negation of speech. It does not entail quietness, stillness, or peace, for that matter. It instead emerges as an inchoate, historically minded enactment of language speaking of its own (im)possibility and thus rendering crisis into the tacit presuppositions of normative discourses. It is a disquieting politics and poetics that performs the simultaneous commitment to saying the unsayable and unsaying the sayable. In addressing the violence involved in the national and international production of memorable lives and deaths, *ŽuC* activists are summoned to assume response-ability but also to cope with the very limits of the available languages of responsibility, as they are haunted by disavowed violence and injustice.

As I have elaborated in the course of this chapter, the silent performance of *ŽuC* is calibrated to convey the aporetic possibility of responsiveness and answerability beside, beneath, and beyond authorised matrices of un/speakability and im/memorability. The violence afflicted by 'their own' national intimates remains, for these activists, an 'unclaimed experience' (Caruth 1996) that opens up a possible niche for producing new nodes of resistance as 'response-ability'. The latter becomes a performative occasion from where to ask who can speak and who cannot speak, who can be heard or cannot be heard, who speaks on behalf of others and who speaks to and with others, who cannot avail herself of an audible voice in the face of incommensurable injustice, and, finally, what eventualities in language would response-ability require. In all, *ŽuC* feminist and antinationalist politics of mourning-otherwise gives us a sense of the aporia between speaking and the unspeakable, between bearing witness and the impossibility of testimonial speech, between contestation and vulnerability. Their practices provoke the possibility of acknowledging the 'not-yet' at the heart of the very political praxis of response-ability for those socially instituted as not response-able within available and authorised idioms. This is, indeed, the eventuality that the disquieting silence of *ŽuC* articulates and makes us listen to.

Notes

1 See <http://www.zenskisud.org/en/o-zenskom-sudu.html> (last accessed 19 August 2015).
2 Women in Black Statement, available at <http://www.womeninblack. net/stats/wibart.html> (last accessed 2 September 2005).
3 The intersection of the 'beyond' and the 'beside' is crucial to the performative grammar I have been describing here. Eve Sedgwick has brilliantly alerted us to the non-dualistic and non-linear modalities of thought enabled by the preposition *beside* (2003: 8). In turn, Homi Bhabha has theorised the condition, or the method, of dwelling 'in the beyond': 'to reinscribe our human, historic commonality; to touch the future on its hither side. In that sense, then, the intervening space "beyond" becomes a space of intervention in the here and now' (1994: 7). Following these reflections, both 'beyond' and 'beside' destabilise the pre-given exteriority/interiority binary.
4 In the same vein of silent protesting, and at the same time as the vigil of the Silent Sentinels, a silent march of about 10,000 African Americans on 28 July 1917, in New York City, protested lynching and anti-black violence. Organised by W. E. B. Du Bois and the National Association for the Advancement of Colored People, the Silent Parade was one of the first public demonstrations for black civil rights.
5 The characteristic practice of silence is not to be understood literally and is not always documented. I recall a demonstration vibrant with slogans, voices, and songs that was staged in August 2005 by the Israeli chapter of Women in Black (with Palestinian and international participants, among which members of *ŽuC*), in Bi'iln, a village of the occupied West Bank, against the occupation of Palestine and the erection of a separation wall. However, the protests carried out in those days at Kalandia, one of the strictest military checkpoints established by the Israeli government in order to control the traffic between Ramallah and the divided city of Jerusalem, were silent.
6 Ever since the initial call for ethnographies of communication (Hymes 1962) and Basso's hypothesis about universal conditions of silence behaviour (1970), a wide array of anthropological work has explicitly addressed the problem of anthropological description when this description reaches its verbocentric limit and encounters the voiceless, the unspeakable, and the inaudible. In the context of the anthropology of the Mediterranean and the cultural complex of 'honour and shame', whereby silence was taken to be a social expression of female seclusion and submissiveness,

reticent or non-verbal forms of resistance have been traced in women's social performances of pain and suffering. Anna Caraveli has documented women's ritual lamentation as a non-lexical communicative event of defiance against circumstances of patriarchal dependency on the island of Crete (1986); Nadia Seremetakis has pointed to women's political use of the affective-performative force of mourning in Inner Mani (1991); and Michael Herzfeld has examined the ironic and inchoate role of the dialectics of silence and garrulousness in the rural Cretan poetics of womanhood (1991). In such ethnographic treatments, women redeploy ambiguously silent comportment in order to deflect and deflate their socially ascribed muteness. The spatial, political, affective, and sexual division of labour into male oratory/rhetoric and female mourning/reticence has occupied an emblematic position in the anthropology of the Mediterranean (Tapper 1987). In other ethnographic contexts, silence has been documented as a strategic means of resistance against the powerful, as when Western Apache men employ it to disconcert white outsiders (Basso 1979). Occasionally, the strategically manoeuvred shift between directness and reticence becomes a communicative device of contesting authorised linguistic forms, as when women in Mendi of New Guinea actively participate in informal discussions, but listen in silence at formally performed, male-dominated meetings (Lederman 1984).

7 Susan Gal has usefully drawn attention to the flaws of the formulation of women's 'mutedness' (Ardener 1975), by insisting that we must focus not on 'mutedness' per se as a static reflex of structural inferiority, but rather on 'the processes by which women are rendered "mute" or manage to construct dissenting genres and resisting discourses' (Gal 1991: 190).

8 A major theme of Derridean deconstruction (1981), phallogocentrism denotes privileging masculine signifying economy in the construction of meaning, which is a structural feature of Western metaphysics. The centrality of *phallus* and *Logos* (as well as phallus *as* Logos) as privileged sites of power plays a fundamental role in the authorisation of heteronormative matrix (Butler 1990), in which the discourse of normative sexuality constitutes and reinforces the status of heterosexuality as natural, original, normal, unmarked, authentic, and viable. Phallogocentrism systematically reduces sexuality to reified and dichotomous ontological categories of active and passive, with clear indications of (active) masculine and (passive) feminine, as well as (active) speech and (passive) silence.

9 'If there is a kind of "proof" of the sincerity of the *parrhesiastes*, it is his *courage*. The fact that a speaker says something dangerous – different from

what the majority believes – is a strong indication that he is a *parrhesiastes*' (Foucault 2001: 15, emphasis in original).

10 The Belgrade Circle was established in Belgrade, in February 1992, as a forum of critical intellectuals opposed to the militarist and nationalist policies of Slobodan Milošević. In the course of the war and disintegration of socialist Yugoslavia, the organisation formed links with like-minded groups and NGOs in other former Yugoslav republics. More specifically, it fostered ties of political friendship with Bosnia and Herzegovina. Members of the groups visited Sarajevo, Mostar, and Tuzla several times during the war, bombing, and occupation. In the period 1992–5, the Belgrade Circle conducted a series of 'Saturday sessions' – public lectures by intellectuals from all former Yugoslavia republics and abroad. Those public gatherings encapsulated the spirit of the group's motto: the 'other Serbia' (i.e. citizens who did not side with the militarist nationalist regime). See <http://www.belgradecircle.org/> (last accessed 23 October 2016).

11 This resonates with what Dimitris Vardoulakis calls 'agonistic monism' (forthcoming), in the context of thinking democracy in agonistic terms, that is, as being involved in a continuous struggle with sovereignty. By agonistic monism, he understands both the ontological condition whereby existence is always a 'being with', and the political insight that democracy is the only constitution and all others are its effects.

12 Such conceptualisation of the political courage of dissent complicates the public–private split as it commonly structures understandings of dissent as courageous political engagement. This split is also present in the way in which Hannah Arendt relates courage to 'leaving one's private hiding place and showing who one is, in disclosing and exposing one's self' (1998: 186).

13 The phrase 'jolted out of their torpor' is from Marina Akhmatova's 'Requiem', <http://www.poemhunter.com/poem/requiem/> (last accessed 20 August 2015).

14 See Agamben 1999a. Also, in her meditation on Claude Lanzmann's film *Shoah* (1985), a film about the witnessing of the Holocaust, Felman considers the unspeakable confession that reverberates throughout the testimonies presented in the film, in the reticence of the Holocaust survivors, who have continued to be 'the bearers of the silence', as though they keep the secrecy of contemporary history. The whole effort of the film, Felman argues, is to cinematically bear witness to this movement between being silenced and retrieving the living voice (Felman and Laub 1992: xix).

15 For an elaboration on witnessing as that which remains from the elimination of the witness, see Agamben 1999a: 34.

16 Seremetakis (1991) delineates the gendered poetics of the body involved in women's labour of lamenting in the male-dominated social order of Inner Mani, southern Greece. Antiphony is the embodied genre of gendered mourning and witnessing that Seremetakis has described as a performative alternation between sound and silence as well as between the individual lamenting subject and the present audience qua community.

17 See also Agamben 1991 and Cavarero 2005. The metaphor of the echo as mutual transposition of silence and resonant voice has also a place in Lacan's consideration of the voice as an embodiment of the psychoanalytic object: the *objet petit a*, which is the object-cause-of-desire. In a reflection about the voice, Lacan elaborates on the physiology of the ear, paying special attention to the acoustic topology, which consists in the form of a cavity, a void; the voice resonates in the void that is the void of the other – the other as a void. Voice takes place as its own echo returning from the other. See Lacan 2004. For a reading of Lacan's reference to the voice, but also an insightful story of the voice in psychoanalysis, see Dolar 2006.

18 For the definition of *Logos* as *phone semantike*, see Aristotle, *Poetics*, 1457a5–30 (Aristotle 1941); for the definition of human as *zoon logon echon*, see Aristotle, *Politics*, 1253a9–19 (Aristotle 1941).

19 According to Derrida's critique of phonocentrism, the primacy of speech and the reduction of writing to a secondary or derivative status is not a natural human attribute, but the result of a metaphysical and historical privileging of voice as presence. The assumption that a unitary subject and a unitary meaning are present in speech is one of the main objects of deconstruction. *Différance*, a word homophonous with *difference* but denoting both 'to defer' and 'to differ', points to the heterogeneous elements that permeate the production of meaning as deferred and differentiated.

20 Such stereotyped perceptions of silence have been famously described in Abbé Dinouart's pamphlet *L'art de se taire* (1771). The fervent supporter of the Church posits the art of keeping silent as an ethical weapon against the overflow of speech in the century of the Enlightenment. For a reading of Dinouart's ethics of silence, see Dolar 2006.

21 Dolar discusses the question of silence in Kafka's short stories 'Before the Law' and 'The Silence of the Sirens'. See 'Kafka's Voices', in Dolar (2006: 171).

22 See also Das and Nandy 1985.

23 The Jasenovac extermination camp (1941–5), operated by the Croatian Ustashe regime during World War II, had been among the largest camps in Europe. The majority of victims were ethnic Serbs, along with Jews,

dissident Croatians, and Roma. The camp was abandoned in April 1945, when, after a prisoners' uprising, the Ustashe killed the remaining prisoners and destroyed the structures in the camp. When the Partisans entered the camp, they encountered ruins and the remains of victims. At the beginning of the 1990s, the numbers of people murdered at Jasenovac became a subject of heated political dispute between conflicting nationalist projects. Prior to the breakup of Yugoslavia, the Croatian side suggested substantially smaller numbers than those indicated in a report commissioned in 1945 by Tito. Serbian officials and scholars, however, wielded Jasenovac as a symbol of Serbian suffering and victimhood during World War II, and claimed that the figures of victims had been suppressed by Tito's government, in the name of the 'brotherhood and unity' principle. Jasenovac is a place evincing a fractured and divided realm of remembrance. With Yugoslavia's breakup, the memorial to World War II atrocities split as well, and each side started remembering events differently.

24 Arendt appropriates the concept of 'a place in the world' from Heidegger and develops it in *The Human Condition* (1998). In her overall political thought, the concept of 'world' is linked to her reflections on common responsibility and the 'right to have rights'.

25 No justice is possible, writes Derrida, without the principle of responsibility before those who are 'victims of wars, political or other kinds of violence, nationalist, racist, colonialist, sexist, or other kinds of exterminations, victims of the oppressions of capitalist imperialism or any of the forms of totalitarianism' (1994: xix).

26 Maurice Blanchot has also addressed the limits of responsibility and its language in the face of disaster: 'That is why responsibility is itself disastrous – the responsibility that never lightens the Other's burden (never lightens the burden he is for me), and makes us mute as far as the word we owe him is concerned' (1995: 27).

27 This conception of responsibility resonates also with Kelly Oliver's account of an ethics of witnessing as response-ability (2001).

28 Laclau has adapted Gramsci's concept of articulation as the configuration of equivalences between different, perhaps even contradictory, unfulfilled demands (2005). In Laclau's work, 'articulation' constitutes a distinct theoretical and political idiom through which to elaborate that discursive formations cannot be taken as unified and self-contained totalities, but rather as contingent, differential, and 'penetrated by a basic instability and precariousness' (1990: 109), and thus susceptible to the possibilities and political strategies of re-articulation. The articulation of a 'demand',

meaning 'request' or 'claim', occupies a crucial position in this perspective: a particular demand that emerges to represent a chain of equivalence and becomes the inscription of all others marks a strategy of hegemonic construction (1996). In Laclau's work on radical democratic populist politics, the unity of a political group – that does not amount to some fixed and pre-established homogeneity but, on the contrary, is itself the outcome of discursively embedded struggles for hegemony – is 'the result of an articulation of demands', which 'present claims to a certain established order' (2005: ix). In their transition from 'requests' to 'claims', 'demands' create a broader space for a plurality of equivalential relations between disparate political actors.

Epilogue: Agonistic Re-Membering of the Political

Throughout the pages of this book, I have been concerned with the performative power implicit in transforming mourning's impossibility into an incalculable and unquantifiable political potentiality, capable of deconstituting the interpellating terms of conventional mourning that are posed by state-nationalist authoritarianism. I have asked how we might understand the politics of contested grievability as a means to refigure agonistic political subjectivity beyond sovereign accounts of agency. I explored these themes by exploring how the feminist and anti-militarist political collectivity *Women in Black* (*Žene u Crnom*) in post-Yugoslavia turns mourning from a proper 'feminine language' into a political performativity critically engaging with the intelligibility of the memorable and its gendered, ethno-national, and militarist configurations.

One of the principal theoretical questions of this book has centred on how this feminist collective, in standing within and against the contexts of nationalism and war, politically wields the possibility of impossible mourning. Differently put, what is at stake is how the conditions of possibility and impossibility set mourning, in all its performative contradiction and undecidability, into motion. The im/possible work of mourning, in its crucial reliance upon the question of 'what the other we have

Srdjan Veljovic, *Women in Black, Republic Square, Belgrade, 2011.*

lost has been to us' (Deutscher 1998: 159), furnishes a sense of *common*, and yet decidedly *uncommon*, susceptibility to loss as a necessarily political experience. It affirms and at once displaces the infinite fusion of divisibility and sharedness that is the mark of finitude. As such, it is about both the impossibility of being one with oneself and the radical corporeal precariousness of being as being-with (Nancy 2000).

As much as these activists' stance is about tracing the incalculable political possibilities of mourning (rather than about counting the dead), it is also, significantly, about acknowledging the interminably unattainable possibilities of mourning. As Derrida had made clear, the affirmation of mourning affirms the impossible (1989). The enduring practice of counter-memory that I have been engaging here implies the awareness that an adequate restitution is impossible: those obliterated by public memory are not appropriable by authorised technologies of representation, recuperation, and recollection. This is the aporetic structure upon which mourning relies: the condition of its possibility is inextricably linked to the condition of its impossibility. Indeed, aporia denotes an affirmative experience of the impossible as indeterminate becoming-possible. It has to do less with passing or surpassing than with non-passive endurance and passionate work on limits (Derrida 1993: 14–15). We might say in this regard that *ŽuC* agonistic mourning, as it performatively attends to the call of the unmournable other, affirms what escapes affirmation. The political work of agonistic mourning that is at the heart of my interlocutors' lived experiences is always becoming-possible – instead of possible as a purely opposite of the impossible (Derrida 2005e: 91). *ŽuC* political anamnesis, in affirming the enduring commemoration of those obliterated by public memory, affirms also the im/possibility of mourning, not as a reconcilable contradiction, but as an interminable event: one which marks a structure of temporality that involves calling the normalising ordinariness of the past and the present into question.

Here we are therefore in a time and space where the notion of the impossible is not to be conceived as negative or impossible *tout court* vis-à-vis the possible, and the possible is not to be conceived as purely positive. Questioning the normative frames that regulate what kinds of losses are authenticated to interpellate witnessing, as *ŽuC* does, does not necessitate reiterating an uncritical account of witnessing as transparent truth-telling; nor is it reduced to making concessions to the protocols of state-sponsored memorialisation (Feldman 2004). It is the very breakdown of witnessing, and also the acknowledgement of this breakdown, that can produce a transformational archive – an archive open to new possibilities for change. Furthermore, in order to be able to tell a different story and create another domain of memorability, those who have been previously injured or jettisoned by established regimes of memory need to transform not only the terms that made possible the inflicted violence but also the terms of remembering and witnessing.

As they mourn impossibly, these activists provide an alternative account of political agonism, one that desists from taking sovereignty – of subject, law, language, memory, grief, and so on – as an absolute presupposition for politics, but also from reverting to the metaphysics of a pure political space outside sovereignty. Thus, attending to these activists' practices, I have sought to account for the possibility of non-sovereign political agency: a notion of critical agency that is not bound to an antecedent sovereign self, attributable to the individual's internal possession, or reducible to intentional self-expression and will. Instead, this notion of critical agency remains interminably immanent to power, socially involved, formed, and compromised. It is at once finite and contingent, potent and vulnerable, powerful in its powerlessness, destituted of its sovereign status:

a modality of sovereignty without sovereignty, and yet always parasitised by it. Occasionally, it becomes other than masterful and indivisible sovereignty, even taking the risk of re-inscribing its logic by means of resisting it.

Thus, critical agency emerges out of this undecidable resist-ability, as an iterable remainder (in Derrida's notion of trace and *restance*) that is never fully present and cannot be subsumed into the normalising matrices of representation and repetition, including the necessary possibility of representability and repeatability that constitutes memory. 'Trace', writes Derrida, 'inscribes in itself the reference to the specter of something else' (2005d: 151). His notion of *restance*, accordingly, indicates the enduring non-present(ational) excess of iterability, which resists appropriation and totalising closure (1988). Articulated for our purposes here, critical agency alludes to what resists and remains inappropriable in memory and thus infinitely challenges the established and iterable realms of memorability. It is precisely this spectral remainder – neither entirely transcendent nor fully embodied as self-present according to the ghost's distinctive ambivalence – that is the indispensable condition of grievability. It is this spectral remainder that is also at work in the contin-gent realm of agonism, conceived in its double valence of *agon* and agony.

As a response to the agonies and injuries imposed by power, agon (in the sense of dispute and struggle) is not about a fully present and realisable event of transcending or overturning power. Rather, it indicates a precarious exercise of subjectivation and de-subjectivation, which haunts, while remaining haunted by, the normalising constraints of power but also the absent presences of other, de-realised subjectivities. Simultaneously con-stituted and constituting, complicit and disengaged, this exercise in subjectivation and de-subjectivation within fields of power strives to subvert regimes of subjection, and, at the same time, risks reproducing and re-enhancing powerlessness. As Judith Butler has shown, in reading Foucault's theory of subjection, to be constituted by and embedded in productive power does not mean to be completely determined by it (1995: 46). Butler attributes to practices of discontinuity and disidentification the possibility to destabilise entrenched terms of subjection and to enact alternative modes of subjectivity (1993). Produced by the non-teleological and incomplete process of the subject's attachment to power, this spectral remainder indicates what remains and persists as a continuous challenge to the ontological claims that govern intelligibility. This is the point of departure for thinking ethical and political potentiality beyond the essentialised and self-contained, sovereign individual. Complicating and perhaps disjointing such claims of sovereignty is a constitutive component of the performativity at work in the spectral remainders of ongoing, incomplete, and imperfect subjectivation.

The critical conception of agonism as what remains a constitutive troubling force, or a spectral challenge, is akin also to how Foucault has theorised agonism in terms of a continuous relationship with power, as a possibility for a 'permanent provocation'. As he writes in his definitive essay 'Subject and Power':

> The relationship between power and freedom's refusal to submit cannot, therefore, be separated. . . . Rather than speaking of an essential freedom, it would be better to speak of an 'agonism' – of a relationship which is at the same time reciprocal incitation and struggle; less of a face-to-face confrontation which paralyzes both sides than a permanent provocation. (1982: 790)

As Foucault abandons the war model for understanding power, while maintaining his critique of the juridical model of sovereignty, he posits 'the relationship between power and freedom's refusal to submit' in terms of mutual susceptibility and ongoing struggle.

If Foucault has proposed agonism as a means to pose the question of resistance and its immanence to power, Chantal Mouffe deploys an agonistic framework to situate dissent at the centre of democratic governance and the political space, in contrast to Habermasian deliberative democracy, which focuses on consensus. Mouffe has proposed 'agonistic pluralism' to present a way to think about democracy that is alternative to the liberal deliberative conception of democracy as a rational negotiation among interests and as a managerial overcoming of particular interests for the purpose of achieving consensus. As a relation between legitimate 'adversaries' rather than enemies, agonism is fundamental to democratic politics, whereby collective passions are channelled through common symbolic spaces in ways that keep democratic contestation alive and operative while keeping the political from transforming into reaction and war. In Mouffe's thought, agonism is a means to indicate the complexity of power relations and the contentious character of political space (2000). This is about a vision of agonistic politics that partly resonates with and partly departs from an Arendtian account of public space as an agonistic place, where plurality and common action can occur as constitutive of the political. Mouffe takes the political to be concerned with the Schmittian distinction between friend and enemy, although she breaks with Schmitt's anti-pluralist politics in reformulating the category of 'enemies' into 'adversaries' – 'legitimate enemies' (1999: 755) – who share minimal liberal-democratic principles of liberty and equality (2000, 2005). For Mouffe, the Arendtian conception of the political neglects and neutralises the element of antagonism in favour of envisaging the public sphere as a place where consensus can be ultimately achieved. In response to this, Mouffe acknowledges the ineradicable character of antagonism and the hegemonic nature of every form of consensus in politics. In this regard, there can be no pluralism without the constitutive role of radical contestation. The latter, however, is but one of the aspects of agonism, according to Mouffe; the second aspect importantly involves the configuration and institution of new hegemonic articulations: 'a profound transformation of the existing power relations and the establishment of a new hegemony' (2005: 52). This transformation, in Mouffe, recognises the impossibility of a final reconciliation and the dangers of a moralistic, pacified administration (2005: 59).

One might ask, with Mouffe, questions such as: Would converting or translating antagonistic enmity into adversarial agonism (2000: 103) not be a way of limiting confrontation and, as such, conducive to an administrative logic akin to deliberative liberal configurations? Aren't the overarching, non-negotiable 'ethico-political principles' (1999: 755) that are required for agonistic democratic coexistence anchored on a consensus-oriented provisional hegemony? What kinds of political subjects do count — and recognise themselves — as 'legitimate opponents' (2000: 102), how is this 'legitimation' determined, and how does the concern with it not reinstate a juridical conception of politics? Indeed, such questions notwithstanding, Mouffe's conception of the political has contributed greatly to theorising the reinvigoration of the constitutive potential for dissent that is not absorbed and dissimulated by a politics impelled by the nexus of antagonistic enmity and depoliticised, post-political reconciliation — both discursive formations particularly salient in the post-Yugoslav space. Her idea of agonistic engagement as adversarial confrontation might allow us to understand how *ŽuC* agonistic politics imagines and generates an alternative to the above formations. In the aftermath of a war that turned 'neighbours' into 'strangers' and 'enemies', these activists spec-tralise the conventional friend/enemy distinction in occupying the subject position of the 'internal enemy', which has been bestowed upon them as a stain of disgrace. They thereby enact a democratic form of agonistic contestation that spectralises the distinction between abjection and agency.

The understanding of agonistic agency is inextricably connected to the understanding of relations of power, conflict, and domination. It is in this regard that Mouffe criticises Hannah Arendt's view of the political that, in insisting on a political that equates with intersubjective being in a 'world in common', it analytically neglects the realities of domination, coercion, and violence, and it eludes the constitutive role of antagonism as the defining and ineradicable feature of the political. Despite Mouffe's justified critique of Arendt's resistance to the element of division, however, it would be overly hasty to reduce the latter's agonistic theory to merely an 'associative' or deliberative politics of consensus. Arendt's affirmative vision of the political as cooperative interrelationality among singular free equals, which has the capacity to create new beginnings, is not without its inner tensions and ambivalences. This vision, which implies the immanent potential for beginning and newness via human action directed toward the world and against absolute domination, is imbued with an awareness of the fragile and unpredictable aspects of action (1998). The possibility to redress 'the inevitable damages resulting from action', however, as Arendt suggests in *Human Condition*, arises out of action itself (1998: 239), most notably the acts of forgiveness, promise making, and communal adjudication. The idea of natality, fundamental to Arendt's political thought, implies the human capacity to bring something new into the world, to set something into motion, or to propel into action: 'Natality not mortality may be the central category of political as distinguished from metaphysical thought' (Arendt 1977: 29). Depending not on an idea of 'human nature', but on a phenomenological account of the 'human condition', Arendt's natality represents her vision of an affirmative relationship between life and politics, which might effectively desist the thanatopolitical violence of absolute domination. In her analysis of the tension – between the twin principles of *initium* and givenness – underlying Arendt's concept of natality, Peg Birmingham has astutely argued for the simultaneity and inseparability of the biological event of birth and the linguistic, public aspect of the 'event of natality' (2006). Significantly, her reading of the theme of givenness in Arendt's thought persuasively alerts against readings of Arendtian action in terms of inception *ex nihilo*.[1]

By way of a rereading of Sophocles' *Antigone*, Bonnie Honig offers an agonistic account that underscores life, instead of mortality, as part of an anti-sovereign politics, although, in attending to Arendt's insistence on the natal trait of the human condition, she usefully disallows a mere reduction of natality to maternity (2013). Seeking to challenge the assumptions of mortalist humanism, which signals, in her perspective, a position premised upon an underlying commonality of finitude and liability to suffering, Honig turns to Arendt in order to propose that focusing on natality – the principle of Arendtian action – 'may generate new commonalities while orienting humanism differently than mortality does' (2010: 9). In previous chapters, I have tried to displace the biopolitical underpinnings of a logic that evokes the trope of natality as a paradigmatic signpost of human action.

In her oeuvre, Arendt has created a space for agonistic action, that is, for courageous acts in concert that address the needs of justice. The legacy of the Arendtian conception of concerted action, plurality, and justice occupies a special position in the *ŽuC* agonistic poetics and politics that defends the other's being-in-the-world. Above all, the connection of performativity and agonism evinced in Arendt's vision of political action is a resource that *ŽuC* effectively engages. I have repeatedly witnessed a powerful interest in Arendtian topics during my research, often finding myself wondering what Arendt might have thought about this feminist engagement with her work, given her dismissive stance toward the feminism of her time, especially toward identitarian definitions of 'woman' (Honig 1995: 2). From the vantage point of my interlocutors, however, their feminism, critical of identity-based feminist politics and occasioned by histories of authoritarian rule, violent displacement, and civil disobedience, is dynamically – albeit complexly – amenable to the challenges offered by Arendt's political thought. Daša Duhaček is a Hannah Arendt scholar who has studied the misfires of (transitional) justice in Serbia and the sustained potential of feminist anti-nationalist struggles, through Arendt's argument on the necessity of acknowledging collective responsibility (Duhaček 2006; Duhaček and Savić 2002), and another *ŽuC* activist, Slavica Stojanović, has translated (with Aleksandra Bajazetov) *The Origins of Totalitarianism* (*Izvori Totalitarizma*), published by Feministička 94. Both Duhaček and Stojanović contributed to a public reading of *The Origins of Totalitarianism* on 26 September 2015, which took place in Belgrade's Center for Cultural Decontamination as part of a transnational 'Why Artivism' action. In their struggles to collectively reclaim, de-masculinise and de-nationalise the space of the agon, these *ŽuC* activists and thinkers share a commitment to the performative deployment of Arendtian agonism for anti-nationalist, cross-border, plural feminism. To be sure, certain aspects of these activists' political work might be at odds with some of Arendt's conceptions: in the context of this feminist activism, categorical distinctions between public and private or social and political do not seem to hold; the body is a differentiated, performative occasion for political-historical eventualisation and contestation rather than an inactive private fact; and the activists' performative public silence, which is meant to agonistically generate and pluralise the realm of action and the appearable, might not be in accord with Arendt's speech–centred political account. In other words, these political subjects look to Arendt's work for inspiration, but at the same time they put it in provocative engagement with the broad array of their own political experience.

The agonistic performativity of the activists with whom I worked might be taken to partly concur with and partly expand or diverge from Arendt's, Mouffe's, and Honig's related but nevertheless distinct accounts of agonism. Such creative intricacies granted, it might be worth addressing here the deleterious effects of reifying the distinction between mortalism as powerlessness and natalism as pure inventiveness, which occasionally undergird certain treatments of agonism. More broadly, the political consequence of turning mortalism and natalism into epistemic devices for politics might be that the ruling assumptions of liberal humanism and moral universalism would thereby be further legitimised. In contradistinction to such assertions, I find it important to resist the appeal to ontological foundationalism in theorising political action. This is why I deem valuable those accounts that disallow readings of Arendt's emphasis on the factuality of new beginning in terms of creation *ex nihilo* and through a biologistic reduction of her Augustinian notion of natality. And so I have been insisting here on interpreting vulnerability, finitude, and courage as thoroughly political and politically contingent themes, indeed as highly contested and differential occasions of agonistic politicisation, rather than as transhistorical liberal humanist touchstones. In that respect, I have been interested in bringing out what is at stake in a performative agonal/agonistic poetics that is not devoid of the multiple potentialities of agony, and points towards a contextually situated – at once limited and incalculable – capacity and desire to engage and intervene in this world. This agonistic politics cuts across the binary between affirmative militancy and regressive grief;[2] a binary often conventionally inscribed in terms of proactive natalism versus reactive mortalism.

The agonistic critique that has been put forward here lays bare and counters the underlying norms upon which the liberal valuation of consensual pluralism is premised. In all its undecidable ambivalences, the commemorative agonism featured in this book fails to comply with a conception of public reason and space as fixed, interactive, and free from constellations of power. For these activists, irreconcilable memories are political and thus contentious and contestable in a context of power relations. The responsibility to take a contestatory political stand with respect to these matrices of un/grievability cannot be displaced by legal and administrative devices of liberal consensus. In reading Arendt's conception of the *polis*'s enactment as a 'space of appearance' (1998), Judith Butler (2011) has argued that, in laying claim to the public, collective actions reconfigure the matter of the body politic. As she has importantly asked: 'how do we make sense of those who can never be part of that concerted action, who remain outside the plurality that acts? . . . what political language do we have in reserve for describing that exclusion?' (2011). In the preceding chapters of this book, I have attended to the ways in which the members of a feminist and antinationalist collective reckon politically with the enforced effacements and delimitations that render political space a restless space for appearing bodies, in the face of loss and its relevance to the normalising constraints of power. And so I have asked what kinds of new and alternative intimate publics would emerge from performing the spectral potentiality of the displaced and disconcerted occurrence of memory that always already complicates 'acting in concert'.

I have drawn from the above theorisations their effective affirmation of a politics of dissent and agonistic re-articulation as a means to challenge established formations of liberalism, but also communitarianism, through the perspective of contingency and unpredictability. Building on this line of enquiry, I have sought to elaborate on a performativity of political subjectivity and engagement beyond masterful sovereignty, construed either as indivisible and irresponsive self-mastery of the subject or as an autarchic modality of power, or, to be sure, as an analogy between the two. So how might we think of agonism and grievability together in putting forward the possibilities for political subjectivity? What new imaginaries and enactments of the political would be prompted by this entwinement? In this book, motivated by the commemorative agonism of the political subjects with whom I worked, I have proposed a means to refigure agonistic political subjectivity beyond foundational, presentist, and sovereign accounts of agency and also beyond the biopolitical duality of natality and mortality.

The commitment to ongoing contestatory and re-articulatory politics, in all its affective and courageous intensity, recurs throughout the practices of the political collective with which I worked. But it also signals a call for a deconstructive, non-sovereign, and counter-sovereign 'affirmative dimension of contestation', in Honig's terms. In affirming contestatory and re-articulatory politics, however, the agonal passion that these activists perform also affirms the impossibility of a final closure in response to political loss and also acknowledges those responses to political loss that have been relegated to the status of the impossible. Owing to others, then, these activists enact a political subjectivity that remains irreducibly heteronomous in its responsive and response-able movement. It is in this sense that I have paid close attention to the concept of agonism, alongside the work of non-sanctioned mourning, as a passionate and precarious means of response-ability, and I have suggested that *ŽuC* activists assume precisely what is unassumable about responsibility and response-ability.

Thus *ŽuC* agonistic mourning renders grievability subject to recurrent struggles over public space, re-presentability, response-ability, and subjectivation. Butler has offered great insight into 'the differential distribution of grievability upon which war depends' (2010: xix) and into the norms that determine 'why certain forms of grief become nationally recognized and amplified, whereas other losses become unthinkable and un-grievable' (2004: xiv). As 'a presupposition for life that matters' (2010: 14), grievability is about the acute political question of whether and how historically specific lives and deaths are accounted for. Through this perspective, the contested terrain of public mourning becomes a site of normalisation, but also an occasion whereby the subjectivity of memory is performatively constituted through the agonistic relationality to others, including, crucially, lost others. Butler's concern is, crucially, with the logic of foreclosure and exclusion through which mourning, as a way of attending to the lives of others, is *made* impossible, and yet is activated as a resource for transformation, in the sense of challenging its inherent injustices and inventing new collective forms of relating to it.

In engaging in the political question of framed and fractured grievability, as a constitutive element of the possibility of war, activists with whom I worked do not just cite the common practice of mourning in their fight. By means of performing mourning in an uncommon and catachrestic affective manner, they also fight over mourning and its scope of iterability. As they are moved by others and with others, they enact disavowed loss and memory as a kind of public good worth fighting over. They do so not in order to establish a universal, conciliatory, and consensual commonality of finitude and injurability, but rather to expose loss and memory as intensely politicised fields of contestation. Countering the disaffected languages of both state bureaucratic proceduralism and non-governmental governmentality, they thus offer a way of thinking about agonism alongside the political intricacies of finitude, courage, and the improper languages of responsiveness to others. As I have argued here, such rethinking of agonistic subjectivity as performing a mode of non-sovereign subjectivity in opposition and resistance to the logics of coercion and abjection would open the space of the political and keep it transformable.

This provides a way of understanding *ŽuC* work of agonistic mourning as an event of democratic contestation that affirms its impossibilities and reactivates its possibilities, albeit without guaranteed outcomes. This work of indefinite, dissident mourning, in its critical connections to national and gender politics, is not to be reduced to the consensual universalism of dutiful or successful mourning, which would establish a fixed and identifiable other, and would render reconciliation and closure possible. Rather, its contingent and spectral potentiality is akin to the weak messianic force 'on which the past has a claim', that Benjamin develops in his theses on the philosophy of history (2006: 390): *weak* messianic in the sense of powerless, inoperative, infinitely yet-to-come. Gillian Rose has unravelled the work of mourning as *'activity beyond activity'* (in juxtaposition to the Levinasian 'passivity beyond passivity'), which involves 'relinquishing *and taking up again* of activity' (1996: 122, emphasis in original). This is a process, however, that exceeds the chronological order of completion and resists the clear distinction between activity and passivity as well as its dependence upon subjective sovereignty. This work of mourning resists its possibility of working and thus pertains to the limit experience of 'unworking' or 'worklessness' (*désoeuvrement*), in Blanchot's terms (2006). And yet, attending to an active process of undoing and unworking the determinations of what 'works', it is unceasingly at work.

I would suggest that what is at stake here is a performative work of eccentric and agonistic mourning, whereby neither self-enclosed subjectivity nor the relation to the other remains in place. What is at stake is the performative work at the heart of the impossibility of working. The political subjects of this study cite mourning in their activism as a way to undo, or render inoperative, the uses of the idealised national and heteronormative grief in the formation of contemporary biopolitical matrices of belonging. They deploy mourning in an uncanny, or *unhomely*, manner. They cite a language they do not entirely possess, and they do so without being fully present in it, or possessed by it. Their mourning – if it can indeed ever be 'theirs' – resists the epistemic violence of lineage, home, and community, even as it is inextricably hardwired into it, always already marked by its own iterability. Staging a not-at-homeness vis-à-vis the inscriptional space of memory as relation to the irreducibly other becomes a performative occasion for these activists to dislocate the proper place of memory while remaining bound to its aporetic condition of possibility.

What does it mean then to work politically through invoking not-at-homeness as resistance to normalisation and abjection and as openness to the other, which always evades completion and recognition? What kind of body politics would such work entail? In the context of the wars in the former Yugoslavia and their aftermath, *ŽuC* activists use the ambivalent sign of mourning, without conforming to its normative ideals, as an affective register of becoming 'beside oneself', in Butler's terms. Becoming 'beside oneself', in the form of imposed but also self-assumed exile, becomes a critical space of political subjectivity through which to call into question the totalising gestures of proper, sovereign, and self-possessed subjectivity. Through the performative registers of dissident belonging and becoming-enemy, these activists mobilise cross-border grievability to counter the biopolitical economy of enmity and disposability, with all its racial, ethnic, and gender inflections.

Their enduring attachments to such affective intensities, as they play out in their commemoration of the annihilated victims of the 'other side', their ongoing relation with the displaced people, their acts of camaraderie, and their alliance with the 'enemy' community, generate spaces for transvaluating afflicted losses into possibilities of critical agency. In hauntingly re-inhabiting and thus estranging the contained place of home, as both kinship and homeland, and in assuming the gender-marked position of the internal enemy, the *ŽuC* activists affirm relationality with unruly others situated out of place and estranged as external enemies. It is through this political performativity of self-estrangement and hauntology that they address the disavowed memory of those who have been absented and effaced from the *polis*.

In enacting such an impropriety, these activists do not merely expose their bodies to the *polis*'s 'space of appearance', in Arendt's terms. Their action – and, arguably, lived experience – of appearing out of place and reclaiming a public space, for remembering others who cannot appear works to spectrally traverse the *polis* and unsettle its order of 'being there' and 'belonging together'. By means of marking those memories and claims that have been disavowed by sanctioned codes of representation, recognition, and remembrance, these political subjects emerge to haunt collectively the national monumental space. The performativity of becoming-ghostly, as I have interpreted it here, conjures the possibility of disruptive re-openings and re-appearings in the present, and thus puts the right of mourning to work: a mourning that signals an infinite demand for a present-to-be-embodied and a political-to-be-re/membered.

In the affective experience of the political subjectivity at hand, 'appearing' involves bodies lingering in spaces rendered uninhabitable, bodies whose presence appears not to be present, and bodies opting out of certain frames of appearance. This is about a political agonism of being moved by and with others as moving towards what is made impossible to present itself in the un/common space of the *polis*. Through their embodied public emergences, these activists wield public space as a register of what Navaro-Yashin has called 'sensing the political' (2003). Their way to 'sense' the political becomes a performative force that registers that not everyone can emerge into the sensuate space of emergence, but also that not all 'appear' – in the sense of being seen and becoming worthy of attention – according to the normalising ordinances of visibility, recognisability, and re-presentability. Accordingly, not all assembling subjects act in concert with one another, nor do they share the same political positionalities and pursuits, nor are they propelled by homogeneous desires to set something in motion. I have tried here to draw attention to the enactments of sensibility, eeriness, and self-dispossession that underlie the subjective experience of the political.

By positioning their bodies at the centre of the city in solidarity with those turned into enemies, these political subjects actualise the multilayered modalities of stasis as a means of embodying their own and others' dissident belonging. Stasis, usually denoting disanimation and disaffection, here signals animating the spectres of unqualifiable loss that haunt, and agitate, the common intelligibility of memorable life. The subjects I worked with in the course of my research actively engage with a labour of repartitioning and reconfiguring the political realm of appearance and presentability through the perspective of those who have become prone to social disposability. Estrangement or erasure from the available space of appearance is often the price for their stasis. At the same time, however, this erasure works as a performative occasion for another collective belonging and worldliness, however precarious this might be, which speaks back to sovereign violence in times of war exigencies and post-war normalisation.

In so 'showing up' to render public space interrupted and uncommon rather than settled and homely, these political subjects become subject to violence, arrest, alienation, or, especially in post-Yugoslav times, state paternalism and demonisation. Their courageous activism affirms a sense of fragility, affection, and camaraderie against the normalising violences that sustain the connections of vulnerability to the ramifications of gendered, nationalised, and racialised subjection. Enacted and sensed in terms of non-essentialist and non-sovereign critical agency, this interminably aporetic political subjectivity is different from, and critical of, the binary terms of agency–vulnerability and activity–passivity. Vulnerability here, it should be noted, is not subsumed into the governmentality of moral universalism, which would compel transubstantiation from vulnerability to safety and securitisation. It entails an alternative to the apparatuses of the self-regulating moral subject and the management of 'vulnerable populations'. Hence, the perspective suggested here entails recognising that vulnerability is always already fraught with modalities of power and differences of location, but also the critical agency related to openness to others. We have been enjoined here to think how a modality of feminist and antinationalist political activism that critically addresses the uneven conditions of grieavability provides ways of producing a zone of indetermination where the epistemological separation of affirmation and negation becomes, effectively, elusive. As in the agonistic grief that has concerned me here, critical agency does not merely either negate or affirm, but rather preserves the register it seeks to negate, or negates the register that it seeks to affirm. Thus conceived, political pursuits become articulated – or, enacted, it should be added, in unarticulated forms – through the conditions of their impossibility (Laclau and Mouffe 1985).[3]

Attending to the im/possible aspects of mourning, beyond any symmetry between possibility and impossibility, has significant effects for avowing vulnerability at the heart of political performativity. In further complicating Foucault's theorisation of resistance as part of the strategic relations of power, Butler's work on performative agency has provided an account of the possibility for re-appropriating a sign in affirmative modes. Butler makes clear that by 'affirmative' she means 'opening up the possibility of agency' (1997b: 15), whereby agency is linked with a spectral plurality of resignifying performative enactments without clear origin and guaranteed outcome, and without the sovereignty of an originating subject. The structural expropriation – or, performative vulnerability – of master discourses offers a site for disrupting the historically sedimented power effects of such normative frames. It is, at the same time, a site of performative fallibility: performativity is 'that which produces events . . . but it is also that which neutralizes the event' (Derrida 2000a: 467). This is about a vulnerability that indicates the originary contamination of the sign, and thus is already implied in any performative event, whereby the latter does not amount to pure and miraculous eventness. What is politically significant about performativity is precisely that it does not entail an absolute rupture between possibility and impossibility, active and passive, or mastery and vulnerability. Rather, the performative event indicates a force that is not merely inherited by a prior convention even if it arises from such limits and defining conditions, even if it does not break with them – yet. In order to be such, performative possibility politically acknowledges – rather than normalises or overcomes – powerlessness and vulnerability that are at work in the performative.

In thinking through the performative, by means of engaging with the lives and words of the activists with whom I worked, I have focused on mourning-work as interminably complicated: both foreclosed and open to political potential. I have sought throughout this text, propelled by my anthropological encounters, to displace the resolute certainty of the unilateral opposition positivity/negativity with respect to radical democratic action, and, instead, explore their mutual contamination, without bracketing the one over the other and without reducing the one to the other. In immersing myself in the phantasmatic configurations emerging from this coextensiveness, my hope has been to problematise the contention that the aporias of political performativity occasion a crisis of 'agency'. Against the grain of a particular routine criticism according to which deconstructive performativity promotes a 'negative' or atrophied model of action, I attempted to draw out how the enactment of conditions of impossibility as conditions of always deferred possibility is what makes performativity political. In this spirit, then, to displace the 'affirmation versus negativity' schema, which often marks particular conceptualisations of political agency that are based upon heroic individualism and the defiant disavowal of finitude, requires a work of critical reconsideration: to acknowledge that vulnerability is inextricable from the domain of agency; to unsettle the idea that agency presumes the emergence of a self-contained, self-preserving, and impassable subject who heroically exceeds (or liberates from) vulnerability; to shift towards an understanding of agonistic agency as necessarily implicated in power and premised upon a suspension of the sovereign 'I' and its humanist tenets; and to imply a mode of being, becoming, acting, and resisting always already traversed by the passions of vulnerability as susceptibility to violation but also disposition to others. Thinking (through) vulnerability together with performative agonism would prompt us to trouble the calculative, individualistic accounts that posit subjectivity in terms of narcissistic sovereign will that masters an array of possibilities in order to confound vulnerability. The thesis I defended here is that vulnerability has to be profoundly rethought in its passionate and expansive possibility of reworking the very defining conditions by which it is persistently and variously marked in contexts of duress, grief, excitement, and desire.

Agonism is beyond active versus passive. It involves and compels being disposed toward others, thinking in action, bearing, responding, resisting, and engaging. As deconstructive performativity before non-passable borders, it is a commitment to infinitely making possible what has been foreclosed by matrices of recognisability that pass as immediately present 'actuality'. As such, agonism complicates the passage *from* potentiality *to* actuality, troubling the rigorous distinction between the two and the 'positive versus negative' matrix that underlies it. How does this aporia come to involve the question of a persistent and resistant politics of remembering otherwise in the face of political loss, despite and against ethno-nationalist formations? How is the aporia of agonistic mourning affirmed and performed in the *here and now* as well as the *there and then* of worldmaking (Muñoz 2009)? Embodying the conflicting and imponderable potentialities of politically engaged performativity, the *ŽuC* agonistic mourning, however suffused with friction and risk, critically and collectively addresses the conventional loyalties that sustain memorability-as-belonging in the transnational context. Such unruly ek-static relationality, predicated on determinate relations of division, bears on the provisional temporality of critical performativity and ongoing global struggles against sovereign violence. It involves the labour of re-membering what is at stake in the intractable political imagination arising from the ordinary criticality of the not-yet-here.

Notes

1 See the reading of Patchen Markell, in *Notre Dame Philosophical Reviews*, <http://ndpr.nd.edu/news/23855-book-1-hannah-arendt-and-human-rights-the-predicament-of-common-responsibility-book-2-hannah-

arendt-and-the-challenge-of-modernity-a-phenomenology-of-human-rights/> (last accessed 23 October 2016).

2 Devoid of the element of agony, the analytics of agonism would risk reiterating the register of biopolitical sovereignty. Significantly for our purposes here, Barder and Debrix (2011) have brought Arendt's language of agonistic engagement to bear on contemporary biopolitical modalities of power, by means of registering practices of war as matters of 'agonal sovereignty'. Taking its cue from Adriana Cavarero's notion of contemporary 'horrorism', agonal sovereignty denotes ultimate devastation of lives and bodies.

3 For an insightful critique of the humanist essentialist penchant for a reduction or normalisation of negativity, from the perspective of Laclau and Mouffe's negative ontology and its implications for radical democracy and the Lacanian Left, see Stavrakakis 2007.

Bibliography

Abraham, Nicolas and Maria Torok. *L'écorce et le noyau*. Paris: Flammarion, 1978, pp. 88–119.

Abu-Lughod, Lila. 'The romance of resistance: Tracing transformations of power through Bedouin women', *American Ethnologist*, 17: 1, 41–55, 1990.

Adorno, Theodor W. 'The meaning of working through the past', in *Critical Models: Interventions and Catchwords*, trans. Henry W. Pickford. New York: Columbia University Press, 2005 [1959], 89–103, p. 97.

Agamben, Giorgio. *Language and Death: The Place of Negativity*, trans. Karen E. Pinkus with Michael Hardt. Minneapolis: University of Minnesota Press, 1991.

Agamben, Giorgio. *Homo Sacer: Sovereign Power and Bare Life*, trans. Daniel Heller-Roazen. Stanford: Stanford University Press, 1998.

Agamben, Giorgio. *Remnants of Auschwitz: The Witness and the Archive*, trans. Daniel Heller-Roazen. New York: Zone Books, 1999a.

Agamben, Giorgio. *Potentialities: Collected Essays in Philosophy*, ed. and trans. Daniel Heller-Roazen. Stanford: Stanford University Press, 1999b.

Ahiska, Meltem. 'Occidentalism and registers of truth: The politics of archives in Turkey', *New Perspectives on Turkey*, 34, 9–29, 2006.

Ahmed, Sara. *Strange Encounters: Embodied Others in Postcoloniality*. London: Routledge, 2000.

Ahmed, Sara. *The Cultural Politics of Emotion*. London: Routledge, 2004.

Ahmed, Sara. 'The skin of the community: Affect and boundary formation', in Tina Chanter and Ewa Płonowska Ziarek (eds), *Revolt, Affect, Collectivity: The Unstable Boundaries of Kristeva's Polis*. New York: State University of New York Press, 2005.

Aleksov, Bojan. *Deserters from the War in Former Yugoslavia*. Belgrade: Žene u crnom, 1994.

Aleksov, Bojan. 'Sudbina dezertera u ratu u bivšoj Jugoslaviji', *Ženezamir*, pp. 282–6. Belgrade: Women in Black, 1996.

Aleksov, Bojan. 'Resisting the wars in the former Yugoslavia: Towards an autoethnography', in Bojan Bilić and Vesna Jankovic (eds), *Resisting the Evil: (Post-)Yugoslav Anti-War Contention*. Baden-Baden: Nomos, 2012, pp. 105–26.

Anderson, Benedict. *Imagined Communities: Reflections on the Origin and Spread of Nationalism*. London: Verso, 1991 [1983].

Anzaldúa, Gloria. *Borderlands/La Frontera: The New Mestiza*. San Francisco: Aunt Lute Books, 1987.

Ardener, Shirley (ed.). *Perceiving Women*. London: Malaby, 1975 [1968].

Arendt, Hannah. *Crises of the Republic*. San Diego and New York: Harcourt Brace Jovanovich, 1972.

Arendt, Hannah. *Between Past and Future: Eight Exercises in Political Thought*. London: Penguin, 1977.

Arendt, Hannah. *On Revolution*. New York: Penguin Books, 1990 [1963].

Arendt, Hannah. *The Human Condition*. Chicago: The University of Chicago Press, 1998 [1958].

Aretxaga, Begoña. *Shattering Silence: Women, Nationalism, and Political Subjectivity in Northern Ireland*. Princeton: Princeton University Press, 1997.

Aristotle. *Basic Works*. New York: Random House, 1941.

Arsić, Branka. 'Queer Serbs', in Dušan I. Bjelić and Obrad Savić (eds), *Balkan as Metaphor*. Cambridge, MA: The MIT Press, 2002, pp. 253–78.

Art Klinika, 'We are returning your tank: Homage to the rebels against war and violence'. Novi Sad, 2010.

Asad, Talal. 'Agency and pain: An exploration', *Culture and Religion: An Interdisciplinary Journal*, 1: 1, 29–60, 2000.

Asad, Talal. *Formations of the Secular: Christianity, Islam, Modernity*. Stanford: Stanford University Press, 2003.

Austin, John L. *How to Do Things with Words*. Cambridge, MA: Harvard University Press, 1975.

Avramopoulou, Eirini. 'The affective language of activism: An ethnography of human rights, gender politics and activist coalitions in Istanbul, Turkey'. Unpublished PhD dissertation. University of Cambridge, 2012.

Azoulay, Ariella. *Civil Imagination: A Political Ontology of Photography*, trans. Louise Bethlehem. London: Verso, 2012.

Bahovec, Eva Dolar (ed.). *Abortus – pravica do izbire?!* Ljubljana: Skupina Ženske za politico, 1991.

Balibar, Etienne. 'The nation form: History and ideology', in Etienne Balibar and Immanuel Wallerstein, *Race, Nation, Class: Ambiguous identities*. London: Verso, 1991, pp. 86–106.

Balibar, Etienne and Immanuel Wallerstein. *Race, Nation, Class: Ambiguous Identities*. New York: Verso, 1991.

Barder, Alexander and François Debrix, 'Agonal sovereignty: Rethinking war and politics with Schmitt, Arendt and Foucault', *Philosophy and Social Criticism*, June 2011.

Barthes, Roland. *Mourning Diary*. New York: Hill and Wang, 2012.

Basso, Keith. '"To give up on words": Silence in Western Apache culture', *Southwestern Journal of Anthropology* 26, 213–30, 1970.

Basso, Keith. *Portraits of the Whitemen*. New York: Cambridge University Press, 1979.

Bell, Vikki. 'On Fernando's photograph: The biopolitics of *aparición* in contemporary Argentina', *Theory, Culture & Society* 27:4, 69–89, 2010.

Benjamin, Walter. 'Theses on the philosophy of history', in Hannah Arendt (ed.), *Illuminations*. New York: Schocken Books

Benjamin, Walter. *The Arcades Project*, trans. Howard Eiland and Kevin McLaughlin. Cambridge, MA: Harvard University Press, 1999.

Benjamin, Walter. 'On the concept of history', *Selected Writings*, volume 4 (1938–40), trans. Edmund Jephcott, ed. Howard Eiland and Michael Jennings. Cambridge, MA: Harvard University Press, 2002, pp. 389–400.

Benjamin, Walter. *Selected Writings*, ed. Howard Eiland and Michael W. Jennings, Vol. 4 (1938–1940). Cambridge, MA: Harvard University Press, 2006.

Berlant, Lauren. *The Anatomy of National Fantasy: Hawthorne, Utopia and Everyday Life*. Chicago: The University of Chicago Press, 1991.

Berlant, Lauren. *The Queen of America Goes to Washington City*. Durham, NC: Duke University Press, 1997.

Berdahl, Daphne. '"(N)Ostalgie" for the present: Memory, longing, and East German things', *Ethnos*, 64:2, 192–211, 1999.

Berlant, Lauren. *The Female Complaint: The Unfinished Business of Sentimentality in American Culture*. Durham, NC: Duke University Press, 2008.

Berlant, Lauren and Michael Warner. 'Sex in public', *Critical Inquiry*, 24: 2, 547–66, 1998.

Bhabha, Homi. 'Remembering Fanon', *New Formations*, 1, 118–24. Spring 1987.

Bhabha, Homi. *The Location of Culture*. New York: Routledge, 1994.

Biehl, João. *Vita: Life in a Zone of Social Abandonment*. Berkeley: University of California Press, 2005.

Bilić, Bojan. *We Were Gasping for Air: (Post-)Yugoslav Anti-War Activism and its Legacy.* Baden–Baden: Nomos, 2012.

Billig, Michael. *Banal Nationalism.* London: Sage, 1995.

Birmingham, Peg. *Hannah Arendt and Human Rights: The Predicament of Common Responsibility.* Bloomington: Indiana University Press, 2006.

Bjelić, Dušan and Lucinda Cole. 'Sexualizing the Serb', in Dušan I. Bjelić and Obrad Savić (eds), *Balkan as Metaphor.* Cambridge, MA: The MIT Press, 2002, pp. 279–310.

Bjelić, Dušan I. and Obrad Savić (eds). *Balkan as Metaphor.* Cambridge, MA: The MIT Press, 2002.

Blagojević, Marina (ed.). *Mapiranje mizoginije u Srbiji: Diskursi i prakse.* Belgrade: AŽIN, 2000.

Blagojević, Marina. *Knowledge Production at the Semiperiphery: A Gender Perspective.* Beograd: Institut za kriminološka i sociološka istraživanja, 2009.

Blanchot, Maurice. *The Writing of the Disaster,* trans. Ann Smock. Lincoln: University of Nebraska Press, 1995.

Blanchot, Maurice. *The Unavowable Community.* Barrytown, NY: Station Hill Press, 2006.

Bloch, Ernst and Theodor Adorno. 'Something's missing: A discussion between Ernst Bloch and Theodor W. Adorno on the contradictions of utopian longing', in *The Utopian Function of Art and Literature,* trans. Jack Zipes and Frank Mecklenburg. Cambridge, MA: MIT Press, 1996.

Bonfiglioli, Chiara. 'The dangerous legacy in the post-Yugoslav space', 1 April 2016, <http://dangerouswomenproject.org/2016/04/01/partizanke-dangerous-legacy/> (last accessed 30 May 2016).

Bonfiglioli, Chiara, Katja Kahlina, and Adriana Zaharijević. 'Transformations of gender, sexuality and citizenship in South East Europe', *Women's Studies International Forum,* 49, 43–7, 2015.

Bougarel, Xavier. 'Death and the nationalist: Martyrdom, war memory and veteran identity among Bosnian Muslims', in Xavier Bougarel, Elissa Helms, and Ger Duijzings (eds), *The New Bosnian Mosaic: Social Identities, Collective Memories, and Moral Hierarchies in a Post-War Society.* Aldershot: Ashgate, 2007, pp. 167–92.

Bougarel, Xavier, Elissa Helms, and Ger Duijzings (eds). *The New Bosnian Mosaic: Social Identities, Collective Memories, and Moral Hierarchies in a Post-War Society.* Aldershot: Ashgate, 2007.

Bourke, Joanna. *An Intimate History of Killing: Face-to-Face Killing in Twentieth Century Warfare.* New York: Basic Books, 2000.

Boyer, M. Christine. *The City of Collective Memory: Its Historical Imagery and Architectural Entertainments.* Cambridge: MIT Press, 1994.

Boym, Svetlana. *The Future of Nostalgia.* New York: Basic Books, 2001.

Braidotti, Rosi. *Nomadic Subjects: Embodiment and Sexual Difference in Contemporary Feminist Theory.* New York: Columbia University Press, 1994.

Braidotti, Rosi. *Metamorphoses: Towards a Materialist Theory of Becoming.* Cambridge: Polity Press, 2002.

Braidotti, Rosi. 'A critical cartography of feminist post-postmodernism', *Australian Feminist Studies*, 20: 47, 169–80, July 2005.

Braidotti, Rosi. *Nomadic Theory: The Portable Rosi Braidotti.* New York: Columbia University Press, 2011.

Brown, Wendy. *Manhood and Politics: A Feminist Reading in Political Theory.* New Jersey: Rowman & Littlefield, 1988.

Brown, Wendy. *States of Injury: Power and Freedom in Late Modernity.* Princeton: Princeton University Press, 1995.

Brown, Wendy. 'Freedom's silences', in *Edgework: Critical Essays on Knowledge and Politics.* Princeton: Princeton University Press, 2005, 83–97.

Brown, Wendy. *Walled States, Waning Sovereignty.* New York: Zone Books, 2010.

Butalia, Urvashi. *The Other Side of Silence: Voices from the Partition of India.* Durham, NC: Duke University Press, 2000.

Butler, Judith. *Gender Trouble: Feminism and the Subversion of Identity.* New York: Routledge, 1990.

Butler, Judith. *Bodies that Matter: On the Discursive Limits of 'Sex'.* New York: Routledge, 1993.

Butler, Judith. 'Contingent foundations', in Seyla Behabib, Judith Butler, Drucilla Cornell, Nancy Fraser, introduction by Linda Nicholson, *Feminist Contentions: A Philosophical Exchange.* New York: Routledge, 1995, pp. 35–58.

Butler, Judith. 'Sexual inversions: Rereading the end of Foucault's *History of Sexuality, Vol. I*', in Susan J. Hekman (ed.), *Feminist Interpretations of Michel Foucault.* Philadelphia: Pennsylvania State University Press, 1996, pp. 59–75.

Butler, Judith. *The Psychic Life of Power: Theories in Subjection.* Stanford: Stanford University Press, 1997a.

Butler, Judith. *Excitable Speech: A Politics of the Performative.* New York: Routledge, 1997b.

Butler, Judith. *Antigone's Claim: Kinship between Life and Death.* New York: Columbia University Press, 2000.

Butler, Judith. 'What is critique? An essay on Foucault's virtue', *Transversal*, 2001.

Butler, Judith. *Precarious Life: The Powers of Mourning and Violence.* New York: Verso, 2004.

Butler, Judith. *Giving an Account of Oneself.* New York: Fordham University Press, 2005.

Butler, Judith. 'Critique, dissent, disciplinarity', *Critical Inquiry*, 35, 773–95, Summer 2009.

Butler, Judith. *Frames of War: When is Life Grievable?* Brooklyn: Verso, 2010.

Butler, Judith. 'Bodies in Alliance and the Politics of the Street.' *Transversal*, October 2011, n.p. <http://www.eipcp.net/transversal/1011/butler/en> (last accessed 18 October 2016).

Butler, Judith. *Parting Ways: Jewishness and the Critique of Zionism.* New York: Columbia University Press, 2012.

Butler, Judith and Athena Athanasiou. *Dispossession: The Performative in the Political.* Cambridge: Polity Press, 2013.

Butler, Judith and Gayatri Chakravorty Spivak. *Who Sings the Nation? Language, Politics, Belonging.* Chicago: The University of Chicago Press, 2011.

Cadava, Eduardo. *Words of Light: Theses on the Photography of History.* Princeton: Princeton University Press, 1997.

Caraveli, Anna. 'The bitter wounding: The lament as social protest in rural Greece', in J. Dubisch (ed.), *Gender and Power in Rural Greece*. Princeton: Princeton University Press, 1986, pp. 169–94.

Caruth, Cathy. *Unclaimed Experience: Trauma, Narrative, and History.* Baltimore: Johns Hopkins University Press, 1996.

Casey, Edward S. *The Fate of Place: A Philosophical History.* Berkeley: University of California Press, 1997.

Cavarero, Adriana. *Relating Narratives: Storytelling and Selfhood.* New York: Routledge, [1997] 2000.

Cavarero, Adriana. *For More than One Voice: Toward a Philosophy of Vocal Expression*, trans. Paul A. Kottman. Stanford: Stanford University Press, [2003] 2005.

Cheah, Pheng. *Spectral Nationality: Passages of Freedom from Kant to Postcolonial Literatures of Liberation.* New York: Columbia University Press, 2003.

Cixous, Hélène. 'The laugh of the Medusa', trans. Keith Cohen and Paula Cohen, *Signs*, 1: 4, 875–93, Summer, 1976.

Cixous, Hélène. 'Castration or decapitation?', trans. Annette Kuhn, *Signs* 7:1, 41–55, 1981.

Clifford, James and George Marcus (eds). *Writing Culture.* Berkeley: University of California Press, 1986.

Cockburn, Cynthia. *The Space between Us: Negotiating Gender and National Identities in Conflict.* London: Zed Books, 1998.

Cockburn, Cynthia. *The Line: Women, Partition and the Gender Order in Cyprus.* London: Zed Books, 2004.

Cockburn, Cynthia. *From Where We Stand: War, Women's Activism and Feminist Analysis*. London: Zed Books, 2007.

Cockburn, Cynthia, Rada Stakic-Domuz, and Meliha Hubic. *Women Organizing for Change: A Study of Women's Local Integrative Organizations and the Pursuit of Democracy in Bosnia-Herzegovina*. Zenica: Medica Zenica, Infoteka, 2001.

Cole, Alyson M. *The Cult of True Victimhood: From the War on Welfare to the War on Terror*. Stanford: Stanford University Press, 2006.

Crimp, Douglas. 'Mourning and militancy', *October*, 51, 3–18, 1989.

Crimp, Douglas. *Melancholia and Moralism: Essays on AIDS and Queer Politics*. Boston: MIT Press, 2004.

Cuéllar, Alejandro C. 'Unraveling silence: Violence, memory and the limits of anthropology's craft', *Dialectical Anthropology*, 29: 2, 159–80, 2005.

Cvetkovich, Ann. 'Legacies of trauma, legacies of activism: ACT UP's lesbians', in David Eng and David Kazanjian (eds), *Loss*. Berkeley: University of California Press, 2003, pp. 427–57.

Cvoro, Uros. 'Remember the nineties? Turbo-folk as the vanishing mediator of nationalism', *Cultural Politics*, 8: 1, 121–37, 2012.

Daniel, E. Valentine. *Charred Lullabies: Chapters in an Anthropography of Violence*. Princeton: Princeton University Press, 1996.

Das, Veena. *Critical Events: An Anthropological Perspective on Contemporary India*. Delhi: Oxford University Press, 1995.

Das, Veena. 'Language and body: Transactions in the construction of pain', in Arthur Kleinman, Veena Das and Margaret Lock (eds), *Social Suffering*. Berkeley: University of California Press, 1997, pp. 67–91.

Das, Veena. *Life and Words: Violence and the Descent into the Ordinary*. Berkeley: University of California Press, 2007.

Das, Veena. 'Action, expression, and everyday life: Recounting household events', in Veena Das, Michael Jackson, Arthur Kleinman and Bhrigupati Singh (eds), *The Ground Between: Anthropologists Engage Philosophy*. Durham, NC: Duke University Press, 2014, pp. 279–306.

Das, Veena. 'On singularity and the event: Further reflections on the ordinary', n.d. <https://www.academia.edu/8237494/On_Singularity_and_the_Event _Furhter_Reflections_on_the_Ordinary> (last accessed 11 February 2015).

Das, Veena and Ashis Nandy. 'Violence, victimhood, and the language of silence', *Contributions to Indian Sociology*, 19:1, 177–95, 1985.

Daskalova, Krassimira, Caroline Hornstein-Tomić, Karl Kaser and Filip. Radunović (eds). *Gendering Post-Socialist Transition*. Vienna: LIT Verlag, ERSTE Foundation Series, 2012.

Dean, Jodi. *Solidarity of Strangers: Feminism after Identity Politics*. Berkeley: University of California Press, 1996.

DeArmitt, Pleshette. 'Resonances of Echo: A Derridean allegory', *Mosaic*, 42:2, 89–100, 2009.

Derrida, Jacques. *Speech and Phenomena*, trans. David Allison. Evanston: Northwestern University Press, 1973.

Derrida, Jacques. 'Cogito and the history of madness', in *Writing and Difference*. London: Routledge, 1978 [1967].

Derrida, Jacques. *Dissemination*, trans. Barbara Johnson. Chicago: Chicago University Press, 1981.

Derrida, Jacques. 'Deconstruction in America: An interview with Jacques Derrida', trans. James Creech, *Critical Exchange*, 17, 1–33, 1985.

Derrida, Jacques. 'Fors: The Anglish words of Nicolas Abraham and Maria Torok', trans. Barbara Johnson, in Nicolas Abraham and Maria Torok, *The Wolfman's Magic Word: A Cryptonomy*, trans. Nicolas Rand. Minneapolis: University of Minnesota Press, 1986.

Derrida, Jacques. *Limited Inc.* Evanston: Northwestern University Press, 1988.

Derrida, Jacques. *Memoires for Paul de Man*. New York: Columbia University Press, 1989.

Derrida, Jacques. 'Force of law: The mystical foundation of authority', trans. Mary Quaintance, *Cardozo Law Review*, 11: 5–6, 1990. Reprinted in: Cornell, Drucilla, Michael Rosenfeld, and David Gray Carlson (eds), *Deconstruction and the Possibility of Justice*. New York: Routledge, 1992a.

Derrida, Jacques. *The Other Heading: Reflections on Today's Europe*. Bloomington: Indiana University Press, 1992b.

Derrida, Jacques. *Aporias*, trans. Thomas Dutoit. Stanford: Stanford University Press, 1993.

Derrida, Jacques. *Specters of Marx: The State of the Debt, the Work of Mourning and the New International*, trans. Peggy Kamuf. New York: Routledge, 1994.

Derrida, Jacques. *Archive Fever: A Freudian Impression*, trans. Eric Prenowitz. Chicago: The University of Chicago Press, 1996.

Derrida, Jacques. *Deconstruction in a Nutshell: A Conversation with Jacques Derrida*. Ed. John Caputo. New York: Fordham University Press, 1997a.

Derrida, Jacques. 'Portrait d'un philosophe: Jacques Derrida', *Philosophie, Philosophie* (Revue des Etudiants de Philosophie Université Paris VIII), 1997b.

Derrida, Jacques. *Archive Fever: A Freudian Impression*. Chicago: The University of Chicago Press, 1998.

Derrida, Jacques. 'Performative powerlessness: A response to Simon Critchley', *Constellations*, 7: 4, 466–8, 2000a.

Derrida, Jacques. 'Et cetera', in N. Royle (ed.), *Deconstructions: A User's Guide*. London: Palgrave, 2000b.

Derrida, Jacques. *The Work of Mourning*. Chicago: Chicago University Press, 2001.

Derrida, Jacques. 'Uninterrupted dialogue: Between two infinities, the poem', *Research in Phenomenology*, 34, 3–19, 2004.

Derrida, Jacques. *Rogues: Two Essays on Reason*. Stanford: Stanford University Press, 2005a.

Derrida, Jacques. 'Poetics and politics of witnessing', in *Sovereignties in Question: The Poetics of Paul Celan*. New York: Fordham University Press, 2005b.

Derrida, Jacques. *The Politics of Friendship*. London: Verso, 2005c.

Derrida, Jacques. *Paper Machine*, trans. Rachel Bowlby. Stanford: Stanford University Press, 2005d.

Derrida, Jacques. 'As if it were possible', in *Paper Machine*. Stanford: Stanford University Press, 2005e.

Derrida, Jacques. *Sovereignties in Question: The Poetics of Paul Celan*. New York: Fordham University Press, 2005f.

Derrida, Jacques. *The Beast and the Sovereign, Volume I*, trans. Geoffrey Bennington. Chicago: The University of Chicago Press, 2009.

Derrida, Jacques with Bernard Stiegler. *Echographies of Television*. Cambridge: Polity Press, 2002.

Deutscher, Penelope. 'Mourning the Other, cultural cannibalism, and the politics of friendship (J. Derrida and L. Irigaray)', *differences: A Journal of Feminist Cultural Studies* 10: 3, 159–84, 1998.

Devic, Ana. 'Women's activism between private and public spaces: The case of the Women in Black in Serbia', in Svetlana Slapšak (ed.), *War Discourse, Women's Discourse: Essays and Case Studies from Yugoslavia and Russia*. Ljubljana: ISH-ŠOU, 2000, pp. 195–211.

Djuric-Kuzmanović, Tanja, Rada Drezgić, and Dubravka Žarkov. 'Gendered war, gendered peace: Violent conflicts in the Balkans and their consequences', in Donna Pankhurst (ed.), *Gendered Peace: Women's Struggles for Post-War Justice and Reconciliation*. New York: Routledge, 2008, pp. 265–91.

Dolar, Mladen. *A Voice and Nothing More*. Cambridge, MA: MIT Press, 2006.

Douzinas, Costas. *Philosophy and Resistance in the Crisis*. Cambridge: Polity, 2013.

Douzinas, Costas. 'Notes towards an analytics of resistance', *New Formations*, 83, 79–98, Winter 2014.

Drezgić, Rada. 'Demographic nationalism in gender perspective', in S. Slapšak (ed.), *Women's Discourses, War Discourses*. Ljubljana: ISH, 1999.

Drezgić, Rada. '(Re)producing the nation: The politics of reproduction in post-socialist Serbia: 1980s and 1990s'. PhD dissertation, University of Pittsburgh, 2004.

Drezgić, Rada. *'Belakuga' među 'Srbima': O naciji, rodu I rađanju na prelazu vekova*. Beograd: Albatros plus, 2010.

Duhaček, Daša. 'Women's time in the former Yugoslavia', in N. Funk and M. Mueller (eds), *Gender Politics and Post-Communism: Reflections from Eastern Europe and the Former Soviet Union*. New York: Routledge, 1993.

Duhaček, Daša. 'Gender perspectives on political identities in Yugoslavia', in Rada Iveković and Julie Mostow (eds), *From Gender to Nation*. Ravenna: Longo Editore, 2002.

Duhaček, Daša. 'The making of political responsibility: Hannah Arendt and/in the case of Serbia', in Jasmina Lukić, Joanna Regulska, and Darja Zaviršek (eds), *Women and Citizenship in Central and Eastern Europe*. Abingdon: Ashgate, 2006.

Duhaček, Daša. *Rasuđivanje u delu Hane Arent*. Belgrade: Belgrade Circle and the Center for Women and Gender Studies, 2010.

Duhaček, Daša and Obrad Savić (eds). *Zatočenici zla: Zaveštanje Hane Arendt* [*Captives of Evil: Legacy of Hannah Arendt*]. Belgrade: Beogradski Krug, Ženske Studije, Biblioteka Collectanea, 2002.

Duncan, Nancy. 'Renegotiating gender and sexuality in public and private spaces', in Nancy Duncan (ed.), *BodySpace: Destabilising Geographies of Gender and Sexuality*. New York: Routledge, 1996, pp. 127–45.

Edelman, Lee. *No Future: Queer Theory and the Death Drive*. Durham, NC: Duke University Press, 2004.

Edkins, Jenny. *Trauma and the Memory of Politics*. Cambridge: Cambridge University Press, 2003.

Eng, David and David Kazanjian (eds). *Loss*. Berkeley: University of California Press, 2003.

Engle, Karen. 'Feminism and its (dis)contents: Criminalizing wartime rape in Bosnia and Herzegovina', *The American Journal of International Law*, 99: 4, 778–816, 2005.

Enloe, Cynthia. *The Morning After: Sexual Politics at the End of the Cold War*. Berkeley: University of California Press, 1993.

Erdei, Ildiko. 'Alice's Adventures in studentland narrative multiplicity of the student protest', *Sociologija: Journal of Sociology, Social Psychology and Social Anthropology*, XXXIX, 111–33, January–March 1997.

Erdei, Ildiko. 'Television, rituals, struggle for public memory in Serbia during 1990s', *Issues in Ethnology and Anthropology*, 3: 3, 145–69, 2008.

Fassin, Didier. *Humanitarian Reason: A Moral History of the Present*. Berkeley: University of California Press, 2011.

Fassin, Didier and Ricahrd Rechtman. *The Empire of Trauma: An Inquiry into the Condition of Victimhood*. Princeton: Princeton University Press, 2009.

Feldman, Allen. 'Memory theatres, virtual witnessing, and the trauma-aesthetic', *Biography* 27: 1, 163–202, Winter 2004.

Felman, Shoshana. *The Literary Speech Act: Don Juan with J.L. Austin, or Seduction in Two Languages*. Ithaca: Cornell University Press, 1983.

Felman, Shoshana and Laub Dori. *Testimony: Crises of Witnessing in Literature, Psychoanalysis, and History*. New York: Routledge, 1992.

Ferris, David S. 'Introduction: aura, resistance, and event in history', in *Walter Benjamin: Theoretical Questions*. Stanford: Stanford University Press, 1998.

Foucault, Michel. *Folie et déraison: Histoire de la folie à l'âge classique*. Paris: Plon, 1961.

Foucault, Michel. *The Archaeology of Knowledge*, trans. A. M. Sheridan. New York, 1972.

Foucault, Michel. 'Counter-memory: The philosophy of difference', in *Language, Counter-Memory, Practice: Selected Essays and Interviews*, ed. Donald Bouchard, trans. Donald Bouchard and Sherry Simon. Ithaca: Cornell University Press, 1977, pp. 113–98.

Foucault, Michel. *Power/Knowledge: Selected Interviews and Other Writings*, ed. Colin Gordon, New York: Pantheon, 1980.

Foucault, Michel. *The History of Sexuality. Volume One: An Introduction*, trans. Robert Hurley. Harmondsworth: Penguin Books, 1981 [1976].

Foucault, Michel. 'Subject and power', *Critical Inquiry*, 8: 4, 777–95, Summer 1982.

Foucault, Michel. 'Governmentality', in Graham Burchell, Colin Gordon, and Peter Miller (eds), *The Foucault Effect: Studies in Governmentality*. Chicago: University of Chicago Press, 1991.

Foucault, Michel. *The Order of Things: An Archaeology of the Human Sciences*. New York: Vintage Books, 1994 [1966].

Foucault, Michel. 'What is critique?' in *The Politics of Truth*. Los Angeles: Semiotext(e), 1997, pp. 41–82.

Foucault, Michel. *Fearless Speech*, ed. Joseph Pearson. Los Angeles: Semiotext(e), 2001.

Foucault, Michel. *Society Must Be Defended: Lectures at the Collège de France, 1975-1976*, trans. David Macey, ed. Mauro Bertani et al. New York: Picador, 2003a.

Foucault, Michel. '17 March 1976', in *Society Must Be Defended: Lectures at the*

Collège de France, 1975–1976, trans. David Macey, ed. Mauro Bertani et al. New York: Picador, 2003b.

Foucault, Michel. *Security, Territory, Population. Lectures at the Collège de France 1977–1978*, trans. Graham Burchell. London: Palgrave Macmillan, 2007.

Freud, Sigmund. 'Mourning and melancholia', in *The Standard Edition of the Complete Psychological Works of Sigmund Freud*, Vol. XIV (1914–1916), trans. James Strachey. London: The Hogarth Press, 1968, pp. 243–58.

Freud, Sigmund. *The Uncanny*, trans. David Mclintock. London: Penguin, 2003 [1919].

Fridman, Orli. 'Alternative voices in public urban space: Serbia's Women in Black', *Ethnologia Balkanica* 10, 291–304, 2006.

Fridman, Orli. 'Javno gradski prostori i alternativni glasovi: Slučaj Žena u crnom', *Ženezamir*. Belgrade: Women in Black, 2009.

Gal, Susan. 'Between speech and silence: The problematics of research on language and gender', in M. di Leonardo (ed.), *Gender at the Crossroads of Kknowledge: Feminist Anthropology in the postmodern era*. Berkeley: University of California Press, 1991, pp. 175–203.

Gal, Susan and Gail Kligman (eds). *Reproducing Gender: Politics, Publics, and Everyday Life after Socialism*. Princeton: Princeton University Press, 2000.

Glynos, Jason and Yannis Stavrakakis. 'Encounters of the real kind: Sussing out the limits of Laclau's embrace of Lacan', *Journal for Lacanian Studies*, 1: 1, 110–28, 2003.

Gordy, Eric. *The Culture of Power in Serbia: Nationalism and the Destruction of Alternatives*. Philadelphia: Pennsylvania State University Press, 1999.

Gordy, Eric. 'Turbo-folk u sjaju devedesetih', in Vladimir Djurić and Goran Tarlač (eds), *Pesme iz stomaka naroda: Antologija o turbo-folku*. Belgrade: Studentski kulturni centar, 2002.

Gordy, Eric. *Guilt, Responsibility, and Denial: The Past at Stake in Post-Milošević Serbia*. Philadelphia: Pennsylvania State University Press, 2013a.

Gordy, Eric. 'What happened to the Hague Tribunal?' *New York Times*, 2 June 2013b, <http://www.nytimes.com/2013/06/03/opinion/global/what-happened-to-the-hague-tribunal.html?pagewanted=all&_r=0> (last accessed 2 January 2015).

Gourgouris, Stathis. *Dream Nation: Enlightenment, Colonization, and the Institution of Modern Greece*. Stanford: Stanford University Press, 1996.

Green, Sarah. *Notes on the Balkans: Locating Marginality and Ambiguity on the Greek-Albanian Border*. Princeton: Princeton University Press, 2005.

Grosz, Elizabeth. *Architecture from the Outside: Essays on Virtual and Real Space*. Cambridge, MA: MIT Press, 2001.

Hacking, Ian. *Historical Ontology*. Cambridge, MA: Harvard University Press, 2002.

Hamilton, Carrie. 'Activist memories: The politics of trauma and the pleasures for politics', in Richard Crownshaw, Jane Kilby, and Antony Rowland (eds), *The Future of Memory*. New York: Berghahn Books, 2010.

Haraway, Donna. 'Situated knowledges: The science question in feminism and the privilege of partial perspective', *Feminist Studies*, 14: 3, 575–99, 1988.

Hayden, Robert, 'Recounting the dead: The rediscovery and redefinition of wartime massacres in late- and post-Communist Yugoslavia', in Rubie S. Watson (ed.), *Memory, History, and Opposition under State Socialism*. Santa Fe: School of American Research Press, 1994, pp. 167–84

Hayden, M. Robert. 'Rape and rape avoidance in ethno-national conflicts: Sexual violence in liminalized states', *American Anthropologist*, 102: 1, 27–41, 2000.

Helms, Elissa. 'Women as agents of ethnic reconciliation? Women's NGOs and international intervention in postwar Bosnia-Herzegovina', *Women's Studies International Forum*, 26: 1, 115–33, 2003.

Helms, Elissa. '"Politics is a whore": Women, morality and victimhood in post-war Bosnia-Herzegovina', in Xavier Bougarel, Elissa Helms, and Ger Duijzings (eds), *The New Bosnian Mosaic*. Aldershot: Ashgate, 2007, pp. 235–353.

Helms, Elissa. *Innocence and Victimhood: Gender, Nation and Women's Activism in Postwar Bosnia-Herzegovina*. Madison: University of Wisconsin Press, 2013.

Herzfeld, Michael. 'Silence, submission, and subversion: Toward a poetics of womanhood', in P. Loizos and E. Papataxiarchis (eds), *Contested Identities: Gender and Kinship in Modern Greece*. Princeton: Princeton University Press, 1991, pp. 79–97.

Hirsch, Marianne, 'Projected memory: Holocaust photographs in personal and public fantasy', in MiekeBal, Jonathan Crewe, and Leo Spitzer (eds), *Acts of Memory: Cultural Recall in the Present*. Hanover: University Press of New England, 1999.

Hirschauer, Stefan. 'Putting things into words: Ethnographic description and the silence of the social', *Human Studies*, 29: 4, 413–41, 2006.

Honig, Bonnie. *Political Theory and the Displacement of Politics*. Ithaca: Cornell University Press, 1993.

Honig, Bonnie (ed.). *Feminist Interpretations of Hannah Arendt*. University Park: Pennsylvania State University Press, 1995.

Honig, Bonnie. *Emergency Politics: Paradox, Law, Democracy*. Princeton: Princeton University Press, 2009.

Honig, Bonnie. 'Antigone's two laws: Greek tragedy and the politics of humanism', *New Literary History*, 41: 1, 1–33, Winter 2010.

Honig, Bonnie. *Antigone, Interrupted*. Cambridge: Cambridge University Press, 2013.

Horvat, Srećko and Igor Štiks (eds). *Welcome to the Desert of Post-Socialism: Radical Politics After Yugoslavia*. London: Verso, 2015.

Hughes, Donna M., Lepa Mladjenović, and Zorica Mršević. 'Feminist resistance in Serbia', *European Journal of Women's Studies*, 2: 4, 509–32, 1995.

Husanović, Jasmina. 'The politics of gender, witnessing, postcoloniality and trauma: Bosnian feminist trajectories', *Feminist Theory*, 10: 1, 99–119, 2009.

Huyssen, Andreas. *Present Pasts: Urban Palimpsests and the Politics of Memory*. Stanford: Stanford University Press, 2003.

Hymes, D. *'The ethnography of speaking', in* T. Gladwin and W. Sturtevant (eds), *Anthropology and Human Behaviour*. Washington, DC: Anthropological Society of Washington, 1962, pp. 13–53.

Ignatieff, Michael. *Blood and Belonging: Journeys into the New Nationalism*. Toronto: Viking, 1993.

Irigaray, Luce. *Speculum of the Other Woman*, trans. Gillian Gill. Ithaca: Cornell University Press, 1985a.

Irigaray, Luce. *This Sex Which is Not One*, trans. Catherine Porter and Carolyn Burke. Ithaca: Cornell University Press, 1985b.

Irigaray, Luce. *An Ethics of Sexual Difference*, trans. Carolyn Burke and Gillian C. Gill. Ithaca: Cornell University Press, 1993.

Iveković, Rada. 'Women, nationalism and war: "Make love not war"', *Hypatia*, 8: 4, 113–26, 1993.

Iveković, Rada. *Le Sexe de la Nation*. Paris: Leo Scheer, 2003.

Iveković, Rada. 'Feminism, nation and the state in the production of knowledge since 1989: An epistemological exercise in political translation', in *Women for Peace*. Belgrade: Women in Black, 2013, pp. 139–65.

Jansen, Stef. 'Victims, underdogs, and rebels: Discursive practices of resistance in Serbian protest', *Critique of Anthropology*, 20: 4, 393–419, 2000.

Jansen, Stef. 'The streets of Beograd: Urban space and protest identities in Serbia', *Political Geography*, 20, 35–55, 2001.

Jansen, Stef. 'Cosmopolitan openings and closures in post-Yugoslav anti-nationalism', in M. Nowicka and M. Rovisco (eds), *Cosmopolitanism in Practice*. Aldershot: Ashgate, 2008, pp. 75–92.

Jansen, Stef and Elissa Helms, 'The white plague: National-demographic rhetoric and its gendered resonance after the post-Yugoslav wars', in Christine

Eifler and Ruth Seifert (eds), *Gender in Armed Conflicts and in Post-War Reconstruction*. Frankfurt am Main: Peter Lang, 2009, pp. 219–43.

Jay, Martin. 'Walter Benjamin, remembrance, and the first world war', in Tetsuji Yamamoto et al. (ed.), *Philosophical Designs for a Socio-Cultural Transformation: Beyond Violence and the Modern Era*. Lanham: Rowman & Littlefield Publishers, 1998, pp. 530–48.

Kaliterna, Tamara. 'Ours and "their" perpetrators: The past is the reality of Serbia', *Women in Black*, 2013, pp. 211–43.

Kandiyoti, Deniz (ed.). *Women, Islam, and the State*. Philadelphia: Temple University Press, 1991.

Kelly, Mark. 'Racism, nationalism and biopolitics: Foucault's *Society Must be Defended*', *Contretemps*, 4, 58–70, 2004.

Kesić, Vesna 'Od štovanja do silovanja ili od majke domovine do hrvatske "posrnule" žene', *Kruh I Ruže* 1: 10–13, 1994.

Kesić, Vesna. 'Muslim women, Croatian women, Serbian women, Albanian women . . .', in Dušan I. Bjelić and Obrad Savić (eds), *Balkan as Metaphor*. Cambridge, MA: The MIT Press, 2002.

Kohn, Margaret. *Radical Space*. Ithaca: Cornell University Press, 2003.

Korac, Maja. 'Understanding ethnic–national identity and its meaning – Questions from women's experience', *Women's Studies International Forum*, 19, 133–43, 1996.

Kronja, Ivana. *Smrtonosni sjaj: Masovna psihologija i estetika turbo-folka* [*The Fatal Glow: Mass Psychology and Aesthetics of Turbo-folk Subculture*]. Belgrade: Tehnokratia, 2001.

Kronja, Ivana. 'Politics, nationalism, music, and popular culture in 1990s Serbia', *Slovo*, 16: 1, Spring, 5–15, 2004a.

Kronja, Ivana. 'Turbo folk and dance music in 1990s Serbia: Media, ideology and the production of spectacle', *The Anthropology of East Europe Review*, 22: 1, 103–14, Spring 2004b.

Lacan, Jacques. *Le Séminaire, Livre X: L' angoisse*, ed. Jacques-Alain Miller. Paris: Seuil, 2004 [1963].

Laclau, Ernesto. *New Reflections on the Revolution of Our Time*. London: Verso, 1990.

Laclau, Ernesto. *Emancipation(s)*. London: Verso, 1996.

Laclau, Ernesto. 'Hope, passion, politics: With Chantal Mouffe and Ernesto Laclau', in Mary Zournazi (ed.), *Hope: New Philosophies for Change*. London: Routledge, 2002, pp. 122–48.

Laclau, Ernesto. 'Discourse and jouissance: A reply to Glynos and Stavrakakis', *Journal for Lacanian Studies*, 1; 2, 278–85, 2003.

Laclau, Ernesto. 'Glimpsing the future: A reply', in Simon Critchley and Oliver Marchart (eds), *Laclau: A Critical Reader*. London: Routledge, 2004, pp. 279–328.

Laclau, Ernesto. *On Populist Reason*. London: Verso, 2005.

Laclau, Ernesto and Chantal Mouffe. *Hegemony and Socialist Strategy*. London: Verso, 1985.

Latić, Nedžad. 'Pobjeda ili časna smrt!' Interview with Mustafa Cerić. *Ljiljan*, 29 September 1993, pp. 26–7.

Lavrence, Christine. '"The Serbian Bastille": Memory, agency, and monumental public space in Belgrade', *Space and* Culture, 8: 1, 31–46, February 2005.

Lazić, Mladen (ed.). *Protest in Belgrade*. Budapest: Central European University Press, 1997.

Lederman, Rena. 'Who speaks here: Formality and the politics of gender in Mendi, Highland Papua New Guinea', in D. Brenneis and F. Myers (eds), *Dangerous Words*. New York: New York University Press, 1984, pp. 85–107.

Lefebvre, Henri. *The Production of Space*, trans. Donald Nicholson-Smith. Oxford: Blackwell, 1992.

Lenhardt, Christian. 'Anamnestic solidarity: The Proletariat and its *Manes*', *Telos*, 25, 133–54, Fall 1975.

Leontis, Artemis. 'The bridge between the Classical and the Balkan', *The South Atlantic Quarterly*, 98: 4, 625–31, 1999.

Loizidou, Elena. *Judith Butler: Ethics, Law, Politics*. London: Routledge, 2014 [2007].

Lopusina, Marko. *Ceca, IzmeduLjubavi I Mrznje*. Belgrade: Euro, 2003.

Loraux, Nicole. *The Divided City: On Memory and Forgetting in Ancient Athens*, trans. Corinne Pache with Jeff Fort. New York: Zone Books, 2002a.

Loraux, Nicole. *The Mourning Voice: An Essay on Greek Tragedy*, trans. E. Trapnell Rawlings, foreword by Pi. Pucci. Ithaca: Cornell University Press, 2002b.

Löwy, Michael. *Fire Alarm: Reading Walter Benjamin's 'On the Concept of History'*, trans. Chris Turner. London: Verso, 2006.

McClintock, Anne. *Imperial Leather: Race, Gender, and Sexuality in the Colonial Contest*. New York: Routledge, 1995.

Mahmood, Saba. *Politics of Piety: The Islamic Revival and the Feminist Subject*. Princeton: Princeton University Press, 2005.

Malkki, Liisa. 'Speechless emissaries: Refugees, humanitarianism, and dehistoricization', *Cultural Anthropology*, 11: 3, 377–404, 1996.

Markell, Patchen. *Bound by Recognition*. Princeton: Princeton University Press, 2003.

Martel, James. *Divine Violence: Walter Benjamin and the Eschatology of Sovereignty*. New York: Routledge, 2012.

Massey, Doreen. 'Power-geometry and a progressive sense of place', in J. Bird, B. Curtis, T. Putnam, G. Robertson and L. Tickner (eds), *Mapping the Futures: Local Cultures, Global Change*. London: Routledge, 1993, pp. 59–69.

Massey, Doreen. *For Space*. London: Sage, 2005.

Matić, Dragan. 'Serbia, antiwar activity 1991–1994', in Roger S. Powers et al. (eds), *Protest, Power, and Change: An Encyclopedia of Nonviolent Action from ACT UP to Women's Suffrage*, vol. 1625. New York: Garland Publishing, 1997, pp. 465–7.

Mayer, Tamar (ed.). *Gender Ironies of Nationalism: Sexing the Nation*. New York: Routledge, 2000.

Mbembe, Achille. *On the Postcolony*. Berkeley: University of California Press, 2001.

Mbembe, Achille. 'Necropolitics', trans. Libby Meintjes, *Public Culture*, 15: 1, 11–40, 2003.

Menon, Ritu. 'Do women have a country?', in Rada Iveković and Julie Mostov (eds), *From Gender to Nation*. New Delhi: Zubaan, 2004.

Mertus, Julie. '"Woman" in the service of national identity', *Hastings Women's Law Journal*, 5: 1, 5–23, Winter 1994.

Messick, B. 'Subordinate discourse: Women, weaving, and gender relations in North Africa', *American Ethnologist*, 14, 210–25, 1987.

Milić, Andjelka. 'Women and nationalism in Yugoslavia', in Nanette Funk and Magda Mueller (eds), *Gender Politics and Post-Communism: Reflections from Eastern Europe and the Former Soviet Union*. London: Routledge, 1993.

Milošević, Milan. 'The media wars: 1987–1997', in Jasminka Udovički and James Ridgeway (eds), *Burn This House: The Making and Unmaking of Yugoslavia*. Durham, NC: Duke University Press, 2000, pp. 110–11.

Miškovska Kajevska, Ana. 'Taking a stand in times of violent societal changes: Belgrade and Zagreb feminists' positionings on the (post-)Yugoslav wars and each other (1991-2000)'. PhD dissertation, University of Amsterdam, 2014.

Mladjenović, Lepa and Donna Hughes, 'Feminist resistance to war and violence in Serbia', in Marguerite Waller and Jennifer Rycenga (eds), *Frontline Feminisms: Women, War, and Resistance*. New York: Routledge, 2001.

Morris, C. Rosalind. 'Returning the body without haunting: Mourning "Nai Phi" and the end of revolution in Thailand', in David Eng and David Kazanjian (eds), *Loss*. Berkeley: University of California Press, 2003, pp. 29–58.

Morton, Stephen. *Gayatri Chakravorty Spivak*. New York: Routledge, 2003.

Mosse, George. *Nationalism and Sexuality: Respectability and Abnormal Sexuality in Modern Europe*. New York: Howard Fertig, Inc., 1985.

Mosse, George L. *Fallen Soldiers: Reshaping the Memory of the World Wars*. Oxford: Oxford University Press, 1990.

Mosse, George. *Fallen Soldiers: Reshaping the Memory of the World Wars*. Oxford: Oxford University Press, 1991.

Mostov, Julie. '"Our women"/"their women": Symbolic boundaries, territorial markers, and violence in the Balkans', *Peace and Change*, 20: 4, 515–29, October 1995.

Mostov, Julie. 'Sexing the nation / desexing the body: Politics of national identity in the former Yugoslavia', in Tamar Mayer (ed.), *Gender Ironies of Nationalism: Sexing the Nation*. New York: Routledge, 2000, pp. 89–110.

Mouffe, Chantal. 'Deliberative democracy or agonistic pluralism?' *Social Research*, 66: 3, 745–58, 1999.

Mouffe, Chantal. *The Democratic Paradox*. London: Verso, 2000.

Mouffe, Chantal. *The Return of the Political*. London: Verso, 1993.

Mouffe, Chantal. *On the Political*. London: Routledge, 2005.

Mršević, Zorica. 'Belgrade's SOS hotline for women and children victims of violence: A report', in Susan Gal and Gail Kligman (eds), *Reproducing Gender: Politics, Publics, and Everyday Life after Socialism*. Princeton: Princeton University Press, 2000, pp. 370–92.

Muñoz, José Esteban. *Cruising Utopia: The Then and There of Queer Futurity*. New York: New York University Press, 2009.

Nancy, Jean-Luc. 'La Comparution / The Compearance: From the existence of "communism" to the community of "existence"', trans. Tracy B. Strong, *Political Theory* 20: 3, 371–98, August 1992.

Nancy, Jean-Luc. *The Experience of Freedom*, trans. Bridget McDonald. Stanford: Stanford University Press, 1994.

Nancy, Jean-Luc. *Being Singular Plural*. Stanford: Stanford University Press, 2000.

Nancy, Jean-Luc. *The Inoperative* Community, trans. P. Connor et al. Minneapolis: University of Minnesota Press, 2004.

Navaro-Yashin, Yael. *Faces of the State: Secularism and Public Life in Turkey*. Princeton: Princeton University Press, 2002.

Navaro-Yashin, Yael. '"Life is dead here": Sensing the political in "no man's land"', *Anthropological Theory*, 3: 1, 107–25, March 2003.

Navaro-Yashin, Yael. 'Affective spaces, melancholic objects: Ruination and the production of anthropological knowledge', *Journal of the Royal Anthropological Institute*, 15, 1–18, 2009.

Navaro-Yashin, Yael. *The Make-Believe Space: Affective Geography in a Postwar Polity*. Durham, NC: Duke University Press, 2012.

Nenic, Iva. 'Ksenija Atanasijevic', in Francisca de Haan, Krasimira Daskalova, and Anna Loutfi (eds), *Biographical Dictionary of Women's Movements and Feminisms in Central, Eastern, and South Eastern Europe: 19th and 20th Centuries*. Budapest: Central European University Press, 2006.

Nichanian, Marc. 'Catastrophic mourning', in David Eng and David Kazanjian (eds), *Loss*. Berkeley: University of California Press, 2003, pp. 99–124.

Nora, Pierre (ed.). *Realms of Memory: The Construction of the French Past*, ed. of English version Lawrence D. Kritzman, trans. Arthur Goldhammer, 3 vols. New York: Columbia University Press, 1996–8.

Novakov, Anna. 'Ksenija Atanasijevic and the emergence of the feminist movement in interwar Serbia', The Free Library, 2011, Slavica Publishers, Inc. 17 September 2014, <http://www.thefreelibrary.com/Ksenija+atanasijevic+and+the+emergence+of+the+feminist+movement+in...-a0357472015> (last accessed 18 October 2016).

Oliver, Kelly. *Witnessing: Beyond Recognition*. Minneapolis: University of Minnesota Press, 2001.

Pandolfi, Mariella. 'Contract of mutual (in)difference: Governance and the humanitarian apparatus in contemporary Albania and Kosovo', *Indiana Journal of Global Legal Studies*, 10: 1, 369–81, 2003.

Panourgiá, Neni. *Fragments of Death, Fables of Identity: An Athenian Anthropography*. Madison: University of Wisconsin Press, 1995.

Panourgiá, Neni. *Dangerous Citizens: The Greek Left and the Terror of the State*. New York: Fordham University Press, 2009.

Papailias, Penelope. *Genres of Recollection: Archival Poetics and Modern Greece*. New York: Palgrave, 2005.

Papanikolaou, Dimitris. 'Archive trouble: Cultural responses to the Greek crisis', in Penelope Papailias (ed.), *Beyond the Greek Crisis: Histories, Rhetorics, Politics*. Hot Spots, published on the Cultural Anthropology website, 10 October 2011.

Papić, Žarana. 'From state socialism to state nationalism: The case of Serbia in gender perspective', *Refuge: Canada's Periodical on Refugees*, 14: 3, June–July 1994.

Papić, Žarana. 'Women's movement in former Yugoslavia: 1970s and 1980s', in *What Can We Do for Ourselves – East European Feminist Conference, Belgrade, 1994*. Belgrade: Center for Women's Studies Research and Communication, pp. 19–22, 1995.

Papić, Žarana. 'The Forging of Schizophrenia'. Interview conducted by Natasa Govedic, *Zarez* 31, 2000.

Papić, Žarana. 'Europe after 1989: Ethnic wars, the fascistization of civil society and body politics in Serbia', in Gabriele Griffin and Rosi Braidotti (eds), *Thinking Differently: A Reader in European Women's Studies*. London: Zed Books, 2002, pp. 127–44.

Parker, Andrew, Mary Russo, Doris Sommer, and Patricia Yaeger (eds). *Nationalism and Sexualities*. New York: Routledge, 1992.

Pateman, Carole. *The Sexual Contract*. Cambridge: Polity Press, 1988.

Pereira, P. P. Gomes. 'Anthropology and human rights: Between silence and voice', *Anthropology and Humanism*, 33: 1–2, 38–52, 2008.

Phelan, Peggy. *Unmarked: The Politics of Performance*. New York: Routledge, 1993.

Prince-Gibson, Eetta. 'Silent screams', *Jerusalem Post*, 23 August 2005.

Pulcini, Elena and Luisa Passerini, 'European feminine identity and the idea of passion in politics', in Gabriele Griffin and Rosi Braidotti (eds), *Thinking Differently: A Reader in European Women's Studies*. London: Zed Books, 2002, pp. 97–109.

Pulkkinen, Tuija. 'Tradition, gender and democracy to come: Derrida on fraternity', *Redescriptions. Yearbook of Political Thought, Conceptual Change and Feminist Theory*, 13, 103–24, 2009.

Rajic, Ljubiša. 'Koliko naroda, toliko neba', *Vreme*, 31 May 1993.

Rancière, Jacques. *Dis-Agreement: Politics and Philosophy*, trans. J. Rose. Minneapolis: University of Minnesota Press, 1999.

Rancière, Jacques. *The Politics of Aesthetics: The Distribution of the Sensible*, trans. Gabriel Rockhill. New York: Continuum, 2004.

Rogel, Carole. *The Break-up of Yugoslavia and the War in Bosnia*. Westport, CT and London: Greenwood Press, 1998.

Rose, Gillian. *Mourning Becomes the Law: Philosophy and Representation*. Cambridge: Cambridge University Press, 1996.

Rose, Jacqueline. '"Dora" – Fragment of an analysis', *m/f*, 2, 5–21, 1978.

Rose, Nikolas. 'The politics of life itself', *Theory, Culture and Society*, 18: 6, 1–30, 2001.

Rose, Nikolas and Paul Rabinow, 'Biopower today', *Biosocieties*, 1, 195–218, 2006.

Sagall, Sabby. 'Reluctant soldiers', *Socialist Review*, 189, September 1995, <http://pubs.socialistreviewindex.org.uk/sr189/sagall.htm> (last accessed 18 October 2016).

Salecl, Renata. 'Nationalism, anti-Semitism, and anti-feminism in Eastern Europe', *New German Critique*, 57, 51–65, Fall 1992.

Salecl, Renata. *The Spoils of Freedom: Psychoanalysis and Feminism after the Fall of Socialism*. New York: Routledge, 1994.

Sanders, Mark. 'Ambiguities of mourning: Law, custom, and testimony of women before South Africa's Truth and Reconciliation Commission', in David Eng and David Kazanjian (eds), *Loss*. Berkeley: University of California Press, 2003, pp. 77–98.

Savić, Obrad. 'Srebrenica: Between denial and recognition', *Eurozine*, 8 July 2005. <http://www.eurozine.com/articles/2005-07-08-savic-en.html> (last accessed 10 August 2009).

Savić, Obrad. 'Memory of war crimes: Can victims speak?',*Belgrade Circle Journal*, 2006, <http://www.eurozine.com/articles/2006-10-05-savic-en.html> (last accessed 29 January 2010).

Sedgwick, Eve Kosofsky. *Touching Feeling: Affect, Pedagogy, Performativity*. Durham, NC: Duke University Press, 2003.

Seremetakis, C. Nadia. *The Last Word: Woman, Death, and Divination in Inner Mani*. Chicago: The University of Chicago Press, 1991.

Simmel, Georg. *The Metropolis and Mental Life*. New York: Free Press, 1976 [1903].

Sklevicky, Lydia. *Konji, Žene, Ratovi*. Zagreb: Ženska Infoteka, 1996.

Slapšak, Svetlana. 'Les alternatives Serbes: y en a-t-il après la Bosnie?' *Migrations Littéraires* 21, 3–17, Summer, 1992.

Slapšak, Svetlana. 'Identities under threat on the Eastern borders', in Gabriele Griffin and Rosi Braidotti (eds), *Thinking Differently: A Reader in European Women's Studies*. London: Zed Books, 2002, pp. 145–57.

Sommer, Doris. *Foundational Fictions: The National Romances of Latin America*. Berkeley: University of California Press, 1991.

Sosa, Cecilia. 'On Mothers and *Spiders*: A face-to-face encounter with Argentina's mourning', *Memory Studies*, 4: 1, 63–72, 2011.

Sosa, Cecilia. *Queering Acts of Mourning in the Aftermath of Argentina's Dictatorship: The Performances of Blood*. Woodbridge, Suffolk: Tamesis Books, 2014.

Southard, Belinda Stillion. 'Militancy, power, and identity: The silent sentinels as women fighting for political voice', *Rhetoric & Public Affairs*, 10: 3, 399–417, Fall 2007.

Sparks, Holloway, 'Dissident citizenship: Democratic theory, political courage, and activist women', *Hypatia*, 12: 4, 74–110, 1997.

Spasić, Ivana and Đorđe Pavićević. 'Symbolization and collective identity in civic protest', *Sociologija: Journal of Sociology, Social Psychology and Social Anthropolog*, XXXIX, 73–93, January–March 1997.

Spivak, Gayatri Chakravorty. 'Can the subaltern speak?', in C. Nelson and L. Grossberg (eds), *Marxism and the Interpretation of Culture*. Urbana: University of Illinois Press, 1988, pp. 271–313.

Spivak, Gayatri Chakravorty. 'Poststructuralism, marginality, postcoloniality and value', in Peter Collier and Helga Geyer-Ryan (eds), *Literary Theory Today*. London: Polity Press, 1990.

Spivak, Gayatri Chakravorty. *Outside in the Teaching Machine*. New York: Routledge, 1993.

Spivak, Gayatri Chakravorty. 'Responsibility', *Boundary 2*, 21: 3, 19–64, 1994.

Spivak, Gayatri Chakravorty. 'Echo', in D. Landry and G. MacLean (eds), *The Spivak Reader*. New York: Routledge, 1995, pp. 175–202.

Spivak, Gayatri Chakravorty. 'The politics of translation', in Tutun Mukherjee (ed.), *Translation: From Periphery to Centerstage*. New Delhi: Prestige Books, 1998, pp. 95–118.

Spivak, Gayatri Chakravorty. *A Critique of Postcolonial Reason: Toward a History of the Vanishing Present*. Cambridge, MA: Harvard University Press, 1999.

Stavrakakis, Yannis. *The Lacanian Left*. Edinburgh: Edinburgh University Press/ Albany: SUNY Press, 2007.

Štiks, Igor. *Nations and Citizens in Yugoslavia and the Post-Yugoslav States: One Hundred Years of Citizenship*. London: Bloomsbury, 2015.

Stojanović, Boban. *Kakvo je vreme u Srebrenici?* Belgrade: Ženezamir, 2009.

Stoler, Ann Laura. *Race and the Education of Desire: Foucault's History of Sexuality and the Colonial Order of Things*. Durham, NC Duke University Press, 1995.

Stoler, Ann Laura. *Along the Archival Grain: Epistemic Anxieties and Colonial Common Sense*. Princeton: Princeton University Press, 2010.

Sturken, Marita. *Tangled Memories: The Vietnam War, the AIDS Epidemic, and the Politics of Remembering*. Berkeley: University of California Press, 1997.

Tapper, Nancy and Richard Tapper. 'The birth of the prophet: Ritual and gender in Turkish Islam', *Man* 22: 1, 227–50, 1987.

Taxidou, Olga. *Tragedy, Modernity, and Mourning*. Edinburgh: Edinburgh University Press, 2004.

Taylor, Diana. *Disappearing Acts: Spectacles of Gender and Nationalism in Argentina's 'Dirty War'*. Durham, NC: Duke University Press, 1997.

Taylor, Diana. *The Archive and the Repertoire: Performing Cultural Memory in the Americas*. Durham, NC: Duke University Press, 2003.

Tešanović, Jasmina. *Istorija Žena u crnom* [*History of Women in Black*]. Belgrade: Women for Peace, 2001.

Tešanović, Jasmina. 'The square and victims', *Women for Peace*, 34–36, Belgrade, 2005, <http://zeneucrnom.org/index.php?option=com_content&task=view&id=48&Itemid=17&lang=en> (last accessed 1 November 2016).

Todorova, Maria. *Imagining the Balkans*. Oxford: Oxford University Press, 1997.

Torov, Ivan. 'The resistance in Serbia', in Jasmina Udovički and James Ridgeway (eds), *Burn This House: The Making and Unmaking of Yugoslavia*. Durham, NC: Duke University Press, 2000.

Torsti, Pilvi. 'History culture and banal nationalism in post-war Bosnia', *Southeast European Politics* V: 2–3, 142–57, December 2004.

Trinh, T. Minh-ha. 'She, the inappropriate/d Other', *Discourse*, 8, Winter 1986–7.

Trouillot, Michel-Rolph. *Silencing the Past: Power and the Production of History*. Boston: Beacon Press, 1995.

Urošević, Miloš and Lepa Mlađenović. 'On duty in all forms of solidarity: Permanent policy of freedom for lesbian and gay activists', in *Women for Peace*. Belgrade: Women in Black, 2013, pp. 295–304.

Vardoulakis, Dimitris. 'Stasis: Beyond political theology?', *Cultural Critique*, 73, 125–47, 2009.

Vardoulakis, Dimitris. *The Doppelgänger: Literature's Philosophy*. New York: Fordham University Press, 2010.

Vardoulakis, Dimitris. *Sovereignty and its Other: Toward the Dejustification of Violence*. New York: Fordham University Press, 2013.

Vardoulakis, Dimitris. *Democracy and the Ruse of Sovereignty: Nine Theses on Agonistic Monism*. New York: Fordham University Press, 2017.

Vardoulakis, Dimitris. *Stasis: On Agonistic Democracy*. New York: Fordham University Press, forthcoming.

Vejvoda, Ivan. 'Not our war', *New Internationalist*, issue 256, June 1994. <https://newint.org/features/1994/06/05/not/> (last accessed 7 November 2016).

Verdery, Katherine. *The Political Lives of Dead Bodies: Reburial and Postsocialist Change*. New York: Columbia University Press, 1999.

Volčič, Zala and Karmen Erjavec. 'Constructing transnational divas: Gendered productions of Balkan turbo-folk music', in Radha Hegde (ed.), *Circuits of Visibility: Gender and Transnational Media Cultures*. New York: New York University Press, 2011.

Wagner, Sarah. *To Know Where He Lies: DNA Technology and the Search For Srebrenica's Missing*. Berkeley: University of California Press, 2008.

Winter, Jay. *Sites of Memory, Sites of Mourning: The Great War in European Cultural History*. Cambridge: Cambridge University Press, 1998.

Women in Black. *Women for Peace*. Belgrade: Women in Black, 1993.

Women in Black. *Women for Peace*. Belgrade: Women in Black, 2001a.

Women in Black. 'Six years since the Srebrenica massacre', in *Women for Peace*. Belgrade: Women in Black, 2001b: 103–4.

Women in Black. 'I am a conscientious objector'. Manifesto. Belgrade: Women in Black, 1998.

Woodward, Susan. *Balkan Tragedy: Chaos and Dissolution after the Cold War.* Washington, DC: The Brookings Institution, 1995.

Woodward, Susan. 'Violence-prone area or international transition? Adding the role of outsiders in Balkan violence', in Veena Das, Arthur Kleinman, Mamphela Ramphele, and Pamela Reynolds (eds), *Violence and Subjectivity.* Berkeley: University of California Press, 2000, pp. 19–45.

Woolf, Virginia, *Three Guineas.* New York: Harcourt Publishing, 1963 [1938].

Yerushalmi, Yosef. *Zakhor: Jewish History and Jewish Memory.* Seattle: University of Washington Press, 2005.

Yuval-Davis, Nira. *Gender and Nation.* London: Sage Publications, 1997.

Yuval-Davis, Nira. 'Human/women's rights and feminist transversal politics', in Myra Marx Ferree and Aili Mari Tripp (eds), *Global Feminism: Transnational Women's Activism, Organizing, and Human Rights.* New York: New York University Press, 2006, pp. 275–95.

Zaharijević, Adriana. 'On trial at the women's court: Gender violence, justice and citizenship', CITSEE Studies website: Citizenship in Southeast Europe, 19 December 2012. <http://www.citsee.eu/citsee-story/trial-women%E2%80%99s-court-gender-violence-justice-and-citizenship> (last accessed 2 January 2015).

Zaharijević, Adriana. 'Being an activist: Feminist citizenship through transformations of Yugoslav and post-Yugoslav citizenship regimes.' The Europeanisation of Citizenship in the Successor States of the Former Yugoslavia (CITSEE). CITSEE Working Paper Series 2013/28. Edinburgh: School of Law, University of Edinburgh, 2013, pp. 1–30.

Zajović, Staša. 'Militarism and women in Serbia', in *Women for Peace Anthology.* Belgrade: Women in Black, 1993 [December 1991].

Zajović, Staša. 'Radjanje, nacionalizam i rat', *Ženeprotiv rata*, I, 6–10, August 1994.

Zajović, Staša. 'Birth, nationalism and war', Women in Black, 1995, <http://www.hartford-hwp.com/archives/62/039.html> (last accessed 18 October 2016).

Zajović, Staša. 'Women in Black: War, feminism and antimilitarism', 2002. http://zeneucrnom.org/index.php?option=com_content&task=view&id=78&Itemid=21&lang=en (last accessed 7 November 2016).

Zajović, Staša. 'Women's activism in conflict and post-conflict areas, and the politics of assistance'. Presentation at the 13th International Conference of Women in Black, 'Women Resisting the Occupation and the War'. Jerusalem, 12–16 August 2005.

Zajović, Staša. 'Feminist ethics, Women in Black resistance: Always disobedient', in *Women for Peace*. Belgrade: Women in Black, 2013a, pp. 14–36.

Zajović, Staša. 'Feminist anti–militarism of Women in Black', in *Women for Peace*. Belgrade: Women in Black, 2013b, pp. 71–108.

Žarkov, Dubravka. *The Body of War: Media, Ethnicity, and Gender in the Break-up of Yugoslavia*. Durham, NC: Duke University Press, 2007.

Zerilli, Linda. *Feminism and the Abyss of Freedom*. Chicago: The University of Chicago Press, 2005.

Ziarek, Ewa Płonowska. *An Ethics of Dissensus: Postmodernity, Feminism, and the Politics of Radical Democracy*. Stanford: Stanford University Press, 2002.

Ziarek, Ewa Płonowska. 'Toward a feminist ethics of dissensus: Polemos, embodiment, obligation', in Claire Nouvet, Zrinka Stahuljak, and Kent Still (eds), *Minima Memoria: In the Wake of Jean-François Lyotard*. Stanford: Stanford University Press, 2007.

Ziarek, Ewa Płonowska. 'Feminine "I can": On possibility and praxis in Agamben's work', *Theory & Event*, 13: 1, 2010.

Ziarek, Ewa Płonowska. 'Feminist reflections on vulnerability: Disrespect, obligation, action', *SubStance*, 42: 3, 2013 (issue 132), 67–84.

Zirojević, Olga. 'Kosovo in the collective memory', in Nebojša Popov (ed.), *The Road to War in Serbia: Trauma and Catharsis*. Budapest: Central European University Press, 2000, pp. 207–8.

Živković, Marko. *Serbian Dreambook: National Imaginary in the Time of Milošević*. Bloomington: Indiana University Press, 2011.

Žižek, Slavoj, 'NATO, the left hand of God?', *Nettime*, Tue, 29 June 1999. Available through <http://www.egs.edu/faculty/slavoj-zizek/articles/nato-the-left-hand-of-god/> (last accessed 20 August 2015).

Žižek, Slavoj, 'The poetic torture-house of language', *Poetry Magazine*, 13 March 2014. https://www.poetryfoundation.org/poetrymagazine/articles/detail/70096 (last accessed 7 November 2016).

Index

EU Authorised Representative:

Easy Access System Europe Mustamäe tee 50, 10621 Tallinn, Estonia

gpsr.requests@easproject.com

Printed and bound by CPI Group (UK) Ltd, Croydon, CR0 4YY

29/04/2026

02099356-0001